"WOMEN LIKE THIS"
NEW PERSPECTIVES ON JEWISH WOMEN
IN THE GRECO-ROMAN WORLD

SOCIETY OF BIBLICAL LITERATURE

EARLY JUDAISM AND ITS LITERATURE

Series Editor
William Adler

Number 01

"WOMEN LIKE THIS"
NEW PERSPECTIVES ON JEWISH WOMEN
IN THE GRECO-ROMAN WORLD

edited by
Amy-Jill Levine

"WOMEN LIKE THIS"
NEW PERSPECTIVES ON JEWISH WOMEN
IN THE GRECO-ROMAN WORLD

edited by
Amy-Jill Levine

Scholars Press
Atlanta, Georgia

"WOMEN LIKE THIS"
NEW PERSPECTIVES ON JEWISH WOMEN
IN THE GRECO-ROMAN WORLD

edited by
Amy-Jill Levine

© 1991
Society of Biblical Literature

Library of Congress Cataloging-in-Publication Data

"Women like this" : new perspectives on Jewish women in the Greco
-Roman world / [edited by] Amy-Jill Levine.
    p. cm. — (Early Judaism and its literature ; no. 01)
    Includes bibliographical references and index.
    ISBN 1-55540-462-6 (alk. paper). — ISBN 1-55540-463-4 (pbk. :
    alk. paper)   ISBN 1-59740-691-0 (pbk)
    1. Women in the Bible. 2. Women in Judaism. 3. Apocryphal books—
Criticism, interpretation, etc. 4. Greek literature—Jewish
authors—History and criticism. I. Levine, Amy-Jill, 1956-
II. Series.
BS680.W7W57 1991
938'.004924'0082—dc20   91-4272
                                                          CIP

08 07 06 05 04 03 02 01 00 99   5 4 3 2

Printed in the United States of America
on acid-free paper

Table Of Contents

Abbreviations

AB	Anchor Bible
AJAH	*American Journal of Ancient History*
ALGHJ	*Arbeiten zur Literatur und Geschichte des hellenistischen Judentums*
ANF	*Ante-Nicene Fathers*
Annales ESC	*Annales Economies Sociétés Civilisations*
ANRW	*Aufstieg und Niedergang der römischen Welt*
Ant.	Josephus, *Antiquities of the Jews*
AP	W. R. Paton, *Greek Anthology*
Bib	*Biblica*
BibOr	Biblica et orientalia
BJS	Brown Judaic Studies
BLE	*Bulletin de littérature ecclésiastique*
CBQ	*Catholic Biblical Quarterly*
CBQMS	Catholic Biblical Quarterly Monograph Series
CIJ	*Corpus Inscriptionum Judaicarum*
CP	*Classical Philology*
Collins	Adela Yarbro Collins (ed.), *Feminist Perspectives on Biblical Scholarship* (Chico, CA: Scholars Press, 1985).
CQ	*Classical Quarterly*
CRINT	Compendia rerum iudaicarum ad novum testamentum
EH	*Ecclesiastical History*
EJ	*Encyclopedia Judaica*
ErIsr	*Eretz Israel*
FRLANT	Forschungen zur Religion und Literatur des Alten und Neuen Testaments
HE	A. S. F. Gow and D. L. Page (eds.), *Hellenistic Epigrams* (Cambridge: University Press, 1965).
HSM	Harvard Semitic Monographs
HSW	Hennecke, Schneemelcher, and Wilson, *New Testament Apocrypha*
HTR	*Harvard Theological Review*
HUCA	*Hebrew Union College Annual*
IG	Inscriptiones Graecae
JAAR	*Journal of the American Academy of Religion*

JBL	*Journal of Biblical Literature*
JEH	*Journal of Ecclesiastical History*
JETS	*Journal of the Evangelical Theological Society*
JJS	*Journal of Jewish Studies*
JLT	*Journal of Literature and Theology*
JSHRZ	*Jüdische Schriften aus hellenistisch-römischer Zeit*
JSJ	*Journal for the Study of Judaism*
JSP	*Journal for the Study of the Pseudepigrapha*
JTS	*Journal of Theological Studies*
LCL	Loeb Classical Library
Legends	Louis Ginzberg, *Legends of the Jews*
Maenads	Ross S. Kraemer (ed.), *Maenads, Martyrs, Matrons, Monastics*
Memory	Elisabeth Schüssler Fiorenza, *In Memory of Her* (New York: Crossroad, 1984).
MGWJ	*Monatsschrift für Geschichte und Wissenschaft des Judentums*
NH	Nag Hammadi
NHS	Nag Hammadi Studies
NTS	New Testament Studies
OTP	J. H. Charlesworth (ed.), *Old Testament Pseudepigrapha I, II*
PG	Patrologiae graecae
PW	Pauly-Wissowa (ed.), *Realencyclopaedie der classischen Altertumswissenschaft*
REB	Revised English Bible
REG	*Revue des études grecs*
RelSRev	*Religious Studies Review*
RSR	*Recherches de science religieuse*
RSV	Revised Standard Version
SANT	Studien zum Alten und Neuen Testament
SBLDS	Society of Biblical Literature Dissertation Series
SBLSCS	Society of Biblical Literature Septuagint and Cognate Studies
SBLSP	Society of Biblical Literature Seminar Papers
Schürer-Vermes	G. Vermes, F. Millar, and M. Goodman (revs. and eds.), *The History of the Jewish People in the Age of Jesus Christ (175 B.C.-A.D. 135). A New English Version*

SecCent	*Second Century*
SEG	*Supplementum Epigraphicum Graecum*
SH	Lloyd-Jones and Parsons (eds.), *Supplementum Hellenisticum*
SNTSMS	Studiorum Novi Testamenti Societas Monograph Series
SPB	*Studia postbiblica*
TAPA	*Transactions of the American Philological Institute*
TDNT	G. Kittel and G. Friedrich (eds.), *Theological Dictionary of the New Testament*
TS	*Theological Studies*
VC	*Vigiliae christianae*
VT	*Vetus Testamentum*
WLGR	M. R. Lefkowitz and M. B. Fant (eds.), *Women's Life in Greece and Rome*
WUNT	Wissenschaftliche Untersuchungen zum Neuen Testament
ZKG	*Zeitschrift für Kirchengeschichte*
ZPE	*Zeitschrift für Papyrologie und Epigrafik*

Preface

> "They admired the Israelites,
> judging them by her,
> and every one said to his neighbor,
> 'Who can despise these people,
> who have women like this among them?'"
>
> (Jdt 10:19)

In 1983, Elisabeth Schüssler Fiorenza lamented the lack of feminist critical analyses of Jewish literature between the Bible and the Mishnah;[1] since then, the task of investigating attitudes toward, lives of, and even possible writings by Jewish women of that period has engaged a number of scholars. The following eleven studies address the literary images and social situations of Jewish women, as well as their Gentile and Christian counterparts, as they appear in and can be reconstructed from the early literature: in philosophy and folktale; Apocrypha and Pseudepigrapha; Classical and Ecclesiastical sources.

The richness of the representations and roles examined — from the problematic presence of women in the public sphere to an emphasis on motherhood, from women as mediators of revelation to women as removed from or ignorant of heavenly matters, from the symbolic use of the female in philosophic vocabulary to the exemplary position of women as martyrs, from their depictions as romantic heroines to the positing of female authorship for these romances — prevents any simple conclusion regarding the Jewish woman of the Greco-Roman period. The difficulty of establishing a normative description of either their literary representations or their social roles is further exacerbated by recent work yielding equally diverse results on rabbinic and epigraphic materials as well as on the writings of Josephus.

Indeed, neither these, nor any essay, should be seen as offering a definitive treatment of women's representations, let alone of any actuality behind them. As the following studies indicate, an investigation merely of "what women do" in a text is insufficient; one

---

[1] *Memory*, 108.

must also include in both narrative analysis and social reconstruction issues such as class, ethnicity, provenance, familial situation, and religious orientation. Aseneth is a member of the upper class and a proselyte; Sitidos and Sarah represent different classes than the slave girl in the *Testament of Job* and the female servants in Tobit; the Maccabean mother lives and dies during a time of persecution, while Mary and Martha live during a time of (relative) peace.

In like manner, representations of women cannot be looked at in a vacuum, because any construction of woman always already implies a construction of man. For example, both for Philo and for Pseudo-Philo, depictions of women, either as symbols or as characters, are most clearly seen when they are compared to their male counterparts. Mary and Martha need to be compared to Jesus' other followers, both male and female. Aseneth's full characterization is only displayed in a comparison with that of Joseph, and Sitidos's often-negativized description is mitigated when she is compared to the three kings who visit Job.

Even with this recognition of the overdetermined nature of these representations, the scholar still does not have a clear path from the literary depiction to the history behind the text. What an author may suggest about women's lives may bear little resemblance to social realities, and the social realities cannot be generalized across all women. Studies of the ancient literature consequently face a host of methodological problems, among which the following questions might be considered rudimentary guides.

Upon what evidence does one determine if a document is prescriptive or descriptive? Applying this question to the *Testament of Job* and to Tobit, one might ask if Sitidos's support of Job and Anna's support of Tobit indicate a strong presence of women in the public sphere, or whether their entry into the marketplace is merely a literary trope, perhaps designed to show the undesirability of women apart from domestic arrangements. To answer such questions, the contributions below by Randall Chesnutt and Beverly Bow and George Nickelsburg provide some guidance. And what of Mary and Martha: should Luke's identification of the house as belonging to Martha (10:38) be seen as an aberration or, as Adele Reinhartz suggests, an indication of an independent Jewish woman.

When dealing with known authors, such as Claudia Camp's study of Ben Sira or Judith Romney Wegner's analysis of Philo, the distinction between the writers and their worlds can more precisely be addressed: do they speak for what is, or for what they think should be? Are wives and daughters confined to the house in Ben Sira's world, or is this his unmet desire? A third alternative is also possible: do the documents address the way the authors *perceive* things to be? In other words, can one determine to what extent the cultural ethos or ideology shape their perceptions?

The essays by Camp and Wegner reveal yet another consideration in the reconstruction of Jewish women's representations: the conjunction of Hellenistic and Hebraic cultures. For Camp, an exploration of the Mediterranean cultural ethos of the honor/shame complex reveals that Ben Sira's attitude toward women is a product of a nexus of socioeconomic conditions and attitudes toward sexuality. For Wegner, Philo's exposition of gender attributes, which is not particularly complimentary toward the female, is "quintessentially Greek." Further, her comparison of Philo's writings to both Greek and Christian as well as biblical and rabbinic thought counters various tendentious studies that view Philo's attitudes toward women as normatively Jewish and that see the Church as promulgating a more egalitarian ideology.

Hellenistic/Hebraic conjunctions and disjunctions influence more than the thoughts of individuals like the Alexandrian philosopher and the teacher of wisdom. Robin Darling Young's study of 2 and 4 Maccabees demonstrates how the figure of the mother of the seven sons embodies Greek as well as Jewish values. The mother's courage in 2 Maccabees is Stoic in form, but it is based in her Jewish hope for the resurrection. Similarly, sounding more like Philo than the Bible, the narrator asserts that the mother awakens the female reason with masculine courage. Fourth Maccabees goes even farther in conjoining the Hebraic with the Hellenistic by emphasizing the paradox of the triumph of reason in the "weakest of rational beings": a mother.

The rewritings of the Maccabean histories lead to the consideration of temporal displacement. As amplifications of biblical narratives, Pseudepigrapha such as Pseudo-Philo's *Biblical Antiquities, Jubilees, The Conversion and Marriage of Aseneth,* and the *Testament of Job* necessarily are set in the past. Apocryphal texts like Tobit and Susanna are similarly backdated. These settings may serve different narrative purposes: either the authors are presenting the way they presume things once were; or they are depicting present social circumstances masked by a fictional setting; or they are prescribing, through an appeal to the legitimation provided by time and tradition, the way they think people ought to behave. Nor are these options mutually exclusive. Further complicating the question

of social setting, a comparison of the various Jewish texts to their
Greco-Roman counterparts indicates that the women characters
may to a great extent be conforming to the literary conventions of
Late Antiquity.

Four essays in this volume consider these problematics. The
first two, the study of Pseudo-Philo's *Biblical Antiquities* by Betsy
Halpern-Amaru and the investigation of women visionaries in *Jubilees*, the *Conversion and Marriage of Aseneth*, and the *Testament of
Job* by Randall Chesnutt, focus specifically on expansions of biblical
materials. Halpern-Amaru's contribution is the first investigation of
the substantial role accorded women by Pseudo-Philo. Her work
reveals not only that the representation of women serves as a key to
a comparison between the *Biblical Antiquities* and *Jubilees*, it also
demonstrates that women serve a theological purpose as either the
instruments or the active agents of God. In addition, she discovers
that all strong female characters are associated with motherhood.

Chesnutt's investigation of revelatory experiences attributed
to women in his three pseudepigrapha reveals quite a different
agenda. Rebekah of *Jubilees* is a moral exemplar, a prominent
proponent of endogamy, and the guardian of salvation history. Like
Aseneth, she overshadows her husband in both action and symbolic
value. And, like Aseneth, she is not defined primarily by her children.
The Hebrew matriarch and the Egyptian convert, as well as Job's
three daughters, obtain otherworldly revelations of diverse natures
and through diverse means. Such portents indicate that women in
the worldviews of these documents could be envisioned as leaders;
more sanguinely, one may propose that they actually assumed
prophetic or leadership roles in their communities.

Both earthly motherhood and heavenly messages are motifs
in Tobit, a text set during the Assyrian exile. But as Bow and Nickelsburg observe, while children are of concern to both male and
female characters, the angel in this apocryphon restricts his
appearances to men. Their conclusion, like that of Chesnutt, is that
the text does not conform to stereotypical assumptions about the
extent or form of Jewish patriarchy. While religious matters remain
largely the prerogative of the male characters, the prayers of women
are also recorded and answered. And while the public sphere is the
domain of men, Anna − like Sitidos in the *Testament of Job* and like
the women Ben Sira fears − ventures, albeit not unproblematically,
into this arena.

The fourth essay to address texts set in times past is offered
by Richard Pervo. Taking a comparative approach, Pervo places the

voyeuristic viewing of Susanna, the emotional and spiritual development of Aseneth, and the deceitful and deadly Judith in the context
of their counterparts in Greek romantic novels. He finds that while
the typical romance is designed to reinscribe traditional sex roles,
the *Conversion and Marriage of Aseneth* and Judith offer challenges
to the established order. The Greek heroines represent what, for the
conservative ideology of the time, women were supposed to want; the
Jewish figures, on the other hand, come closer to describing what
Pervo suggests many women actually wanted.

Pervo's focus on plot and characterization is extended in Adele
Reinhartz's literary-critical study of the Mary and Martha narratives. And her essay raises as well an essential question for both
historiography and hermeneutics: to what extent do the biases of
the investigators influence the interpretation of texts? Her careful
analysis of the Lucan and Johannine narratives challenges the
reconstructions of such scholars as Witherington, who posits that
the sisters' depiction counters negative evaluations of women prevalent in Formative Judaism, and Schüssler Fiorenza, who sets the
material within the early Christian housechurch. Her essay offers,
in addition, some serious guidelines on the dangers in as well as the
possibilities of moving from the text to the history behind it.

As Reinhartz's study indicates, feminist criticism, like biblical
criticism in general, travels along the hermeneutical circle: one will
frequently first determine the social situation on the basis of internal evidence and, once that determination is made, proceed to interpret the text on the basis of the hypothetical *Sitz*. For women's
history, the ruts in the circle are deepened by the question of authorship. For example, the thesis that the first section of the *Testament of Job* was written by a man might lead to the conclusion that
the author had a negative view of women; claiming a woman's authorship might lead to the opposite theory: the first section condemns the exploitation of Sitidos and shows her ultimately to be
more heroic than her husband.

Equally problematic are the conditions of the document's
production and reception. One might distinguish between a work
written by a woman for the community at large and a work written
primarily for women readers. Here the question of intent versus
effect appears, for a document may call a community into being,
preserve one that is already intact, or do a bit of both. And how are
such communities to be reconstructed? One might begin with the
presupposition that the women are somewhat or even completely
removed from men (e.g., various reconstructions of the setting of the

Apocryphal Acts), or one might posit a woman's *Havurah* (cf. Acts 16), or even a woman's group within a larger movement (e.g., the Therapeutrides). Such considerations underlie Stevan Davies's methodological essay on the authorship and audience of Luke's two volumes and of the Apocryphal Acts.

But as Davies, Pervo, and Mary Lefkowitz make clear, a preponderance of women characters or even sympathy for these characters alone cannot be used to advance the theory of woman's authorship. Lefkowitz directly addresses the question of composition in her comparison of the *Testament of Job* and the *Conversion and Marriage of Aseneth* — texts often posited as women's compositions — to classical sources written by both men and women as well as to early Christian writings such as the Acts of Thecla and the Martyrdom of Perpetua. Her conclusion not only provides an intriguing foil to Pervo's article, it counters those who would argue for women's authorship on the basis of a narrative's point of view. Lefkowitz's additional observations on motifs associated with known women writers offers additional clues for the quest for Jewish and Christian women writers.

In part a response to Davies and Lefkowitz, and in part a reconstruction of the circumstances within which women might have written, Ross S. Kraemer's contribution ties together the questions of women's history and the study of religion. Her analysis of women's education and the dissemination of literature in Greco-Roman antiquity, the stylistic techniques posited by Lefkowitz for women writers, and the constraints imposed on the *Conversion and Marriage of Aseneth* and the latter half of the *Testament of Job* by their biblical models establishes a considered argument for women's authorship of the two pseudepigrapha. Her analysis of *Mary the Proselyte to Ignatius* and of the *Debate of a Montanist and an Orthodox* extends the discussion to Christian texts and explores the conditions under which some women might mask their authorship.

The value of these essays goes far beyond the already broad base of biblical studies, Formative Judaism, Early Church History, and Classics. These works have as well substantial implications for Christian hermeneutics and Jewish feminism. For example, as several of the articles observe, some feminist reconstructions of early Christianity have not merely occluded the presence of Jewish women, they have indirectly contributed to anti-Judaism within the Church. In discussions of "women in the Church," scholars often rarify and relegate to background material the richly varied lives and images of Jewish women in the Hellenistic and Roman periods. Further, some writers suggest that for Jesus to liberate women *to* their full potential, he had to liberate them *from* something; this "something" is then described as the repressive, patriarchal, Jewish system.[2] These essays reveal at the very least the impossibility of stereotyping Jewish women in the Greco-Roman period, and they suggest that the Jewish systems in both Palestine and the Diaspora may not have been as repressive as has been claimed. As more Christian feminists recognize the richly varied lives of these women, they will be able to produce a more historically faithful reconstruction of those Jewish women who decided to join the Church. As Bernadette Brooten has observed, "Writing the history of Jewish women in the Roman period is an urgent task for Christian theology."[3] For Jewish women, the essays recover a part of their own history disencumbered from canonical considerations. Although they do not indicate an egalitarian society, they reveal the variegated representations of Jewish women — as symbols, as role models, as real people — available in the ancient world.

The impetus for this collection was provided by a panel discussion at the 1987 annual meeting of the Society of Biblical Literature. Entitled "*Testament of Job* 46-55 and *Joseph and Aseneth*: The Possibility of Female Authorship and its Exegetical Implications," the panel was organized and moderated by Shaye J. D. Cohen. Thanks are due to him, as well as to the co-chair of the section, William Adler, who proposed this collection originally to the Septuagint and Cognate Studies Division of Scholars Press. I thank Professor Adler as well for his warm heart and his sharp eyes. Appreciation is also extended to Mary Hasbrouck for developing the program for this copy, Lori Kenschaft for undertaking the final copyediting, proofreading, and indexing, Swarthmore College for providing the funding to prepare the camera-ready manuscript, and, especially, to Jay Geller, for good advice and for patience.

Amy-Jill Levine
Swarthmore, Pennsylvania
7 January 1991

---

[2]See the discussion in J. Plaskow, "Blaming the Jews for the Invention of Patriarchy," *Lilith* 7 (1980): 11-12; Fiorenza, *Memory*, esp. 106ff; Bernadette Brooten, "Jewish Women's History in the Roman Period: A Task for Feminist Theology," in G. W. E. Nickelsburg and G. W. MacRae (eds.), *Christians Among Jews and Gentiles* (Philadelphia: Fortress, 1986), and, most recently, Susannah Heschel, "Anti-Judaism in Christian Feminist Theology," *Tikkun* 5.3 (1990): 25-28.

[3]Brooten, "Jewish Women's History," 22.

Understanding a Patriarchy:
Women in Second Century Jerusalem Through the Eyes of Ben Sira

Claudia V. Camp

Introduction

In a previous article, I attempted a brief sketch of Ben Sira's view of women toward the end of discerning the role of the "female sage" in second-century Palestine.[1] This sketch deserves deepening if our understanding of women's lives and their place in a man's world — and in a man's symbol system — is to grow. The barriers to learning about women when our only data come from men are notorious and legion; they need no rehearsal here. It may indeed be the case that women's history is irretrievable from a document like the text in question. Nonetheless, Ben Sira not only has much to say about women, he stands self-consciously in a tradition that at one point defined itself in female terms, as the Book of Proverbs witnesses.

The present study proposes a set of questions more complexly formulated than the straightforward issue of women's social roles. The root question asks whether we can discern the intellectual-affective process by which Ben Sira transcribed women into his book. By "intellectual-affective process" I do not intend something individualistically defined. To the contrary, I assume that the sage's work was embedded in his own cultural context, and that this context both elucidates and is elucidated by his masterwork.[2] It is, of

---

[1]"The Female Sage in Ancient Israel and in the Biblical Wisdom Literature," in J. Gammie and L. Perdue (eds.), *The Sage in Ancient Israel* (Winona Lake, IN: Eisenbrauns, forthcoming).

[2]A very useful study of the connection of Ben Sira to his text and context is B. Mack's *Wisdom and the Hebrew Epic* (Chicago: University of Chicago, 1985). Mack describes his interpretation of Sir 44-50 as an analysis of the connections between different "systems of signs": the system within the poem itself to that of the book, from there to "precursor texts," and then to the cultural context. The present article does not allow space to reprise this intellectual journey with Ben Sira's women (even if this author could hope to match Mack's scholarly achievement!). Issues that beg for attention include, especially, those of the relationship of "real" women discussed by Ben Sira to his Wisdom figure, and of both of these to their precursors in Proverbs. In other words, men's writing and thinking about women — particularly though hardly exclusively in a society as "gendered" as the Mediterranean — may be seen as part of the system of signs through which they encode and create the world. To understand better how this has been done may or may not tell much about women's actual lives. It may, however, tell a great deal about the

course, this embeddedness that provides hope, however slim, of recovering aspects of women's lives.

Critical to this analysis is the recent work in cultural anthropology that focusses on social-psychological patterns in the circum-Mediterranean area.[3] Though details remain debated, there is a wide consensus that variations of what is called the "honor-shame complex" is a determinant feature of contemporary Mediterranean life. In its older and less nuanced form, the "honor-shame" concept suggested that social identity is construed with particular attention to sexual relationships, such that male "honor" — the highest, and a highly contested, good — is determined essentially by the control men exercise over women's "shame," that is their sexuality. Recent anthropologists temper this picture with reference to more positive values at stake in male honor, but the dynamic's sexual dimension remains significant. Even more recently, a number of biblical scholars have suggested that Mediterranean cultural continuity, at least in the villages, allows us to consider ancient society and persons from this framework.[4] Part of this essay, then, will be to test whether an analysis of the Book of Sirach under this aegis will yield clues to that intellectual-affective process by which the author encoded women.

Shame and Honor

To describe Ben Sira's concept of honor and shame and how it relates to male-female relations, let me first present David Gilmore's three-point summary of the traditional anthropological categoriza-

---

dynamics of the symbolic world men create for women to live in.

[3]For an excellent recent overview of the field, see the nine essays in D. D. Gilmore (ed.), *Honor and Shame and the Unity of the Mediterranean* (Washington, DC: American Anthropological Association, 1987). Gilmore's introduction includes an extensive bibliography indicating a predominance of publications from the mid-1970s on. Of particular interest for the present essay are: J. Davis, *People of the Mediterranean* (London: Routledge and Kegan Paul, 1977); S. Ortner, "The Virgin and the State," *Feminist Studies* 4 (1978): 19-33; J. Schneider, "Of Vigilance and Virgins," *Ethnology* 9 (1971): 9-24; J. and P. Schneider, *Culture and Political Economy in Western Sicily* (New York: Academic, 1976). I thank Bruce Malina, Victor Matthews and Gale Yee for their encouragement and assistance in my own entry into the field of Mediterranean anthropology.

[4]Bruce Malina has graciously shared with me portions of a book manuscript written by him and J. Neyrey on the first-century Mediterranean person. A useful focus on wisdom literature will soon be available in John Pilch's *Introduction to the Cultural Context of the Old Testament* (Mahwah, NJ: Paulist, forthcoming). I obtained Pilch's manuscript too late to include reference to its insights here.

tion:[5] (1) Honor and disgrace are acquired by men through women, especially through women's sexual misconduct. Women are, therefore, both a "weak link" in the chain of honor, but also powerful because of their "potential for collective disgrace." (2) Shame is mainly a property of women, but it governs the relationship between the sexes. (3) Honor is a zero-sum game: a man gets it by taking it from others. More recently, Gilmore and others have noted in field studies less aggressive aspects of honor such as economic success, physical prowess, family autonomy, hospitality, integrity, and generosity. Although economic success and generosity are key values for Ben Sira, as Brandes states:

> The connection between honor or esteem, on the one hand, and social masculinity on the other, is also an inescapable part of the Mediterranean value system. ... [E]ven where the concern for expressing virility and masculine prowess coexists with other evident aspirations ... a man's performance in the non-sexual domain confers upon him a coveted manliness. *To be respected is to achieve gender-specific goals* (my emphasis).[6]

Crucial within the web of connected values that comprise male honor is the "rather unusual (ethnographically speaking) connection between erotic and economic power, the latter being largely contingent on the former."[7] Gilmore describes as "an almost universal thread in the [anthropological] literature" the "organic connection between sexuality and economic criteria in the evaluation of moral character."[8] He notes further D. O. Hughes's terms "economics of shame" and "fiscal sexuality," which refer to "the conceptual identification of erotic with tangible resources and a correlative belief that sexual access represents a convertible or 'marketable' commodity."[9] The last point helps distinguish the Mediterranean ethos from other societies where affluence derives from control of women and their labor. A strictly functionalist view of such male control would presumably place primary value on women's health or proven reproductive capacity, perhaps even making a pregnant bride a desirable commodity. In Mediterranean culture, however, the issue is not just sweat and babies but an almost fetishized chastity

---

[5]"Honor, Honesty, Shame: Male Status in Contemporary Andalusia," *Honor and Shame,* 90.
[6]"Reflections on Honor and Shame in the Mediterranean," *Honor and Shame,* 122.
[7]Gilmore, "Introduction," *Honor and Shame,* 4.
[8]Ibid., 6.
[9]Ibid., citing Hughes, "From Brideprice to Dowry in Mediterranean Europe," *Journal of Family History* 3 (1978): 285.

"arbitrarily elevated to central position as an exchange value."[10]

The direction of this anthropological research thus leads us to examine the bases for honor and shame in Ben Sira, especially as they relate to gender and to the socio-economic realm.

Shame. Ben Sira's concern for shame is evident both in the number and frequency of words within this semantic field.[11] The Greek uses nominal and verbal forms of αἰσχύνω (23X), ἀτιμάζω (16X), and ἐντρέπομαι (3X); verbal forms of καταισχύνω (7X); and the noun ἀσχημοσύνη (3X). The Hebrew equivalents are variants of the roots בוש‎, קלה‎, כלם‎, בוז‎, מזה‎, אול‎ and כמע‎.

Further, J. T. Sanders has delineated a crucial nexus of themes. He demonstrates that one of Ben Sira's principal concerns was to teach that the wise man is the cautious man, a concern evidenced in his use of נפש שמר‎ and שמר‎ in the niphal, "to guard or keep oneself" (6:13; 13:8, 13; 29:20; 32:22, 23, 24; 37:8, 31), and פחד‎, "to fear", in the sense of showing reverence and discretion (4:20; 18:27; 23:18; 37:12; 41:12).[12] This equation of wisdom with caution is extended theologically by Ben Sira's identification of wisdom with the Torah, "keeping" the commandment (שמר מצוה‎; 15:15; 32:22; 37:12), and his relentless recourse to "fear of the Lord." The double-edged motivation for this caution lies in preserving one's good name (5:15-16; 15:6; 37:26; 41:11-13; 44:8, 14; 49:1 and *passim*) and in avoiding shame. Indeed, "shame is the key ethical sanction in Ben Sira."[13]

Sanders makes two other observations relevant to the present discussion. First, he posits a significant "distinction between a

---

[10]Ibid., 4. The origin of this cultural reality is obscure, although well-developed hypotheses by such anthropologists as Ortner and the Schneiders are much discussed in the literature. For the present essay, origin is of less concern than the function of this nexus of values within Ben Sira's own context.

[11]For consistency, in most cases I adopt the translation in the recent, carefully annotated *Anchor Bible* commentary by P. Skehan and A. DiLella, *The Wisdom of Ben Sira* (New York: Doubleday, 1987). Where I offer my own translation, this fact is either noted explicitly or, where a single word or two is at issue, by inclusion of the original language(s) in the citation. I use the texts found in F. Vattioni, ed., *Ecclesiastico. Testo ebraico con apparato critico e versioni greca, latina e siriaca* (Naples: Istituto Orientale di Napoli, 1968). For word counts and comparison of Hebrew and Greek vocabulary, I use R. Smend, *Griechisch-Syrisch-Hebraeischer Index zur Weisheit des Jesus Sirach* (Berlin: Georg Reimer, 1907), and D. Barthelemy and O. Rickenbacher (eds.), *Konkordanz zum Hebraeischer Sirach* (Göttingen: Vandenhoeck & Ruprecht, 1973).

[12]"Ben Sira's Ethics of Caution," *HUCA* 50 (1979): 73-106.

[13]Ibid., 83.

proper and an improper shame."[14] Although he notes two passages offering extensive instruction on the two kinds of shame, 4:20-28 (part of a larger unit extending to 5:16) and 41:16-42:8, he comments only on the first, which concerns situations in which one should control one's speech. Although language, in both its practical and symbolic dimensions, is a critical aspect of Ben Sira's view of shame (which space will not permit attention to here), Sanders ignores the two other topics related to proper and improper shame that predominate in the second passage: sex and money. Contemporary anthropology's highlighting of *women's* shame as *a* (if not *the*) defining locus of the shame-by-which-one-must-be-bound in order to avoid the shame-that-destroys demands a closer look at 41:16-42:8, as well as at 26:15 and 32:10 where "shame" is used in its positive sense of "modesty."

Sanders's second useful, though undeveloped, notion is the implicitly psychologizing comment that "for Ben Sira, shame lurked everywhere...."[15] Sanders finds the motivation for this pervasive anxiety in the author's stated concerns for the quality of one's life and the immortality of one's name. While these are surely significant factors, more may be at stake. Concern for reputation is a consistent feature of the biblical ethos, but nowhere in the Hebrew Bible is there the concentration of shame vocabulary that occurs in Ben Sira.[16] Further, nowhere in that canon (except perhaps in Ezekiel) is there the virulent attack on women that occurs here: not only against traditionally "evil" women (harlots), but also against one's wife and daughters.[17]

While Sanders provides points of departure, he stops short of a full analysis of Ben Sira's multi-dimensional concept of shame. Our lens adopted from contemporary Mediterranean studies sug-

---

[14]Ibid., 84.

[15]Ibid., 99-100.

[16]The roots בוש‎, כלם‎, חפר‎, and קלה‎ II appear a total of 277 times in the Hebrew Bible, not an insignificant number (cf. C. Muenchow, "Dust and Dirt in Job 42:6," *JBL* 108 [1989]: 603). Although Muenchow does not include in his count all relevant Hebrew roots that appear in Ben Sira, בוש‎, כלם‎, and קלה‎ account for the vast majority of extant translational choices from the Greek. We can, then, make a rough comparison between the concentration of shame vocabulary in Ben Sira, where Greek equivalents occur 52 times, and the rest of the Hebrew canon: our sage has added almost a nineteen percent increase to the canonical works.

[17]While Proverbs emphasizes the symbol of the "strange woman," which is missing from Ben Sira, the earlier editor(s) had little negative to say about real women, except for the typical man's complaints about nagging wives (Prov 19:13; 27:15). Shame may come from an archetypal female danger "out there" (Prov 5:8-14), but nowhere evident in Proverbs is the fear of such a danger inside the circles of one's professional and family life.

gests that shame itself (not merely as a subset of "caution ethics") is a crucial category for understanding this ethos. Indeed, the sheer quantity of Ben Sira's shame vocabulary — especially compared to the occasional, if significant, occurrences of שמר and פחד — supports this perception. Anthropologists seeking to distinguish the Mediterranean honor-shame complex from notions of honor that occur in all societies note its importance to this culture's psychology of masculinity. Such a social-psychological perspective may help us to hear what Ben Sira does *not* say about shame — that is, what issues of identity and power are ideologically masked by the shame concept — and thus help to explain why, for this sage, "shame lurks everywhere." The rather static picture of the shame-name-wisdom-Torah ideational nexus painted by Sanders can thus be enlivened through attention to the social particulars of shame and how these interact with the authorizing concepts of Wisdom and Torah. The present essay thus will focus its anthropological lens upon the possible connections among shame, sexuality, and economics.

Before proceeding, however, we must look briefly at the concept of honor in Ben Sira.

Honor. Because of this essay's interest in women, I have chosen to concentrate primarily on shame. I will, however, often refer to shame's correlative, honor, a word also important to the sage. The concept of honor is closely related to the values Sanders discusses with respect to one's name. However, the quantity of the text's honor vocabulary suggests that this concept is actually the controlling category. Nominal and verbal forms of the Greek δόξα occur no fewer than 85 times, along with τιμή (14X) and ἔντιμος (3X). In the Hebrew manuscripts, these three words translate a variety of roots, most often כבד (21X) and הדר (7X). The honor concept itself can refer to the Lord, the stars, wisdom, and one who fears the Lord — in which case it is usually translated into English as "glory"; it can also refer to a human status, recognized by other humans, in which case it is usually translated "honor." Δόξα is, then, a quintessential ideological term serving not only as a religious symbol valorizing the worshiper and the object of worship in the cultic context, but also as a cultural symbol defining the worshiper's status goals within society. Although Mack sees the attribution of כבד to the hasidim as "bordering on profanity,"[18] an understanding of the cultural significance of "honor" in the Mediterranean makes such an assignation fully comprehensible. Although only occasionally in contemporary Medi-

---

[18]*Wisdom and the Hebrew Epic,* 167.

terranean anthropological literature is the honor-shame complex linked explicitly to the religious symbol system.[19] In Ben Sira, the linkage is unmistakable.

Honor, Shame and Wealth in Ben Sira: The Ideal and the Real

Ambivalence Regarding Wealth and the Sage's Social Status. The view of wealth in wisdom literature is anything but coherent. In Proverbs, a theory of retribution dominates: those who work hard and are faithful obtain material success; the lazy and the foolish suffer want. But exceptions exist. The poor (presumably those who cannot help themselves) are under divine protection and must be aided. Similarly, some things are better than wealth: notably wisdom, but also love. Despite such exceptions, the retribution theory lends the book an optimism: good things in life are available to those who seek wisdom.

Ben Sira presents a shift in perspective. No longer can he express confidence in a correlation between hard work and material success: neither work nor sloth yields predictable results. The search for wealth only increases anxiety, for "if you chase after it, you will never overtake it" (11:10c). Moreover, "wakefulness over riches wastes away the flesh/more than a serious illness, it washes out sleep" (31:1-2).

> One may toil and struggle and drive,
> and fall short all the same.
> Another goes his way a broken-down drifter,
> lacking in strength and abounding in weakness;
> Yet the eye of the Lord looks kindly on him;
> he shakes him free of the stinking mire,
> lifts up his head and exalts him
> to the amazement of many.
> Good and evil, life and death,
> poverty and riches are from the Lord. (11:11-14)

Although Ben Sira states that "the Lord's gift remains with the just/ his favor brings lasting success" (11:17; cf. 20:28), this vague affirmation precedes commentary on the miser who, having accumulated much, dies before he can enjoy his savings (11:18-19). Thus, Ben

---

[19]An excellent analysis is that of Carol Delaney, "Seeds of Honor, Fields of Shame," *Honor and Shame*, 35-48.

Sira sounds considerably more like Qohelet than Proverbs on the matter of wealth. The Lord gives, the Lord takes away (cf. 11:21; 18:25-26; 31:1-4; 33:11-15), and death levels all (11:28; 38:16-23; 40:1-7; 41:1-4). But while Ben Sira can no longer express the optimism of Proverbs, neither does he, like Qohelet, resign himself to the mysteries of uncontrollable destiny. Rather, the effort to gain and teach control over one's economic status pervades his book. References to wealth and economic dealings appear in 31 of his 51 chapters, sometimes a verse or two but often more extended discussions. To the particulars of his teaching we now turn.

Beyond the fundamental ambiguity embedded in God's unpredictable conferring of wealth, another ambivalence appears in the sage's evaluation of the rich and poor. This, in turn, leads to questions concerning Ben Sira's own economic status. One point, at least, is clear: the absoluteness of the divine command to give alms (29:8-9). Almsgiving atones for sin (3:30), protects from evil (12:3; 29:12), earns God's favor (16:4; 17:22), and functions, in effect, as a sacrificial offering (35:4). Indeed, without the Greek translation's specification, the Hebrew צדקה, "righteousness," could be read with a more general meaning. With almsgiving, as with other matters of textual concern, we may question whether the sage is expressing a widely held sentiment or encouraging a practice he finds his contemporaries lack. Whatever his social reality, the richness and variety of his admonitions suggest a sincere commitment to almsgiving specifically, and to a more general concern for care of the poor (3:30-4:10 and *passim*).[20]

A similar prophetic-style teaching emerges in Ben Sira's attacks on the injustice and pride of the powerful (5:1-8; 9:17-11:6; 11:22-26; 21:4). Unlike the almsgiving material which admonishes his actual audience, threats against those who put their faith in wealth rather than in fear of the Lord may provide more an ideological reinforcement to Ben Sira's other teachings than pragmatic moral instruction. The sage is all too aware that reward and punishment seem arbitrary or, at best, delayed. There will be a "time of vengeance" (5:7) or a "day of wrath" (5:8) against those deceived by their own wealth and power, but repayment may not come until "the day of death" (11:26). Although Ben Sira's words may be addressing his own students and colleagues, it is equally possible that they are directed primarily (as were the biblical prophets' similar teachings) to those over whom the speaker has little real influence, whether the Syrian rulers or, more likely, that newly emergent class of Jews who

---

[20]Cf. Skehan and DiLella, *Wisdom of Ben Sira*, 88-90.

were taking advantage of opportunities for commerce in the Hellenistic world.[21] I do not mean to imply that Ben Sira thought such people would read his book. Rather, the guarantee of God's eventual action against those with real power would have had the most impact on those with little power; this message would reinforce the point that one's relationship with the deity makes a difference, in spite of appearances to the contrary. The same principle operates among modern preachers who condemn the heathen — that is, anyone who does not believe as they do! — to hell. Such rhetoric functions not to convert the heathen, who would not be listening anyway, but to reassure the faithful.

If Ben Sira's views of salvation through almsgiving and damnation through self-reliance seem unequivocal, he presents substantial evidence that bespeaks a certain tension, either between his personal ethics and those of his society or within the society itself. The sage appears caught between wealth and poverty; he must contend with those who have more, and learn how to live appropriately with less. Adding to the difficulty of financial instability was the need to control appearances as well as reality, a concern still alive in the Mediterranean where the former often counts for more than the latter.[22]

This ambivalence between appearance and reality, both in the culture and in Ben Sira's own mind, is nowhere more evident than in his discussions of wisdom and poverty. Clearly, this sage *wants* to put forth a valuation of wisdom over wealth, a valuation he contends will be socially recognized.

Be it sojourner, wayfarer, alien or pauper,
his glory is the fear of the Lord. (10:22)
When the free serve a prudent slave,
the wise person does not complain. (10:25)
The poor person's wisdom lifts his head high
and sets him among princes. (11:1)
The poor is honored for his wisdom
as the rich is honored for his wealth. (10:30)

Already in 10:30 social norms are confronted: it is a given that the rich will be honored for his wealth, much less so that the poor will be honored for his wisdom! Thus, in spite of the confidence in the preceding sayings, the sage must also admonish: "It is not just to

---

[21]On the latter, see V. Tcherikover, *Hellenistic Civilization and the Jews* (Jewish Publication Society, 1959; reprint: New York: Atheneum, 1970), 149.
[22]R. Patai, *The Arab Mind* (New York: Charles Scribner's Sons, 1973), 101-106.

despise a person who is wise but poor/nor proper to honor any oppressor" (10:23). And, is it hard-headed realism or an unwitting acceptance of the appearance of honor he wants to undercut when he says: "Honored in poverty, how much more in wealth!/dishonored in wealth, in poverty how much the more!" (10:31).

Indeed, Ben Sira seems to be as concerned about the proper comportment of the poor as he is about the pride of the wealthy:

> Do not consider yourself wise in doing your work,
> and do not glorify yourself (תתכבד/δοξάζου)
>   in your time of need.
> Better the worker with left-over wealth
> than the self-glorifier in need of sustenance (10:26-27).
> (my translation)

While these verses may be simply a general allusion to a particular type of fool, the lazy self-deceiver (cf. 25:2c; Prov. 12:9), the direct address of 10:26 indicates otherwise. Ben Sira seems to be confronting the phenomenon of scribes who are poor but who, like the sage himself, view manual labor as incapable of conferring honor and immortality (cf. 38:24-39:11). Thus, while this sage holds an idealized vision of the poor man honored for his wisdom, he also, realistically, advises his students not to wrap sheer laziness in such a flag. Better to be wise *and* wealthy (10:31a).

Perhaps Ben Sira's most revealing comment about wealth comes in 26:28, where he identifies two things that "bring grief" to his heart: a wealthy person reduced to want and the intelligent held in contempt. The parallelism, which sets wisdom and wealth on the same level, also expresses the fundamental anxiety of one who earns his bread with his brain. Wisdom is the one claim to honor a poor man has, but poverty endangers the claim. This sense that a sage could live at, and sometimes fall over, the edge of economic ruin is vividly displayed in the larger context of 26:28-27:3.

> These two things bring grief to my heart,
> and the third rouses my anger:
> A wealthy person reduced to want;
> the intelligent held in contempt;
> and the person who passes from righteousness to sin —
> him the Lord makes ready for the sword.
> A merchant can hardly remain without fault,
> or a salesman (κάπηλος) free from sin.
> For the sake of profit many sin,
> and the struggle for wealth blinds the eyes.

Like a peg driven between fitted stones,
between buying and selling sin is wedged in.
Unless one holds fast to the fear of the Lord,
with sudden swiftness, one's house will be thrown down.

The complete passage suggests the following scenario: A well-to-do sage has met with economic misfortune. He sees an advantage to be had, however, in the small but fast-rising class of merchants. He moves to one of the Greek cities on the coastal plain where he can be near the highly profitable international trade lines. (The Greek for "merchant" [26:29a] is ἔμπορος, meaning "one who travels on business.") In so doing, in Ben Sira's view, he has lost his honor; he is a κάπηλος (26:29b), a "petty tradesman" or, alternatively, a "cheat." To capture the tone, I have changed Skehan and DiLella's "shopkeeper" to the sometimes more pejorative "salesman."[23]

Loss of honor has social as well as religious connotations for Ben Sira, and given the historical context, both may be evident in this passage. Explicitly, sin is defined in 27:1-2 as economic bad faith. If, however, Ben Sira associates merchants with Hellenizers like the Tobiads, sin may also carry the connotation of religious faithlessness. Precisely this combination of loss of honor before both God and men is indicated by the punchline of the pericope's opening saying (26:28). If two things cause grief, a third brings anger: the person who moves from righteousness to sin. Here, as elsewhere, we also get sense of the failure of the honor-shame ethos to control those who abandon traditional norms in search of wealth: the work of the Lord is needed to bring them to justice.

The concluding verse might allow a slight reprieve to those entering the world of trade. Sir 27:3 could be interpreted: "granted the difficulty for a merchant to remain honest, one who fears the Lord (that is, retains the honor integral to his wisdom) can do so." Alternatively, it may simply define "fear of the Lord" as the wise man's acceptance of poverty in spite of the lures of mercantile profit.

In sum, while Ben Sira evinces a strong moral obligation to care for the poor (26:28c) and expresses his grief over the wealthy reduced to want, he leaves no doubt that his sympathies lie with

---

[23]We might also note the crude sexual allusion in Ben Sira's cutting remarks about trade. Sir 27:2 describes buying and selling as having "sin wedged in" "like a peg driven between fitted stones." The other reference to the placement of tent-pegs occurs in the immediately preceding poem on the ways of a wife who "sits down before every tent peg and opens her quiver to every arrow" (26:12bc). This sage, as we shall see, habitually mixes sexual and economic language.

those who live within striking distance of wealth yet without the security of economic excess. Indeed, his own role as scribe, which he exalts above other professions, requires wealth enough to be "free from toil" (38:24).

These inductive impressions of Ben Sira's social standing are supported by several studies showing him to have been not only a "scribe," but a priest.[24] Tcherikover assumes a contrast between poor, rural priests who come to Jerusalem only for assigned periods, and "rich Jerusalemite priests."[25] Conversely, Mantel assumes that all priests except the High Priest — who had access to agricultural products appropriated to the Temple — were dependent on voluntary contributions because of the proscription on their owning land.[26] Neither assessment is entirely satisfactory. Tcherikover himself notes the existence of wealthy land-holders in rural areas;[27] though there was certainly a large secular aristocracy, there is no reason some of these could not have been of priestly families. Against Mantel, it seems improbable that only the immediate family of the High Priest would have benefitted from Temple-state acquisitions. Maintenance of effective power would have required some sharing of wealth. Notable here is Mack's commentary on the "striking claim" that the descendents of the hasidim have prosperity by virtue of their ancestors' righteousness (42:10-11; cf. 42:6). These verses "reflect a social and economic concern for the security of property" and "may indicate the degree to which Ben Sira understood the history and model of Second Temple Judaism to include given social structures and economic institutions."[28] Considering the tensive, existential ambiguity of Ben Sira's teachings about wealth, I would even suggest that 44:6, 10-11 represent ideological justification of an economic system from which the sage benefits, but which he does not control, a position from which he can see both losers and winners among those who also play the tricky game.

This status and the anxiety it generates result from a combi-

---

[24]Mack, *Wisdom and the Hebrew Epic*; S. Olyan, "Ben Sira's Relationship to the Priesthood," *HTR* 80 (1987): 261-86; H. Stadelmann, *Ben Sira als Schriftgelehrter* (WUNT 2. Reihe, 6; Tübingen: J. C. B. Mohr [Paul Siebeck], 1980).
[25]"Social Conditions," in A. Schalit (ed.), *World History of the Jewish People*, 1st ser., vol. VI (New Brunswick, NJ: Rutgers University, 1972),110.
[26]"The High Priesthood and the Sanhedrin in the Time of the Second Temple, in M. Avi-Yonah (ed.), *World History of the Jewish People*, 1st ser., vol. VII (New Brunswick, NJ: Rutgers University, 1975), 267-68.
[27]"Social Conditions," 95.
[28]*Wisdom and the Hebrew Epic*, 75.

nation of factors. In particular, a long-standing feature of Mediterranean culture is that of patronage, a system closely connected to concern for honor. It occurs:

> whenever men adopt a posture of deference to those more powerful than they and gain access to resources as a result. It is associated with honour because honour is a moral code in which rich and poor are ranked and in which their interdependence is emphasised as in no other idiom of stratification; because the language of honour is that used by the weak to mitigate the consequences of their helplessness in this relationship; and because honour aids choice: it is at least potentially an absolute differentiator; and a patron, choosing among several would-be clients, chooses the more honourable. It is in this way that honour is an allocator of resources, and creates conflict among those "equals" who struggle for a livelihood.[29]

This understanding of patronage illumines the many passages in which Ben Sira discusses the problematic relationship of his students to the rich (see below). Moreover, the tension of the jockeying of clients before patrons was undoubtedly compounded for Ben Sira by his changing social and religious environment. Although Jerusalem had yet to experience the full weight of the Hellenistic reform begun in 175, the city was already rife with factionalism.[30] Such instability was particularly trying for a member of the scribal class, whose existence was predicated upon service to a stable upper class in the context of a complex bureaucracy.[31] Hoffer's general observation, that only in the midst of social decay does a scribe turn writing talents toward a "new role as sage, prophet, and teacher,"[32] finds striking testimony in Mack's analysis of Ben Sira's integrated social vision: his "praise of the ancestors," in the face of his disjunctive social reality.[33] That latter reality is much in evidence elsewhere in his book.

To this point, we have observed two competing tendencies in Ben Sira's views on wealth. On the one hand, he idealizes and ideologizes the extremes of wealth and poverty: the proud who rely on

---

[29]Davis, *People of the Mediterranean*, 132.
[30]Much of this tension was apparently focussed on the ambition of the Hellenistized Tobiad family, some of whom remained Ptolemaic allies even after the Seleucid takeover of Palestine in 198. Tcherikover, "Social Conditions," 96-104 and "The Hellenistic Movement in Jerusalem and Antiochus' Persecutions," also in *World History*, VI.118-21.
[31]E. Hoffer, *The Ordeal of Change* (New York: Harper & Row, 1964), 101-11.
[32]Ibid., 105.
[33]*Wisdom and the Hebrew Epic*, 179-80.

their material resources will be struck down by God who, in turn, pays special and speedy attention to the prayer of the poor. Thus is validated the ethic of almsgiving as a definitive mode of righteousness. Yet in what seems to be "real life," the sage lives without financial security in an unstable environment that identifies wealth with honor.

The Pragmatics of Economics. Caught between the rich and the poor, the sage requires standards for dealing with both and takes precautions against the hazards confronted in each direction. In turn, within these economic modalities lie opportunities for honor and shame. Whatever the full range of duties of a sage/scribe/priest like Ben Sira, he clearly anticipates regular contact with the rich and powerful, in a relationship that seems to be that of client to patron. The dangers are manifold.

> As long as the rich can use you he will enslave you,
> but when you are exhausted he will have nothing to do with
>   you.
> While you own anything, he will be part of your household,
> then reduce you to penury without a qualm.
> As soon as he needs you, he will trick you,
> and with smiles he will win your confidence.
> He will make gracious promises, and ask what you need,
> and shame you with gifts of delicacies;
> twice or three times he will intimidate you,
> and finally laugh you to scorn.
> Afterward he will gloat over you,
> pretend to be angry with you,
> and shake his head at your downfall. (13:4-7)

A primary danger in consorting with the rich, then, is the perception that one might be able to turn the relationship to one's own advantage, as evidenced in the gifts the rich man gives. But only the fool is unaware that unreciprocated gifts are forms of incurred debt; a gift in itself is a form of intimidation. The wise person, therefore, must interpret properly economic fortune and adversity, including the traffic in gifts (20:9-17). To save face, one might even have to loan the rich money with no hope of repayment (8:12). Thus, shame inheres in the relationship itself; one's downfall is a proleptic reality, and it is a sorry picture Ben Sira paints of those dependent on the hospitality (and subject to the insults) of others (29:21-28). Only the shameless could enjoy such a life (40:28-30).

These dire warnings to accept one's life as is, whether with

much or little (29:21-23), face an opposing pull from both the culture
and the author himself: to honor the rich over the poor. Ben Sira's
cautions about dealing with the powerful do not mean utterly
avoiding such persons. The point, rather, is to learn how to function
effectively in dangerous encounters. Immediately after the passage
quoted above about the gifts and tricks of the rich, the sage adds:

> Guard against being easily upset,
> and do not come to grief with those lacking astuteness
> (חסירי מדע/ἐν ἀφροσύνῃ σου).
> When approached by a person of influence, keep your distance;
> then he will urge you all the more.
> Be not too forward with him lest you be rebuffed,
> but be not too standoffish lest you be taken for an enemy.
> (13:8-10)

While it is dangerous to contend with a powerful man (8:1-2), those
wise in both speech and resource management will "please the great"
(20:27-28) and thus, presumably, advance. Similarly, although Ben
Sira bemoans that "in our prosperity we cannot know our friends"
(12:8), he advises handling one's enemies (12:10-12) rather than
forsaking wealth.

The honor-shame concept provides one way to understand
this apparent ambivalence. Difficulties involved in owing favors or
loans are readily apparent, and advice to avoid situations that might
tempt one in this direction can be generally understood. Yet in the
Mediterranean, honor and shame are conflictual categories won and
lost in contests between actors on the social stage. However much
Ben Sira idealizes the wisdom of the poor, he deals realistically in a
world where wealth and influence are part of how one makes one's
name. Thus, while consorting with the powerful is dangerous, it is
also a challenge. Even the cautious wise take risks to maintain or
increase social status. Avoiding shame means playing the power
games of society. The author's comments on the anxiety involved in
chasing wealth would seem to come from experience that was both
first-hand and unavoidable.

Perhaps the topic of greatest ambivalence in Ben Sira's
economics is that of making loans and going surety for another. The
significant Mediterranean values of generosity[34] and loyalty, which
prompt his urging to enter such transactions, conflict with his fear
of losing his own wealth. Unlike almsgiving, which by endebting
others brings unmitigated esteem, honor gained by making loans or

---

[34]Patai, *Arab Mind*, 87-88 and *passim*.

standing surety is countered by the danger of losing status.

Hence Ben Sira's ambivalence about friendship. On the one hand, friends are more valuable than wealth: "Barter not a friend for money, nor a true brother for the gold of Ophir" (7:18; cf. 6:5-17; 9:10; 19:13-17; 22:19-24; 25:1c, 9; 27:16-21; 37:5-6; 40:12; 41:18c, 21ab). With a poor man, associational caution is not needed; indeed, one should befriend a person while he is poor and remain true in his times of trouble, for then one will share in his prosperity and inheritance (22:23-24). Concretely this demanded show of loyalty means making loans (29:1-2a). Failure to do so brings shame (22:25-26). There is no little irony in Ben Sira's advising a wealthier person to seek out the benefits of such a relationship — essentially, a patronage — which he advises the poorer man to avoid![35]

The matter of loans and surety reveals fully the tension friendship can engender. Chapter 29 is a fascinating mix of idealism and less sanguine advice offered to potential lenders and borrowers. While the fundamental values remain generosity and loyalty to the needy (29:1-2a; 20a), the sayings are complicated by a two-sided warning: first to repay loans (29:2b-3, 14-15) and, second, not to go surety beyond one's means, to "take care lest you fall thereby" (29:20; cf. 8:13). These warnings are accompanied by disquisitions on the shamelessness of and danger posed by the fraudulent borrower (29:4-6, 14-18), although problems can also occur when "sin" rather than compassion motivates the lender (29:19). There is a perilous necessity to this system: a lender is due honor for his generosity, but a shameless borrower may give abuse instead (29:6). Ben Sira's sympathies are again manifest when he observes without judgment: "Many refuse to lend, not out of meanness, but from fear of being cheated to no purpose" (29:7).

Thus, despite ideals that might point him elsewhere, Ben Sira is committed to the cultural game of honor and shame. But this observation does not entail an accusation of insincerity, since he also persistently remonstrates against taking wrongful advantage of one's position (13:24a; 19:20-25; 21:8; 31:5-11; 34:21-31; 40:11-17; 41:21b). There is a fine balance present, not only of actions but also of values. Indeed, riches are seen not as a reward for righteousness, but as a *test* of righteousness (31:8-11). Given such an anxiety level, it is small wonder the sage needs *also* advise readers not to forget to enjoy what they have before death takes all (14:3-19)!

---

[35]Similarly, while one should resist the temptation of delicacies from the avaricious rich, the reader is advised to be generous with his own food (31:23-24).

Underneath all this one may hear a rather poignant personal plea from the sage: "Please don't make me renege on my fundamental values of loyalty and generosity — and thus fail in my own quest for honor or else risk my material well-being — by acting like a shameless fraud." Beneath this plea is an even more subconscious one: "Please don't make me face the fundamental contradiction in my own values, namely, that honor located in wealth is not in full harmony with the honor found in loyalty and generosity. Please don't make me choose, for I might fail the test that wealth presents to righteousness." In light of this analysis, Ben Sira's advice in 11:29-12:6, to know well the person whom you financially support so that you will do good only to the just and not the sinner (for "God himself hates sinners") emerges as a moralizing rationalization for the protection of one's honor along with one's possessions.

Our discussion of the complicated and hence anxiety-producing clash and re-weaving of values as they relate to loans and surety would be incomplete without considering Ben Sira's meditation on language, lies, and loans (20:1-26). The poem opens with counsel on knowing when to speak (20:1-8). Such ability is contextually connected to the correct interpretation of economic fortune and adversity (20:9-12), which segues into a commentary on the fool's inability to understand proper traffic in gifts and loans (20:13-17). This passage picks up directly on the concern in 18:15-18 for aligning one's attitude (charitability, not reproach) with one's gift-giving (cf. 41:22d). The wise person's word may be better than a gift, though "both are to be found in a gracious man." Gifts are means of political and economic intercourse, and thus of status. But as noted above, when gifts are received more than given they can incur a debt which in turn can threaten one's honor. "There are losses on account of honor (δόξης)" (20:11) means that either one seeking honor by making loans may lose his shirt, or that (false) honor gained by receiving gifts will end in shame.

Concerns for graciousness and proper timing of speech are united in the following pericope, which also introduces the theme of the succeeding section, namely, the perverse use of language:

A slip on the pavement rather than a slip of the tongue!
thus the downfall of the wicked will occur speedily.
An ungracious man is a tale untimely told,
which is continually on the lips of the ignorant.
A proverb from a fool's lips will be rejected,

for he does not tell it at its proper time (20:18-20).[36]

The first proverb introduces what follows (20:21-26) by intimating the connection between an accident (slip of the the tongue = slip on the pavement) and outright wickedness. An understanding of the competitive dynamic of shame explicates the logic by which Ben Sira develops this notion.[37] First, by ironic coincidence, poverty might prevent one from sinning (20:21). The next verse, seemingly a *non-sequitur*, suggests that a man might lose his life through shame (22a) or a foolish countenance (22b).[38] The repetition of the verb "lose" (ἀπολλύων, ἀπολεῖ) and the object "his life (it)" (τὴν ψυχὴν αὐτοῦ, αὐτήν) in the two cola indicates that "shame" and "foolish countenance" form a hendiadys. The vague reference to shame gains some specificity in v. 23: "One may for the sake of shame make promises to a friend, and needlessly make him an enemy" (my translation).

The full meaning becomes apparent only when all three verses are understood together. Poverty may keep a man from sin *unless* for shame's sake he promises a friend economic help. The shame involved here is not that of being poor (i.e., a value connected to the abstraction of "poverty"), nor does it reflect a judgment that the poor have been punished by God. Rather, shame derives from the poor individual's inability to compete in the granting and receiving of gifts, that is, in the social interchange that defines a man. Such shame, argues Ben Sira, is one a man simply has to accept, secure in the honor that comes even to a poor wise man (though see above!). Failure to accept this situation (i.e., the accident of shame) can lead to shame of a different sort: real wickedness, the lie of vv. 24-26. Again, "lying" is not condemned in an abstract sense. The context demands that the lie be read as the false promise (v. 23) of economic assistance a poor man makes to maintain face (the foolish countenance of v. 22) with a friend, and therefore before society. Such distortion of the discourse upon which society rests is worse than thievery, though both bring ruin (20:26) and shame (5:14). Inability to walk the fine economic line between honor and shame may lead one into outright evil.

---

[36]This translation reads the Greek text. Skehan and DiLella argue that the Syriac of 20:19 provides a more original rendition (*Wisdom of Ben Sira*, 297, 298), but the point is not crucial to this discussion.

[37]Note that αἰσχύνη, "shame," appears three times in these few verses (22, 23, and 26) and is accompanied by ἀτιμία, "disgrace," in 20:26.

[38]Cf. Skehan and DiLella's very accurate translation of ἄφρονος προσώπου as "foolish posturing."

Speech, Associates, Sexuality and Household:
The Sage's Struggle for Control

In presenting Sanders's argument regarding caution, I suggested an unplumbed mine in his comment that "for Ben Sira, shame lurked everywhere...." Having elucidated the sage's economic status with reference to his values and to the mediating concepts of honor and shame, we are now in a position better to understand shame's omnipresence. Who could live in a situation where values clashed so intensely yet so subliminally, where status and security were so fragile, and not feel enormous anxiety? The natural response to such a situation is to exert control where one can, even if the arena of control has little effect on the actual pressure source. For Ben Sira, possible control existed over a man's speech, his associates, his sexual behavior, and his household. The first three, at least, were of concern in the wisdom tradition to which he was heir. In this book, however, they emerge as specific and interrelated responses to the problem of maintaining honor and avoiding shame.

Speech and Associates. The concern for proper speech is so widespread in the wisdom tradition (especially Proverbs and Job, but also elsewhere in the ancient Near East) as to be almost definitive of the tradition. Its function in the book of Sirach deserves an essay of its own. Here we shall consider but one salient passage: one of the more pragmatic counsels on fitting speech concerns behavior at banquets (32:1-13; G, 35:1-13). The setting itself indicates the high but perilous status of the sage.

His instruction includes the following (32:10; G, 35:10): "Before a hailstorm flashes lightning/and before shame (or, Gk., a shame-bound man), favor (חן, χάρις)." Again we find the two-sided sense of shame. Controlled speech yields proper shame in the sense of modesty and thus, implicitly, helps one avoid the costs of improper shame when dealing with superiors (cf. 20:27). The one other place associating grace or favor (חן, χάρις) with shame is 26:15, where shame also carries the meaning of modesty. However, the word here applies to the wife who is silent, disciplined and chaste, and so able to maintain a well-ordered home.[39] Control of speech is, in some

---

[39]The Greek understanding of this passage as referring to the wife in her "home" (οἰκίας) is not inappropriate, but it does not capture the double entendre of the Hebrew דביר בחזר. The דביר was the innermost room of the Temple of Solomon, the holy of holies. The Hebrew thus reminds us of P. Skehan's proposed "Temple structure" of the book of Proverbs, which literarily "builds" a cella for Woman Wisdom ("Wisdom's House," *Studies in Israelite Poetry and Wisdom,* CBQMS 1 [Washington, DC: Catholic Biblical

measure, control of one's economic destiny, though the context is gender-specific. With the wife, the *topoi* of controlled speech and controlled wealth merge with that of controlled sexuality. Female chastity is thus an overdetermined locus of two-sided shame.

A second category of control concerns dealing with associates. As seen above, dealing with the powerful is both dangerous and necessary. A similar discernment in the midst of ambiguity is necessary in relating to friends. "There is nothing so precious as a faithful friend" (6:16; cf. 6:14-17; 37:5-6), yet only "one in a thousand" should be trusted for counsel (6:6). Friends must be tested and, tragically, many will fail in time of trouble (6:7-13; 37:1-4). The same difficulties occur in exercising generosity. Although one should give alms and befriend the poor, peril exists in bringing a stranger into one's home, for many are the slanderers and the wicked who would make one a stranger there himself.

Sexuality. Poor Ben Sira! He can't trust anyone — rich or poor, stranger or neighbor — and yet he must deal with them all, each one capable and perhaps even desirous of bringing about his downfall before God and men. One of life's few relational dimensions he can control is his own sexuality. Regulation of sexual activity within the patriarchal family was always part of the Israelite effort to maintain social cohesion. But rarely if ever in Hebrew Scripture does one find such intense concern for *men's* personal sexual control. As we shall see, a man's ability to control his own sexual desires has ramifications both in private and public spheres.

The tenuousness of Ben Sira's socially acknowledged manliness manifests itself in a psychology of weakness with respect to the relationships he can control, most notably, those with women outside his family.[40] The fear of losing *self*-control can be seen in the poem on sexual relationships in 9:1-9. Sir 9:2 states: "Do not desire (δῷς τὴν ψυχήν σου) any woman, lest she trample down your 'high places'" (במתיך, ἰσχύν).[41] 9:3-9 provide a fairly complete list of female

---

Association, 1971], 27-45). The reference to the wife's (Wisdom's) "chosen cella" then segues nicely into the comparison of the wife's beauty with the Temple objects in 20:17-18.

[40] I thank Toni Craven for pointing out one other controllable group not mentioned but implied throughout his book, namely, the students Ben Sira teaches. It is difficult to contemplate what their lives may have been like!

[41] In Greek and emended Hebrew (see Skehan and DiLella, 216), 9:2a literally reads "do not give (תן אל/μὴ δῷς) your life (or self) to any woman." Both נפש and ψυχή can connote "desire" as well, however, which is the understanding demanded by the context. Sir 9:2a thus closely parallels 9:1a and so makes the apparent dittography of אל תקנא, which appears in both 9:1a and 9:2a quite

nemeses: strange woman, singing girl, virgin, prostitute, comely woman, and married woman. To an extent these warnings are clichés. The sexual unavailability of virgins and other men's wives was a long-standing stricture in Israel, while the wisdom tradition had a particular concern for prostitutes and the "strange woman." The rationale is consistent: such liaisons lead to loss of inheritance (9:6) and possibly death (9:9).

Ben Sira's list is, nonetheless, notable in at least two respects. One is its cultural specificity: as is evident elsewhere in the book, the sage regularly attends banquets, and it is here that entanglements with performers, as well as the arousal of reclining (and whatever else!) at table with married women, arise.[42] Inclusion of such warnings distinguishes the list from traditional biblical paranesis and gives it an existential thrust. Moreover, central to this teaching is not simply the possibility of disrepute and loss of fortune. The sage's ultimate concern is the very real possibility that a man's body — one of the few arenas not subject to external control — will betray him. "Through woman's beauty many have perished/and love of it burns like fire" (9:1bc).

Revision of the usual translations of 9:1a reinforces this reading. The standard rendering is "Do not be jealous (אל תקנא, μὴ ζήλου) of the wife of your bosom." The motivation is to avoid having her "learn evil against you" (9:1b). But how does not being jealous of your own wife relate to avoiding sexual contact with other women (vv. 3-9)? Efforts to providing an answer lead to disagreements about whether the אשה/γυνή in 9:2 refers to one's own wife (suggested by 9:1) or to the other women enumerated in 9:3-9. Following Box-Oesterley, Skehan and DiLella suggest that jealousy "might promote the realization of the thing feared."[43] Trenchard, conversely, argues that a groundlessly jealous husband might be discovered by his wife

---

understandable (see below for a translation of אל תקנא as "do not feel ardor"). In 9:2b, Skehan and DiLella render במה/ἰσχύν as "dignity." Again, the meaning is sexual as well as economic, and a literal translation of במה as a metaphorical reference to the various sorts of male "high places" seems quite appropriate.

[42] W. C. Trenchard, Ben Sira's View of Women (Chico, CA: Scholars Press 1982), 112, believes that 9:9a, "do not stretch out the elbow" with a married woman, implies more indecent activity than merely reclining at table (see below, n. 59). In 26:8-9, Ben Sira connects the harlotrous wife's shameless behavior to drunkenness. One of the few places that public drunkenness could occur for a woman would have been at banquets, which may explain 9:9. Conjoining these two passages yields a two-fold anxiety, first of a man confronted with lascivious but proscribed women; second of a man whose own wife might behave in a similar manner.

[43] Wisdom of Ben Sira, 218.

in his own infidelity, that is, she will be taught jealousy itself.[44]

Both interpretations stretch needlessly. The problem can be resolved by translating קנא/ζήλου not as "jealous of" but rather as "zealous, or passionate, for." Thus: "Do not feel passion for the wife of your bosom lest she learn evil against you." The "evil" is neither jealousy nor rebellion against unfair suspicion. Since the fundamental problem of 9:3-9 is the man's control of his desire when in proximity to women, the same is likely present in the opening verse. The issue is not, in the first instance at least, control of his wife's sexuality (as "do not be jealous" would suggest), but of his own. Thus, the evil a wife learns from her husband's ardor is sexual desire itself. The dangers are not spelled out, but at least two are plausible. First, she may find that other men also inspire her ardor. If, with Skehan and DiLella, we take Sir 26:10-12 to refer to the wife rather than the daughter,[45] we find Ben Sira capable of virtually pornographic lewdness in describing the sexual activity of an adulterous woman. Although his expression might seem extreme, his belief about the indiscriminate sexuality of women is typical among men in contemporary Mediterranean culture.[46]

The second negative outcome of a wife's learned passion is her potential to use her husband's desire to manipulate him, sexually, economically, or both. This possibility seems the dominant nuance. If strange women present snares and singers intrigues, if virgins bring penalties and harlots loss of inheritance, if comely women kindle fires and married women plunge one to destruction, of what might a sexually adept wife be capable? With women other than his wife, the admonition is one of avoidance. The wife presents the greatest problem, and hence heads the list, precisely because one cannot

---

[44]*Ben Sira's View of Women*, 30.

[45]Although θυγάτηρ, "daughter," appears in 26:10, the context describes wives. Because the identical opening words appear in 42:10, where the subject is daughters ("keep a strict watch on..."), Skehan and DiLella argue that the θυγάτηρ from the latter passage has been mistakenly transposed into 26:10. Trenchard, however, suggests a rearrangement of the whole section on women in 25:13-26:18, such that the passage would move from a treatment of the good wife to the bad wife, and end with the daughter, in a manner similar to 42:9-14 (*Ben Sira's View of Women*, 10-11, 140-141). Thus, he retains the reference to the daughter in 26:10. I prefer the former argument, for the following additional reasons. First, the reference to the "impudent eye" in 26:11a reiterates the "eyes/eyelids" of the harlotrous wife in 26:9. Second, the sexual activity rather obscenely described in 26:12 is a representation of the harlotry mentioned in 26:9. Third, the verb πλημμελέω in 26:11 ("sin against you") is the same as that in 23:23, where the offender is clearly a woman who commits adultery.

[46]See Delaney ("Seeds of Honor," 41), whose description of male views of women's indiscriminate "openness" to sex is vividly represented by Sir 26:12.

avoid her. By a terrible twist of fate, one might lose control of oneself *and* lose control of this signal possession in one weak moment.

Given this interpretation, 9:2 provides a logical transition from consideration of one's wife to that of other women. Although the Hebrew Ms A reading of 9:2a, אל תחקן, may be a secondary dittography from 9:1a (cf. the Greek of 9:2a, μὴ δῷς = אל תחן), it is consistent with the whole passage. Just as one should not feel ardor for one's wife, neither should one feel ardor for these other sorts. While the wife may learn evil (i.e., sexual desire), the others may also find one's "high places" good grounds for stomping. Loss of fortune may well be the result of any of these relationships, but the sage has even more to worry about. With loss of fortune comes public loss of face. The shame becomes as much a motivational factor as the threat of economic loss although, as we have already seen, the two are finally for Ben Sira inseparable.

Unlike the case of loans and surety, however, the problem with women does not pose a conflict of values. Indeed, the sage's radical concern for self-control with respect to women is likely a psychological defense against the bifurcation of values produced by the extreme lack of control he experiences in the other areas of his life. But anxiety breeds anxiety, and precisely where there are no arbitrary external forces, where everything is "in his control," the uncontrollable workings of his own body threaten self-betrayal.

Household. There is one final arena in which Ben Sira seeks to overcome the random and powerful mechanisms which threaten both his material well-being and his values. This lies in the management of his personal possessions, his money, wife, children, slaves, land, and livestock, in sum, his household (cf. 7:19-28; 20:28). Two features of the household are of particular interest to the present discussion: the connection of the wife to money and shame, and Ben Sira's concern for controlling his daughters.

Women, money and shame. It is obvious that the sage has an idealized notion of a good wife's benefits. Along with a man's loyal friends, she is among the premier blessings for those who fear the Lord (6:14-17; 7:18-19; 25:1; 40:23). If she meets the ideals of beauty, prudence, chastity and disciplined speech, her husband will double his years with fat on his bones (25:8a; 26:1-4, 13-18; 36:21-26). In this view, even poverty is acceptable in the presence of her good heart and cheerful (Hebrew: "radiant") countenance (26:4). However, just as Ben Sira's statements about the acceptability of poverty in the name of higher values mask real ambivalence in a man whose society honors the wealthy, so his romantic portrayal of wedded bliss in the midst of poverty is problematic. The danger of a bad wife, and thus of losing control of his household — and loss of face in public — haunts Ben Sira as much as the other anxiety-producing associations he must maintain.

To appreciate the force of his problem, we begin by deromanticizing his view of the marital relationship which is promulgated by many English translations.

1. A good wife — congratulations to her husband!
   the number of his days will be doubled.
2. An industrious wife will bring fatness to her husband,
   and the years of his life she will gladden.
3. A good wife is a good portion
   in the share assigned to one who fears the Lord.
4. Be he rich or poor — a good heart (καρδία ἀγαθή),
   and at all times an upbeat appearance (πρόσωπον ἱλαρόν).
   (26:1-4, my translation)

This translation's emphasis contrasts with the usual renditions which find here an appeal to wedded bliss that will keep one content even in poverty. First, the translation of אשרי, μακάριος as "congratulations" rather than "happy" draws attention to the public nature of the husband's status.[47] The point is not that he feels internally happy but that he has attained an honor worthy of societal notice. Second, retaining the Hebrew Ms C reading in 26:2a (חדש, make fat) instead of the Greek's εὐφραίνει (be cheered) emphasizes the material gains the husband hopes to have from his אשת חיל (cf. Prov 31:10-31), as does the literal translation of מנה, μερὶς // חלק as "portion" and "share" in 26:3. Third, and perhaps the most striking revision of usual translational nuances, is my rendition of καρδία ἀγαθή as "good heart" in v. 4. The RSV is more typical: "Whether rich or poor, his heart is glad, and at all times his face is cheerful." As with the usual "happy" in v. 1, this translation suggests that the husband's feelings (his "glad heart") count most. There is, however, no basis for translating ἀγαθή as "glad" rather than "good" in the sense of "virtuous." Indeed, in both Hebrew and Greek, the same word describes the wife in vv. 1 and 3. The whole passage directly recalls 13:24-26a:

> Riches are good (טוב, ἀγαθός) when there is no sin,
> but evil is poverty in an insolent mouth.

---

[47] Cf. D. Schmidt, "Congratulations, You Poor!" *The Fourth R* 3:2 (1990): 13-14.

A man's heart (לב, καρδία) changes his face (פניו, πρόσωπον),
whether for good (מוב, ἀγαθά) or for evil.
The sign of a good heart is a radiant face (פנים אורים, πρόσωπον
ἱλαρόν).

There can be no question, then, that the καρδία ἀγαθή of 26:4a
concerns goodness or evil, not gladness. This stich has nothing to
do with the bliss of marriage overcoming poverty. Rather, it reiterates Ben Sira's point that the good may experience poverty. Similarly, as 13:26a indicates, the "radiance" in 26:4b (πρόσωπον ἱλαρόν)
does not concern personal happiness brought about by marital
affection. Rather, it is the sign *to others in the society* that, even
though "poverty is evil in the mouth of the insolent," one is nonetheless virtuous. Hence my somewhat colloquial translation of
πρόσωπον ἱλαρόν in 26:4 as "upbeat appearance."

The fourth change from the usual translations occurs in v. 4,
where I note that the Greek text (the Hebrew is lacking) does not
specify the owner of either the good heart or the upbeat appearance.
Although the husband may be implied by the masculine inflection of
the immediately preceding adjectives (πλουσίου, πτωχοῦ), the spare-
ness of expression allows for the possibility that it is the *wife's*
countenance that retains honorable radiance in the face of poverty,
secure in the knowledge that *her* heart is good. Such an understanding suggests that Ben Sira's society was not unfamiliar with
the practice, reported by anthropologist John Davis, of poor wives
engaging in sex with wealthy men in order to support their families.
Indeed, even when actual adultery does not occur, there is a tendency to suspect that, when a man cannot support his family in the
usual manner, his wife and daughters may not be chaste in the
usual manner.[48] As we have seen, appearance can be as important
as reality in the game of honor. There is little doubt that Ben Sira
would prefer poverty to an unchaste wife. But as 26:4 suggests, an
"upbeat appearance" — whether of husband or wife — is the first
guardian against loss of honor.

If love means little for the "happiness" a woman brings to her
husband, sexual and economic control means everything. Ideally, a
good wife will help ensure her husband's prosperity. Yet Ben Sira
can imagine any number of less-than-ideal situations, and all
concern loss of household control.

In the first place, a man may not find (or perhaps not even

---

[48]*People of the Mediterranean*, 92.

seek?) what the sage considers to be "his richest treasure" (36:29).[49]
"A vineyard with no hedge will be overrun/and a man with no wife
becomes a homeless wanderer," part of "an armed band that skips
from city to city" (36:30-31). Although Ben Sira offers this
instruction in hopes of preventing his students from losing status
and inheritance, it strikes as well a note of personal unease that is
also heard in his threats to adulterous men in 23:18-21. Because
darkness is such an effective cover for this sinner (v. 18), the sage
has to make a rather desperate recourse to "the eyes of the Lord" (vv.
19-20) as the means of apprehension. The issue underlying both
passages is this: if the next generation does not accept the values of
the old, it might be this sage's own property that gets plundered or
his own women shamed. Moreover, he might face a whole new generation of impoverished con artists testing his values of generosity
and loyalty! What better way to prevent such a situation than to
shepherd his charges inside the marital fence and so gird them with
the same strictures of honor and shame that he himself wears.

The foregoing does not suggest that Ben Sira invented this
plan for his own self-protection. Marriage was an expected part of
adult male status. But de-mystifying the adult male anxiety that
this teaching only barely conceals helps to explain the fears that
roar back when the marital cure for the dangerous shame of root-
lessness produces its own potential for shame. One of the most
obvious problems is an adulterous wife.

Having described the inevitable detection and shame of the
unfaithful husband, in 23:22-26 Ben Sira turns to the wife.

> So also with the woman who is unfaithful to her husband
> and offers as heir her son by a stranger.
> First, she has disobeyed the law of the Most High,
> second, she has wronged her husband;
> Third, in her wanton adultery
> she has raised up children by another man.
> Such a woman will be dragged before the assembly,
> and her punishment will extend to her children;
> Her children will not take root;
> her branches will not bring forth fruit.
> She will leave an accursed memory;
> her disgrace will never be blotted out.

---

[49]The verse numbers indicated for 36:29 and 36:30-31, just below, are from
Skehan and DiLella. The manuscripts are more confused here than usual,
however; thus, e.g., the RSV and the REB enumerate 36:29-30 as 24-26.

As in the immediately preceding teaching against male adultery, here lies an implicit assumption that the woman might actually get away with her action. If she can get to the point of "offering as heir" her son by a stranger, then she has succeeded in undetected adultery. The threats against her and her children ring as hollow as they do loud; they are punishments God must inflict, not society.

But what social reality lies behind this rhetoric? Does the wife's "offering" a stranger's child imply that her husband might "accept" it? Although the potential punishment falls on the wife and her children, one must recall that Ben Sira's teachings in general are directed toward men. Thus the possibility, or even the probability, stands that he is warning men not to collude with their wives in such an affair. But why would such a warning be necessary? Two possibilities, both quite remarkable, emerge. First, Trenchard (following Frankenberg) suggests that the passage may reflect a common practice in which a childless wife seeks to produce an heir for the household, a practice condemned by Ben Sira though accepted by most people in his society.[50] This interpretation is the most straightforward reading of the text, which does not present a woman sneaking about like the adulterous man (23:15) but rather openly offering her extramarital issue as heir. The difficulty is that, given what we know about social strictures in both the ancient and contemporary Mediterranean worlds, it is difficult to imagine widespread acceptance of such a practice by the heads of patriarchal families.

The issue is not one of inheritance laws per se. As Trenchard notes, Israelite fathers did adopt as heirs whomever they chose, regardless of biological relationship. But he cites no instances of intentional surrogate fathering, and there is a strong constraint against its being an accepted practice: that of the typical belief in monogenesis, of only one active *and male* principle in fertility. Carol Delaney's field work points to the tight interweaving in Mediterranean culture of belief in monogenesis (a single principle of procreation), monotheism (a single principle of creation), and the requirement that a woman be able to "guarantee the seed of a particular man" (that is, be a virgin at marriage and faithful thereafter). Ben Sira's citation of the wife's disobedience to the "law of the Most High" preceding "an offense against her husband" (23:23) is thus quite predictable. Delaney further argues that, in this context, "the honor/shame complex is not just a function of male dominance and authority. ... Rather it is a distinctive system in which power,

---

[50]*Ben Sira's View of Women*, 99-102.

sex, and the sacred are interrelated and seen to be rooted in the verities of biology."[51]

Delaney's work would lead us to suspect, *contra* Trenchard, that Ben Sira's instruction represents less a voice in the wilderness than the roar of his society. To comprehend his extreme rhetoric on what should be an obvious point, one must imagine a situation so extreme as to force men, in a culturally atypical way, to accept strangers' sons as heirs. A possible scenario is that suggested above in our discussion of 26:4, namely, that the wives of poor men engage in sexual activity with wealthy patrons in order to help support their families. The issue here not would be the desire of childless women for heirs, but the shameful necessity for a man — in order to avoid shame! — to accept as legitimate the fruit of his wife's labor for another.

A background of financial instability also seems to lie behind Ben Sira's excoriations of the evil wife in 25:13-26. This passage, too, must first be de-romanticized. 25:13 begins: "Worst of all wounds is that of the heart, worst of all evils is that of a woman." It is doubtful that by "the wound of the heart" Ben Sira means the pain of a broken relationship. His many uses of the "heart" metaphor refer either to the heart's capacity as the organ of choice or, less often, as the source of feelings such as gladness, fear or grief, but never "love" in our modern romantic terms. The "wound of the heart" caused by a woman, then, is the loss of "happiness" in the sense described above; it is the loss of the honor and the attendant benefits his culture tells him marital status should confer.

A similar imprecation against the wrath of enemies appears in the next verse. Although at first glance, 25:14 seems to take the burden off women by suggesting there might be something on a par with women's wickedness, this is not the import of the reference to enemies. Raymond van Leeuwen's study of Proverbs 25-27 shows how the introduction to a proverb-poem can mention a topic other than the one to which the passage is devoted.[52] This seemingly extraneous reference is not intended to call attention to itself, but rather to provide another example of or analogue to the main topic in order to reinforce the poet's point. Thus, the reference to the enemy's vengeance, following directly the introduction of the main theme, does not ameliorate the attack on women's wickedness but rather shows how bad it really is: it incorporates, as it were, all the

---

[51]"Seeds of Honor," 45; cf. 39.
[52]*Context and Meaning in Proverbs 25-27*, SBLDS 96 (Atlanta: Scholars Press, 1988). An example would be Prov 26:2 in the context of 26:1-12.

evil one associates with enemies. And, as the book asserts elsewhere, the danger from enemies lies in their ability, often by slander, to cause the loss of honor and wealth (5:13-6:1; 28:13-26; 51:2, 5-6).

The connection of shame with failure to control one's women and money gains particular focus in 25:21-22 — "Stumble not through a woman's beauty/nor be greedy for her wealth; Harsh is the slavery, great is the shame/when a wife supports her husband." Thus, to "marry well" means, for a man, to "marry down," a situation Ortner associates with increased hostility towards women.[53] In the next verse, two more generally descriptive phrases refer to the woman who causes her husband personal and social disability: she is the "evil wife" and the "one who does not make her husband happy." Sir 25:26 reinforces the message: "If she does not walk by your side, cut her away from your flesh." Skehan and DiLella add "with a bill of divorce" to the end of the verse.[54] Based on the Gen 2:24 allusion to wife and husband as "one flesh," divorce is certainly to be understood here. But "one flesh" also implies, specifically, an exclusive *sexual* relationship. Thus, the particular way in which the wife has not walked by her husband's side is also suggested. A husband who cannot control his wife will suffer shame, and a woman's control of her own resources makes the husband's task more difficult.

Ben Sira authorizes his teaching about women in this context with 25:24-25. Verse 24 reads: "From woman is the beginning of sin, and because of her, we all die." Given the setting of this verse in a poem about evil wives, Levison argues that we should not interpret a reference to Eve, but rather more narrowly, to those offensive real women one is in danger of marrying.[55] I prefer to see this as a case of "both-and" rather than "either-or". The author is certainly concerned with evil wives, but he is also, at this point, concerned to justify his teaching. The skillful double entendre of 25:24, in which one cannot help but hear an allusion to Genesis 3, succinctly both

---

[53]"Virgin and the State," 32. Ortner's analysis, applied to Ben Sira, puts women in an excruciating double-bind. On the one hand, having a wealthier wife who supports you is a bad thing, in Ben Sira's view. On the other hand, if his society is indeed one like Ortner describes, in which a family's virgin women are the ticket to social advancement through marriage, then there is also a generalized hostility to women because of their mediating position. In Ortner's analysis, "female purity ... is oriented toward an ideal and generally unattainable status. The unattainability may in turn account for some of the sadism and anger toward women expressed in these purity patterns, for the women are representing the over-classes themselves."
[54]*Wisdom of Ben Sira*, 344, 349.
[55]"Is Eve to Blame? A Contextual Analysis of Sirach 25:24," *CBQ* 47 (1985):

re-states and authorizes his point.

Sir 25:25 (only in Greek) provides another mode of authorization, employing in classic wisdom style a proverbial expression as a simile that reinforces the paralleled admonition: "Allow water no outlet, nor let an evil wife give the orders in your house (παρρησίαν)." Again, a man's control of his household, both sexually and economically, is at stake. The "water" in 25:25a recalls most directly the poem on marital fidelity in Prov 5:15-19, where the wife's sexuality is imaged as water in a cistern//flowing water in a well. Verse 25b shifts the focus to economics. The only other use of παρρησι- ("freedom of speech") occurs in 6:11, where, in verbal form, it refers to the unacceptable authority a (false) friend assumes in giving orders to the household of the prosperous.[56] Thus, here again, the problem with wives parallels the problem with friends: good ones are very good; but the effort to find a good one, while avoiding those who will bring shame and economic ruin, is a source of anxious desperation. Critical in each case is a man's capacity to control his own household.[57]

Ben Sira's advice in 33:20-24 (G, 30:28-32) is not, then, unexpected:

20 Let neither son nor wife nor kin nor neighbor
   have power over you while you live.
   Do not give your goods to another
   lest you must turn and entreat his favor.
21 While you are still alive and have breath in you,
   do not let any one take your place.
22 Better to have your sons entreat you
   than that you should look to the hands of your sons.
23 Stay in charge (עליון היה, γίνου ὑπεράγων) of all your affairs,
   and bring no stain (מם, μῶμον) upon your honor (כבד, δόξῃ).
24 When your few days of life reach their limit,
   at the time of death, distribute your inheritance.
   (my translation)

Verse 23, which seems particularly to have the wife in mind, once again interweaves sex and money. The admonition to "bring no stain

---

617-23.
[56]Παρρησίαν occurs only in the Sinaiticus and Alexandrinus of 25:25. The important Vaticanus reads ἐξουσίαν, "authority" or "resources." Either, indeed both, of these connotations reinforces the point.
[57]In the situation of dowry marriage apparently envisioned in 25:21-22, the loss of control might come not only to the wife, but also to her family who, if we may extrapolate from the evidence of some late medieval cities, may have claimed the right to manage the dotal fund. Cf. Hughes, "Brideprice to Dowry," 284.

upon your honor (or glory!)," in the context of economic instruction, implies "keep control of your financial resources." The undertone of sexual control, however, can be seen by comparison with 47:19-20. The one person Ben Sira accuses of bringing a "stain upon his honor" is none other than Solomon, who laid his loins beside women and gave them power over him (cf. Prov 31:3). Just in case we missed this point, the Greek translator provides another clue in the preceding stich (23a), with ὑπεράγων. The only other use of this term appears in 36:24, which asserts that a good wife is "chief (ὑπεράγει) over all the yearning (ἐπιθυμίαν) of man." Ἐπιθυμία can be "lust" as well as "yearning," and lust is a certain path to losing control of one's affairs and possessions. A good wife may provide a proper outlet for one's lust, but even here danger lurks. Our present text puts the sage's priorities in order: γίνου ὑπεράγων!

The last major pericope that defines shame in terms of control over women and wealth appears in the summary teachings of 41:14-42:8. Immediately preceding this material, Ben Sira's meditation on death concludes:

> The human body is a fleeting thing,
> but a virtuous name will never be annihilated.
> Have respect for your name, for it will stand by you
> more than thousands of precious treasures;
> The good things of life last a number of days,
> but a good name, for days without number. (41:1-13)

As Sanders has demonstrated, having a good name is identical with having avoided shame. Thus, 41:14-42:8 offers summary remarks on how to achieve that good name with a two-stanza poem on proper and improper shame. Again the connection of women and economics is plain. Following the introduction in 41:14-16, the stanza on proper shame can be divided into two sub-units, 41:17-19a and 41:19b-23. The first lists the shame one should avoid in terms of those who will bring it to judgment. It begins, strikingly, with "be ashamed of fornication before your father or mother." Shameful behavior is catalogued in the second sub-unit. Concern for women and wealth predominates, with particular focus on the key values of avoiding πορνεία and exercising generosity.

41:19b [Be ashamed] of breaking an oath or agreement,
    and of stretching your elbow at dinner;[58]

---

[58]"Stretching one's elbow" (מטה אציל) may refer merely to poor dining etiquette (so Skehan and DiLella, *Wisdom of Ben Sira*, 481). However, as Trenchard observes (*Ben Sira's View of Women*, 112), the same phrase occurs in Sir 9:9a in the admonition not to "stretch out the elbow with a married woman." The

       of refusing to give when asked,
21a and of rebuffing your own kin;
  b of defrauding another of his appointed share,
20a and of failing to return a greeting;
21c of gazing at a man's wife,
20b and of entertaining thoughts about another woman;
  22 of trifling with a servant girl of yours,
       and of violating her bed;
       of using harsh words with friends,
       and of following up your gift with an insult....[59]

In the last item (41:23), Ben Sira interjects another central concern, that of proper speech: "of repeating what you hear, and of betraying any secret."

     The second stanza lists those things one should not be ashamed of, "lest you sin to save face" (42:1e). A religious allusion appears prominently at the outset, and the unit concludes with a reference to proper speech. The rest is devoted to controlling of one's resources. The sage should not be ashamed

2 of the law of the Most High and his precepts,
    and of justice to acquit the ungodly;
3 of sharing the expenses of a business or a journey,
    and of dividing an inheritance or property;
4 of accuracy with scales and balances,
    and of tested measures and weights;
    and of acquiring much or little;
5 of bargaining in dealing with a merchant;
    and of constant training of children,
    and of beating the back of an evil servant (עבד רע);
6 Upon an evil (foolish?) wife, a seal![60]
    and upon a place of many hands, a lock!
7 Upon a place where you deposit, a number!
    and what you give and take — all in writing!
8 of chastisement for the silly and the foolish,
    and for the tottering old person occupied with immorality.

---

issue of illicit sexuality thus lurks in the background of 41:19, whether or not the connotation of lasciviousness inheres in the phrase itself.
[59]Following Skehan and DiLella, the order of the cola in the translation follows the Hebrew Ms M; the numbering is from G, which has jumbled the order (*Wisdom of Ben Sira*, 478).
[60]In 42:2-5 and 8, I follow Skehan and DiLella. In 42:6, 7, however, the Hebrew word order changes; thus, the English syntax should not, as theirs does, simply repeat that of 42:2-5 and 8. See below on a possible wordplay in these verses.

The Greek of 42:5c-6 contains a fascinating wordplay. Whether it stems from Ben Sira himself or enters in only in his grandson's translation is open to debate. The Jerusalem sage certainly knew Greek, however, and it is not impossible that is was he who verbally played with his human possessions. Verse 5c refers to an evil male servant (οἰκέτε πονερῷ). In v. 6a, it is the wife who is evil (γυναικὶ πονερῷ),[61] and thus requires a good seal (καλὸν σφραγίς). Pomeroy has pointed out, however, that Sphragis was a common name for female slaves.[62] Thus, to maintain the double entendre introduced by the reference to the male slave in v. 5c, we should read in 6a: "an evil wife requires a good Sphragis." For what purpose? The second colon gives a clue. "Where there are many hands, lock things up" could suggest that the wife's evil consists of embezzling from the household accounts. Thus, the σφραγίς could be a literal seal on the money box, or it could be a female slave faithful to her master, who would report on her mistress. The language of hands, seals and locks also carries with it strong sexual connotations. In the Song of Songs, the woman is described as "a garden locked, a fountain sealed" (4:12). In her own romantic reverie, the woman imagines:

My beloved put his hand to the latch....
I arose to open to my beloved,
and my hands dripped with myrrh,
my fingers with liquid myrrh,
upon the handles of the bolt. (5:4-5)

If the husband is concerned to seal his wife off from "many hands," a watchful Sphragis could do the trick. Alternatively, a Sphragis who is just a little too good to the husband might induce a wife to faithfulness. We note, of course, that earlier in this very poem Ben Sira remonstrates against liaisons with female servants!

In sum, the emphasis on control of sex and of money in this summary teaching on shame reinforces the importance, and the essential interconnectedness, of these two issues. Whether or not the Jerusalem sage is himself responsible for the wordplay on seals and slaves, this example does not stand alone; his work includes many such verbal compressions of the sex-money control issue. Indeed, it becomes difficult to know whether he creates them as a

---

[61]There is variance in the Hebrew manuscripts with respect to the adjective used to describe the woman. In Ms Bixt, רעה corresponds to the Greek. In M, it has been restored by Strugnell to read ממש[וטה], "woman who plays the fool," picking up the root from Ms Bmg's מטשה ("Notes and Queries on 'The Ben Sira Scroll from Masada," ErIsr 9 [1969]: 109-19). If the wordplay is to be attributed to Ben Sira, רעה would presumably be the original reading.
[62]Women in Hellenistic Egypt (New York: Schocken, 1984), 129.

matter of conscious artistry, or whether, in his own mind, he is incapable of separating the two realms.

Daughters. There is but one further topic dealing with household control: Ben Sira's rather extreme commentary on controlling the sexuality of one's daughters. Three main passages concern daughters. The first, 7:24-25, occurs within a common-sense list of admonitions (7:18-28) on dealing with close associates, that is, one's household and friends. On the surface, the advice about daughters is no worse than patriarchal norms: be concerned for their chastity, and marry them to sensible men. But the virulence observed in other remarks about women's sexuality is also evident here. The admonition to guard their chastity is expressed with surprising baldness, literally, "guard their flesh" (שאר, σώματι).

The second stich of 7:24 reads "do not let your face shine towards them." This phrase may simply advise fathers not to indulge their daughters.[63] In typical Mediterranean family arrangements, however, there is "an unusual absention of Mediterranean males generally from domestic affairs" and "a rigid spatial and behavioral segregation of the sexes."[64] Thus, there would have been little opportunity for such paternal indulgence. Moreover, as discussed above, elsewhere a "shining face" is the sign not of happy feelings but of a virtuous heart (13:25-26; 26:4; 35:9). Since the actions of children, virtuous or otherwise, advert to their parents, we should probably read our present stich to mean something like "do not count on your daughters' capacity to bring you honor."

A second passage, 22:3-6, reinforces this connotation. While "it is a disgrace to be the father of an undisciplined son," the mere "birth of a daughter is a loss." Ben Sira at one point refers to the possibility of a "sensible daughter" (v. 4a), but, if Trenchard is correct, he defines "sensible" here in the perversely narrow sense of "faithful to her husband."[65] Unlike the adulterous woman of 23:22-26, whom Ben Sira fears his daughter will emulate (43:10b), the sensible daughter will "receive"[66] her husband, and not repudiate him in acts of adultery. The best one can hope for is the relief of

---

[63]So Skehan and DiLella, *Wisdom of Ben Sira,* 203.
[64]Gilmore, "Introduction," 14.
[65]*Ben Sira's View of Women,* 138.
[66]The verb is κληρονομήσει, which literally means "obtain a portion, inherit." Trenchard notes, however, its frequent metaphorical and/or general uses as "acquire, obtain, receive" (ibid., 292). I would not reject, as he does, a possible reading of "obtain her husband." This, too, is part of the sage's worry (42:9c). Whether the issue is "obtaining" or "receiving," however, the root

anxiety that marrying off a daughter will bring (7:25), but even then a father may still be shamed by her licentiousness (22:5).

The fullness of Ben Sira's anxiety about daughters comes to expression in 42:9-14. He is robbed of sleep, worrying

> lest in her youth she remain unmarried,
> or when she is married, lest she be childless;
> While unmarried, lest she be defiled
> or lest she prove unfaithful to her husband;
> lest she become pregnant in her father's house,
> or be sterile in that of her husband. (42:9c-10)

This concern immediately narrows, however, in 42:11-14 to the question of the daughter's sexual misconduct. The father is instructed to keep a strict watch on an "impudent daughter," lest he be shamed before the people; not to allow windows in her room, lest she display her beauty before men; and not to let her talk with married women, lest she learn about sexuality. This last point is reinforced by a proverb: "[Let her not] spend her time among married women; for just as moths come from garments, so a woman's wickedness comes from a woman" (42:12b-13).

In context, "woman's wickedness" must refer to woman's sexuality.[67] However, because of the proverb (14:13a), the point moves from the particular focus on what virgin daughters will learn from married women (14:12b) to the more universal concern about goodness and evil (14:13b). Ben Sira carries through on this level in the next stich (42:14a): "Better a man's wickedness than a woman's goodness." He then returns to his teaching about daughters: "And a daughter causes fear regarding disgrace more than a son."[68] Although this final line is a rather awkward reversion to the daughter-*topos*, it marks clearly the structure of Ben Sira's thinking about goodness and evil: these are inherently tied to the "shame of women," that is, their sexuality.

Two broader points can be made about this pericope. The first concerns its position in the book of Sirach as a whole; the second regards the significance of daughters in light of Mediterranean anthropology. Ben Sira's poem on the two kinds of shame in 41:14-42:8, following the reference to a "good name" in 41:13, provides a well-integrated summary of his book's moral instruction. Appropri-

---

problem of female sexual purity is the same.
[67]So Trenchard in ibid., 158.
[68]This is Trenchard's translation of a textually problematic verse (ibid., 147). Very different translations are possible, but his arguments seem to me

ately, then, this poem stands almost — but not quite! — immediately
preceding what may be considered the book's two-fold finale, the
praise of Yahweh (42:15-43:33) and the praise of famous men (44:1-
50:21). But one small pericope is unaccounted for: the poem on
daughters in 42:9-14 intercedes between the shame poem and the
Yahweh-hymn. Is this an "afterthought"[69] in an otherwise carefully
constructed text? I propose that it is anything but. Occurring
immediately after the summary lesson on shame, and just before
Ben Sira "turns up the music" to praise the works of the Lord and
the everlasting name wisdom bestows, the passage indicates one
last time the most dangerous obstacle on a man's path to honor/
glory. It is as if, in Ben Sira's drive to master life amid anxiety and
arbitrary reversals of fortune, women — especially as sexual beings
— epitomize all that is potentially out of control.

Why, then, does he move so directly and easily from instruction about *daughters* in particular to women in general in 42:12-14?
The anthropologist's perspective sheds light here. First, students of
the Bible, and of Ben Sira in particular, generally recognize that each
family member is affected by the shameful acts of another. What we
have often failed to see, or at least to articulate, is the enormous
reality of shame in Mediterranean culture. Shame is not a personal
feeling of failure that may be potent today but diminished tomorrow.
It is, rather, a culturally defined prison which affects one's abilities
to relate as an equal to others; indeed, it is a stigma that may even
attach to the next generation.[70]

This description of shame applies to all those arenas of a
man's life where he stands to lose control, whether of wealth,
speech, wives, sons, or daughters. He can learn to control himself,
however, and his wives and sons both stand to gain from adopting
the ideology of shame (security of marital status and children, and
inheritance, respectively). Daughters, however, are a wild card. As
his property, he is honor-bound to prevent encroachment on them;
as women, they share the "woman's wickedness" of indiscriminate
sexual inclination; unmarried, they have no stake in regulating their
own honor;[71] awakened to their own sexuality in marriage, they

---

persuasive.
[69]So Sanders, "Ben Sira's Ethics of Caution," 13.
[70]Schneider and Schneider, *Culture and Political Economy*, 87.
[71]Under normal circumstances, a father ought to be able to assume that his
daughter will be able to discern her own future with sufficient clarity that she
will accept her restrictions as in her own interest (cf. J. Schneider, "Of
Vigilance and Virgins," 20; and Delaney, "Seeds of Honor," 42). Whether Ben
Sira's anxiety on this point results from an extreme view of women's un-

may have even less restraint. Thus, the father of a daughter has an almost impossible task. The danger goes far beyond the economic loss posed by a nonvirginal and thus unmarriageable daughter, whom her father will have to support. Writing about contemporary Sicily, the Schneiders state:

> The loss of a daughter's virginity spelled failure of the family in two ways. First, by assuming the complicity of the woman, the community suspected her of treason, of aiding and abetting the expansionist policy of a competing family, and of subvert-ing the interests of the group to which she owed allegiance. Thus, the solidarity of the family — its capacity to control and protect its members — was brought into question. Second, the outsider who successfully attacked the sanctity of the family by violating one of its women was, in effect, publicly and most dramatically proclaiming his disregard for the honor and dignity of its men. For these men faced with dishonor there were few remedies.[72]

Throughout the contemporary Mediterranean, at least where more traditional values shine through the veneer of Catholic teaching, it is daughters (not mothers) who fulfill the role of the family's "reposi-tories of honor."[73] This is no less true for our sage. An adulterous wife can be divorced, but a sexually deviant daughter has no place to go but home. She is an everlasting blot on her father's name, which is all, in the sage's view, a man has to live for.

Conclusions

The question with which I opened this essay was that of the intellectual-affective process by which Ben Sira encoded women. Through the use of insights gained from contemporary Mediter-raneanists' study of the honor-shame complex and its relationship to other cultural values, I have attempted to get beyond the mere identification of misogyny to analyze the form of patriarchy evidenced in this book. Rather than reading for direct evidence of women's roles, I have read for evidence of females' function as part of the cultural symbol system embodied in the concepts of honor and shame.

---

restrainable lust (cf. 26:9-12) or from the changing social conditions created by a newly profound Hellenistic influence needs further consideration.
[72]*Culture and Political Economy*, 90.
[73]Ibid., 90, 96.

There are, I believe, two major gains from this analysis: first is the recognition of Ben Sira's consistent link between sexual and economic issues; second is an enhanced ability to relate the system of signs which constitutes the text to that of its cultural milieu. Repeatedly, the topics of sex and money are joined, occasionally with language so condensed that it is hard to determine which is the referent (if not both). The issue is not that "woman has been reduced to chattel," but rather that both money and women are overdetermined symbols of male honor, which has to do, in this case at least, with the need for external signs of control: they are the sigla of manliness. Such signs have become the *sine qua non* of contemporary Mediterranean anthropology. Consequently, we might be able to understand Ben Sira's shrill, sometimes virulent, instructions on women to be no more than an expression of the culture in which he lives (though we have now specified the nature of that culture further than previously has been done).

If we consider the sage's particular historical setting, however, further reflections arise. It is worth asking, for example, whether stress generated by the profound cultural, political, and ultimately religious flux of Ben Sira's day augmented the coinage of honor and shame. This analysis suggests such might be the case. Two forces seem to have been at work. One is the loss of control that the sage experienced in the larger social realm, which may have translated into an obsession for control in the closer sphere, specifically his sexuality and his household. The second is the conflict of values which social stress exacerbates.

It is true that no person or society ever operates with full integrity in terms of values; it is rare even for a society's members to become conscious enough of value discrepancies to apply what has become known as "situational ethics." Rather, what seems to be a universal human determination to believe in an orderly world usually shields us from noticing its moral disorder. Such a mind-set may be even firmer in Mediterranean culture where the orientation toward valuing appearance over "reality" has been elevated to a high art. The writings of Ben Sira manifest anxiety precisely on this point. He fears the deception of appearances, while at the same time he teaches the necessity of maintaining face. Moreover, he expresses with existential clarity the tangle in which a man can ensnare himself as he attempts to maintain both face and fortune. Although such tensions always exist in a "shame-culture," it is hard to ignore the possibility that the extremely unsettled conditions of Ben Sira's time exacerbated the *awareness* of such value discrepancies.

The intensity of this awareness may be seen in the fact that the author is not just worried about his honor before men, but his glory before God, the two facets of כבד, δόξα uniting in the concern for his "name." When confronted with the consciousness of a lack of integrity that cannot be easily suppressed, humans turn to the realm of symbols to work out the tension and ambiguity caused by such a state. And, in a shame-culture, the symbol most readily available to bear the load is "woman." Whether one's own wife or another's, a daughter or a prostitute, this sage perceives that women in all their roles threaten a man's ability to control not only his possessions, but his very self and thus, ultimately the memory of his name before God and eternity.

Philo's Portrayal of Women — Hebraic or Hellenic?[1]

Judith Romney Wegner

Introduction

In 1982, with the field of women's studies still in its infancy and historical data on the position of women in the ancient world still largely in the hunting-and-gathering phase, I collected a representative selection of Philonic statements about "women" and "female" attributes. Classifying them in a somewhat *ad hoc* fashion, I made a few comparisons with classical Greek texts on the one hand and rabbinic texts on the other, and then asked whether one could "discern either specifically Greek or specifically Jewish influences" on Philo's attitudes toward women. Could one state definitively that Philo's depiction of women in his scriptural exegesis owed more to his Jewish roots or to his Alexandrian Hellenistic environment? Or does one find features common to all patriarchal cultures, which tend to produce similar results for the image and status of women? My stated goal was "to stimulate comparative exploration of the image of women in the two ancient cultures — Hellenistic and Judaic — which together have shaped attitudes to women in the predominantly Christian West."

In the past decade, much information on attitudes concerning women in ancient cultures was published, and historical studies of women began to progress beyond mere description to analysis and interpretation.[2] In the context of the study of religion, information about women of antiquity has been used in the service of various political agendas. Religious feminists of a more radical stamp, convinced that patriarchal religion was utterly beyond repair, pursued the quest for evidence of pre-patriarchal societal structures in which women called the shots — or at least enjoyed a more favorable posi-

---

[1]This essay is a revision of a paper read at the SBL Annual Meeting, Anaheim, November 1989. In turn, it is an expanded version of a paper first presented to the SBL Philo Seminar in 1982. See my "Image of Women in Philo" in K. H. Richards (ed.), *SBLSP* 1982 (Missoula: Scholars Press), 551-63.

[2]See, for instance, Sarah B. Pomeroy, *Goddesses, Whores, Wives and Slaves: Women in Classical Antiquity* (New York: Schocken 1975); M. R. Lefkowitz and M. B. Fant, *Women's Life in Greece and Rome* (Baltimore: Johns Hopkins, 1982); Jane F. Gardner, *Women in Roman Law and Society* (Bloomington: Indiana University, 1986); Carol Meyers, *Discovering Eve* (New York and Oxford: Oxford University Press, 1988); and Judith Romney Wegner, *Chattel or Person? The Status of Women in the Mishnah* (New York and Oxford: Oxford University Press, 1988).

tion. Various versions of this hypothesis (matriarchy, maternalism or mother-right, based in part on Bachofen's *Mutterrecht*) were proposed;[3] but scant evidence has emerged, and much of that has been equivocal.[4] Some radical feminists have concluded that modern women have no choice but to develop new forms of religion (either gynocentric or gender-neutral) and to create new liturgies, if not new Scriptures, to express these new forms.

Less radical religious feminists, reluctant to throw out the baby with the bath water, believe that even the most androcentric Scriptures can be saved by a new *midrash*: a gender-neutral exegesis can purge the texts of the accidents of sociology, recover women's essential role in religions of antiquity, and restore their "rightful" place in contemporary practice of these religions. Such a place would include the capacity to serve as ministers, rabbis and priests.

Christian feminists who have analyzed the status of women in the New Testament similarly follow two main trends. One group claims that the coming of the Christ brought an improvement to women's position: the early Church is seen to have displaced the "archaic" Jewish perception of women with a "progressive" Hellenistic stance. Thus Constance Parvey adduces Philo as evidence that "first century Judaism" emphasized the weakness of women.[5] But can we assume that the writings of Philo in first-century Hellenistic Alexandria reflected society in first-century Judaic Palestine? And should we beg the question of whether Philo's downgrading of women was "Judaic" rather than "Hellenistic"?

Parvey calls Philo "the most universally read Jewish philosopher of the time." But there is no evidence whatsoever that the first-century Pharisees (forerunners of rabbinic Judaism) had even heard of Philo; his name appears nowhere in rabbinic literature. Josephus fails to mention him when reporting on the legation to Gaius in which Philo participated and about which he wrote an entire book (which Josephus apparently never saw). Nor does Philo, for his part, mention either "rabbis" or "Pharisees."[6] Parvey may be

---

[3]An overview appears in Gerda Lerner, *The Creation of Patriarchy* (New York: Oxford University Press, 1986), 21-35.
[4]Thus, steatopygic figurines may depict goddesses, or they may be simply sympathetic magic symbols used in fertility rites of patriarchal cults; the layout of the site recently unearthed at Çatal Hüyük may or may not reflect a more egalitarian culture. See ibid., 31-35.
[5]"The Theology and Leadership of Women in the New Testament," in R. R. Ruether (ed.), *Religion and Sexism* (New York: Simon and Schuster, 1974), 117-47.
[6]The Index to "Translator's Notes" in Vol. X (469, 473) of the LCL lists entries for both "Pharisees" and "rabbinic tradition," but close scrutiny of those

on firmer ground in claiming that the Apostle Paul "reflects with Philo *the thought of his time*" (emphasis added). But here too, the assumption that the *thought* reflected by Philo and Paul is Judaic rather than Hellenistic is at least questionable. These methodological problems were less obvious in 1974 than today, when it is well understood that many competing Judaisms (including the Nazarene sect itself) co-existed during the first century of the Common Era.

There are, further, methodological problems of another kind. One widely cited book on the status of women in Judaism, notable for its selective references, includes many talmudic strictures on women while ignoring many rabbinic statements that present women in a positive light.[7] This is particularly unfortunate because stylistic peculiarities make the primary texts of rabbinic literature virtually inaccessible (even in translation) to most scholars of religion, who must perforce rely on secondary sources. And equally deplorable is the opposite tendency of some Jewish apologists to emphasize rabbinic praise of women while ignoring the strictures.[8]

More recently, a second trend has developed among Christian feminists. Some now argue that the evangelists, and even Paul, had a more favorable attitude to women than appears on the surface; that the Nazarene movement developed within Palestinian Judaism rather than Hellenistic culture (hence was unequivocally Jewish in its origins); that women played a far more active role in early Christianity than appears in the canonical texts (whose patriarchal writers tended to suppress women's role); and that the later decline in Christian women's favorable position can be attributed to tendencies in the Roman Empire stemming from Greco-Roman pagan (i.e., neither Jewish nor Christian) culture.[9]

---

references reveals no mention of either Pharisees or rabbis even in the Notes, let alone the text. The Index seems to reflect its maker's uncritical assumption that Philo's text refers by indirection to his acquaintance with Pharisees and/or rabbis.

[7]Leonard Swidler, *Women in Judaism: The Image of Women in Formative Judaism* (Metuchen, NJ: Scarecrow, 1976). For examples of both kinds of statements, see Judith Romney Wegner, "The Image and Status of Women in Classical Rabbinic Judaism," in J. R. Baskin (ed.), *Jewish Women in Historical Perspective* (Detroit: Wayne State University, 1990, forthcoming).

[8]E.g., Moshe Meiselman, *Jewish Women in Jewish Law* (New York: KTAV, 1978); Menahem Brayer, *The Jewish Woman in Rabbinic Literature* I, II (New York: KTAV, 1986). The main usefulness of these works lies in their listing of many talmudic and midrashic references Swidler ignores.

[9]See, e.g., R. R. Ruether, *Sexism and God-Talk: Toward a Feminist Theology* (Boston: Beacon, 1983); Florenza, *Memory*; John Temple Bristow, *What Paul Really Said About Women* (New York: Harper and Row, 1988); Catherine

Those who claim that first-century Christianity treated women far better than did contemporaneous rabbinic Judaism attribute Paul's strictures on women in I Corinthians, Ephesians, I and II Timothy, and Colossians to his Jewish background (particularly his Pharisaic training at Gamaliel's Academy, Acts 22:3), rather than to his early upbringing in Hellenized Tarsus.[10] It seems to have been virtual dogma to credit to Hellenistic influence any improvements in women's image and status in the transition from Jewish sect to Gentile *Ecclesia.* Yet the possibility that the status of both first-century Jewish and Christian women might exhibit features common to all patriarchal cultures, including Judaism and Hellenism alike, has scarcely been explored.[11]

Against this backdrop, I shall consider the extent to which Philo's attitudes regarding women are traceable either to his Jewish heritage or to his Greek education. In examining Philo's thoughts on "female" attributes, I shall explore the extent to which these statements match the image of women either in the Scriptures Philo expounds or in the classical Greek sources with which he was equally well acquainted.

Woman As Allegory

Philo has no interest in women as a topic for sustained discussion; despite ample scriptural material on the subject his many volumes include no special book on women. Yet Philo expresses opinions on "the female" at every turn. His strictures on women are scattered throughout his work, often in the form of gratuitous comments in unrelated contexts.

Kroeger, "The Apostle Paul and the Greco-Roman Cults of Women," *JETS* (1987): 25-38. Some Muslim feminists have made analogous claims about women in early Islam, whose initially favorable treatment is said to have degenerated because of "non-Islamic" influences from Iran, Turkey, or some other "retrograde" non-Arabic culture. In both early Christianity and early Islam, more attention might profitably be paid to the thesis that women tend to receive better treatment in situations where they are in short supply. See also, for the case of Judaism, S. D. Goitein, *A Mediterranean Society,* Vol. 3 (Berkeley: University of California, 1978), 346-83.
[10]For example, Parvey, "Theology and Leadership," 127: "The general lines of Paul's argument in 1 Cor 11 follow the religious presuppositions of the Judaism of the time." Quite apart from the unclarity of the reference to "*the* Judaism" — in a century which knew several competing Judaisms (Pharisees, Sadducees, Essenes, Zealots, the Nazarenes themselves, etc.) — one cannot simply assume that Paul's discussion does not at least equally reflect the status of women in Hellenistic culture.
[11]But cf. Ruether, *Sexism and God-Talk,* 33.

Gender and Human Attributes. A basic theme of Philo's alle-gorical *midrash* is the relationship between gender and certain characteristics of the soul. Identifying the mind or intellect (the "sovereign element of the soul") with the image of God in which man (ἄνθρωπος) was created (*Op. Mund.* 69 on Gen 1:26-27), Philo speci-fies mind (νοῦς) as a male attribute and feeling or sense-perception (αἴσθησις) as a female attribute: "for in us, mind corresponds to man, the sense to woman" (*Op. Mund.* 165). Mind is superior to sense-perception (*Leg. All.* 3:222). For Philo, νοῦς is the soul's ratio-nal, αἴσθησις its irrational quality. The relationship between this polarity and the male-female polarity in the corpus is explicated by Richard Baer:[12]

> That the male-female polarity is associated with the irrational part of the soul, not with the higher νοῦς finds further confir-mation in *Rer. Div. Her.* 133ff., a description of the division of all things into equal parts and opposites through the agency of the λόγος τομεύς. In *Rer. Div. Her.* 138-9 ... Philo points out that just as God separated the living from the lifeless, so he further divided the living into rational and irrational species. The rational species he divided into mortal and immortal, "and *of the mortal* he made two portions, one of which he named men and the other women." Here it is clear that the male-female polarity originated from the sphere of the mortal, not from that part of man which was created in the image of God.

Νοῦς, the soul's rational quality, is the immortal part, made in the image of God. Woman, fashioned from the mortal aspect, has no part in νοῦς, but only in αἴσθησις, the soul's irrational quality. Philo frequently makes this point — always to the detriment of the female.

The distinction appears from the outset in Philo's exegesis of the two biblical creation myths. In discussing Gen 1:1-2:4a, he sep-arates "And God created man in his image; in the image of God he created him" (Gen 1:27ab, as traditionally punctuated) from the statement that follows: "male and female created he them" (1:27c).[13] Though the now-standard punctuation treats Gen 1:27c as the conclusion of what comes before, the rules of Hebrew prosody strongly suggest that this phrase was not intended as the end of the preceding statement but rather as the beginning of a separate and distinct thought — as Phyllis Bird has convincingly argued.[14]

---

[12]*Philo's Use of the Categories Male and Female* (Leiden: Brill, 1970), 19.
[13]Like the Masoretic text, the Septuagint was not punctuated until well after Philo's day.
[14]"Male and Female, He Created Them: Genesis 1:27b in the Context of the

Following his own punctuation, Philo explains that male and female (ἄρρεν τε καὶ θῆλυ) are two physical species (φήσας) of the genus "man" (τὸ γένος ἄνθρωπον), which, though mentioned at this point, had not yet taken shape (*Op. Mund.* 76). This statement has no basis in Scripture, but rests squarely on classical Greek biology.[15] Here we note the significant fact (often missed by native English-speakers, who wrongly assume that "woman" is simply "man" with a prefix) that in Greek as in Indo-European and Semitic languages generally, the words for "man" and "woman" usually (if not invariably) stem from *different etymological roots.*[16]

Philo's taxonomy of male and female as separate species enables him to discuss the relationship between man and God without addressing the division of humankind into male and female. But this discussion blurs the conceptual distinction between "humankind" (ἄνθρωπος) and "man" (ἀνήρ, ἄρρεν), the human male. The effect of dropping the female from the discussion at this point, while continuing to speak of the supposedly sexless ἄνθρωπος in masculine terms, is not evenhanded, as we see from the following passage:[17]

... there is a vast difference between the man thus formed [at Gen 2:7] and the man that came into existence earlier [at Gen 1:27] after the image of God; for the man so formed [i.e. at Gen 2:7] is an object of sense-perception (αἰσθητός) ..., consisting of body and soul, man or woman, by nature mortal, while *he* [emphasis added: masc. pronoun ὁ] that was after the (Divine) image was an idea or type or seal, an object of thought (only), incorporeal, neither male nor female.... (*Op. Mund.* 134)

Philo's definition of ἄνθρωπος as "neither male nor female" is somewhat at odds with his general tendency to speak of man in his relationship to God exclusively in masculine terms. This is partly

---

Priestly Account of Creation," *HTR* 74 (1981): 129-59.
[15]Cf. Plato's *Timæus* 91aff.; Aristotle's *De Generatione Animalium* 775aff. See below for further discussion.
[16]For instance, Greek: ἄνθρωπος, ἀνήρ, γυνή; Latin: *homo, vir, femina / mulier*; French: *homme, homme, femme*; German: *Mensch, Mann, Weib*; Russian: *chelovek, muzhchina, zhenshchina*; Hebrew: *adam* (אדם), *'ish* (איש), *ishshah* (אשה); Arabic: *adam, rajul, mar'a*; Aramaic: *enash* (אנש), *gabra* (גברא) *itteta* (אתתא); English: humankind (from homo), man, woman (from wifman = female-human). This differentiation of the sexes is equally common in the names of domestic animals, e.g., hound/bitch; bull/cow; stallion/mare; boar/sow. Hebrew and Arabic terminology differentiate likewise between male and female animals, like the camel, that were domesticated in Semitic cultures (but not between male and female dogs or pigs, which were not domesticated).
[17]This and all subsequent citations are from the LCL.

dictated by the grammatical gender of ἄνθρωπος. But the use of masculine generic terms for "humankind" in Greek (as in other languages, like Latin and German, which possess the neuter and so could have developed a neuter term for this concept) begs an important question by obscuring the equal relationship of male and female to humankind.[18] When coupled with the exclusion of the female in his discussion of mankind's reception of the rational faculty, this creates an inextricable nexus between rationality and masculinity that virtually makes Philo's point for him.

Philo's definition of the ἄνθρωπος created in God's image as "neither male nor female" directly contradicts traditional Jewish/ Christian exegesis, based on the Masoretic punctuation that has God creating humankind "in the image of God ... male and female" (κατ᾽εἰκόνα θεοῦ....ἄρρεν τε καὶ θῆλυ). The Talmud asserts that because both male and female were created in God's image, both partake of the divine spirit; Augustine and Aquinas wrestle with the conflict between this viewpoint and that of classical Greek science, which perceives woman as an imperfect or defective man.[19] The *Midrash* interprets Gen 1:27 to mean that God's first human creation was androgynous,[20] which is at odds with the Philonic view of a genderless ἄνθρωπος. This divine spirit, breathed into the *man* at Gen 2:7 (LXX πνοήν) corresponds with the πνεῦμα, which Philo asserts is the essence of the rational faculty:

> To the faculty which we have in common with the irrational creatures, blood has been given as its essence; but to the faculty which streams forth from the fountain of reason, breath (πνεῦμα) has been assigned. ... By "man" (ἄνθρωπος) I mean not the living creature with two natures, but the highest form in which the life shows itself; and this has received the title of "mind" (νοῦς) and "reason" (λόγος). This is why he [the Scrip-

---

[18]Although linguistic theorists consider speculations on the reasons for the development of a particular gender for nouns signifying referents for which sex has no relevance generally futile, sex has obvious relevance in the present case. Hence, the development of a *masculine* rather than a *neuter* noun to denote "humankind" is not necessarily arbitrary.

[19]For the rabbinic notion that the Adam of Gen 1:27 included both male and female, cf. *b. Ketub.* 8a, b; *b. Ber.* 61a; b; *b. 'Erub.* 18a. Commenting on Gen 1:27, Nahmanides says that "the creation of man was, from the first, male and female, and his divine spirit (*nishmato*, נשמתו) was included in them both." *Neshama* (נשמה) is the word translated as πνοήν in Gen 1:27. For the fathers, see Kari Elisabeth Børreson, *Subordination and Equivalence: The Nature and Role of Women in Augustine and Aquinas* (Lanham, MD: University Press of America, 1981). The classical Greek view is discussed below.

[20]*Gen. Rab.* 8:1, which takes "male and female" in Gen 1:27 to refer to the creation of a single creature.

ture-writer] says that the blood is the life of the flesh [Gen 9:4],
being aware that the fleshly nature has received no share of
mind, ... but man's life he names "breath," giving the title of
"man" (ἄνθρωπος). ... to *that God-like creation with which we
reason* (*Det.* 83-84, emphasis added).

The connection here established between "male" and "reason"
follows not only the classical Aristotelian science but also classical
Pythagorean dichotomies. Thus, in discussing the second creation
myth, which presents the fleshly man of Genesis 2:7ff., Philo
specifically associates "good" qualities with the male and "bad"
qualities with the female. Man has the "male" attributes of mind and
reason (νοῦς and λόγος); woman the "female" attributes of body and
sense-perception (σῶμα and αἴσθησις). Σῶμα is a "bad" thing: for the
creation of woman "begat bodily pleasure, which is the beginning of
wrongs and violation of law" (*Op. Mund.* 152). Likewise, αἴσθησις is
a female attribute:

> "He built it to be a woman" (Gen 2:22) proving that the most
> proper and exact name for sense-perception (αἴσθησις) is
> "woman." For just as the man shows himself in activity and the
> woman in passivity, so the province of the mind (νοῦς) is
> activity and that of the perceptive sense (αἴσθησις) passivity....
> (*Leg. All.* 2:38)

Unfortunately, mind becomes the slave of sense-perception
when the man succumbs to the desire for intercourse. Commenting
on "Therefore shall a man ... cleave to his wife" (Gen 2:24), Philo
concludes:

> For the sake of sense-perception the mind, when it has become
> her slave ... cleaves to and becomes one with sense-perception
> and is resolved into sense-perception so that the two become
> one flesh and one experience. Observe that it is not the woman
> that cleaves to the man, but conversely the man to the woman,
> mind to sense-perception. For when that which is superior,
> namely mind, becomes one with that which is inferior, namely
> sense-perception, it resolves itself into the order of flesh which
> is inferior, into sense-perception.... (*Leg. All.* 2:50)

It was because of the power of sense-perception over mind that
the serpent spoke first to Eve rather than to Adam:

> Pleasure [i.e., the serpent] does not venture to bring her wiles
> and deceptions to bear on the man, but on the woman, and by
> her means on him. This is a telling and well-made point; for in
> us mind corresponds to man, the sense to woman; and

pleasure encounters and holds parley with the senses first, and through them cheats with her quackeries the sovereign mind itself.... (*Op. Mund.* 165)

A second explanation exploits the notion of woman's inferior intellect from yet another angle. The serpent:

> ... deceives by trickery and artfulness. And woman is more ac-customed to be deceived than man. For his judgment, like his body, is masculine and is capable of dissolving or destroying the designs of deception; but the judgment of woman is more feminine, and because of softness she gives way and is taken in by plausible falsehoods which resemble the truth. (*Quæst. Gen.* 1:33)

As for the question, "Why did the woman, rather than the man, pick the fruit from the tree (Gen 3:6), Philo answers: "It was fitting that the man should rule over morality and everything good, and the woman over death and everything vile" (*Quæst. Gen.* 1:37). By picking the fruit of the tree of knowledge, the woman becomes responsible for God's barring man's access to the Tree of Life and thus condemns humankind to mortality. Philo's exegesis once again corresponds with the Pythagorean table of opposites, in which the desirable member of any pair of polar attributes (like "good") always appears on the right-hand, "male" side of the list, and the undesir-able member (like "vile," here synonymous with "evil") on the left-hand, "female" side." Although the ten dichotomies found in the table do not include life/death, Philo's allegorical definition of "life" as a male and "death" as a female attribute is consonant with the Pythagorean scheme.[21]

Here, for good measure, Philo adds a second explanation that again connects woman with sense-perception and man with mind. It had to be the woman who picked the fruit because:

> In the allegorical sense ... woman is a symbol of sense[-percep-tion], and man of mind. Now of necessity sense comes into contact with the sense-perceptible and by the participation of sense, things pass into the mind; for sense is moved by objects, while the mind is moved by sense. (ibid.)

Here the lofty male principle of mind is so far above noticing material things that only the mediation of feminine sense-perception can

---

[21]The Pythagorean table is conveniently listed in Genevieve Lloyd's excellent exposition of the problem exemplified by Philo *inter alia,* in *The Man of Reason: "Male" and "Female" in Western Philosophy* (Minneapolis: University of Minnesota, 1984), 3.

bring the man "down" to that level.

A final question on this subject is asked and answered in the interpretation of Gen 3:8:

> Why, when they hid themselves from the face of God, was not the woman, who first ate of the forbidden fruit, first mentioned, but the man; for (Scripture) says, "Adam and his wife hid themselves"? ... It was the more imperfect and ignoble element, the female, that made a beginning of the transgression and lawlessness, while the male made the beginning of reverence and modesty and all good, since he was better and more perfect. (*Quæst. Gen.* 1:43)

Hence, while the woman initiates sin, the man initiates atonement. His guilt is thus mitigated in two ways: first, he sinned only because the woman seduced him; second, he was the first to repent.

These examples demonstrate Philo's pronounced male bias. Indeed, the only context in which he treats the sexes with relative impartiality is when acknowledging the indispensability of both for reproduction: "Equality too divided the human being into man and woman, two sections unequal indeed in strength, but quite equal as regards what was nature's urgent purpose, the reproduction of themselves in a third person" (*Quis Her.* 164).

In one rare instance, Philo does assign some positive value to sense-perception:

> ... the mind was docked of all its powers of sense-perception, thus truly powerless. It was but half the perfect soul, lacking the power whereby it is the nature of bodies to be perceived, a mere unhappy section bereft of its mate without the support of the sense-perceiving organs, whereby it could have propped as with a staff its faltering steps. And thus all bodily objects were wrapped in profound darkness and none of them could come to the light. For sense, the means whereby they were to become the objects of knowledge, was not. God then, wishing to provide the mind with perception of material as well as immaterial things, thought to complete the soul by weaving into the part first made the other section, which he called by the general name of "woman" and the proper name of "Eve" thus symbolizing sense. (*Cher.* 59-60)

This acknowledgment that in real life (as opposed to symbolic systems) men cannot function without women may suggest that Philo's true attitude to women was one of ambivalence — perhaps even cognitive dissonance — rather than the misogyny that seems to inform most of his theoretical statements about the female. But complementarity does not imply equality, and clearly Philo's perception of the female as categorically inferior to the male reflects her subordinate position in the real-life, Hellenistic culture.

How closely, then, can we relate Philo's stance to that of the classical Greek sources? Philo's statements on biological science, "male" and "female" principles, and "masculine" and "feminine" attributes offer overwhelming evidence that he modeled his work closely on Greek authorities. Not only are the dichotomies underpinning his distinctions between male and female precisely those featured so prominently in the classical Pythagorean and Aristotelian schemes: form/matter; activity/passivity; soul/body; intellect/sense-perception; good/evil; life/death; and so forth, but Philo also draws on such works as Plato's *Timæus* and Aristotle's *De Generatione Animalium*. Thus, his account of woman's inferiority in the passages from *Quæst. Gen.* cited above evokes the *Timæus* far more than Genesis. Here I quote from the *Timæus* (42a-b; 91a, LCL, Plato VII):

> ... since human nature is two-fold, the superior sex is that which hereafter should be designated "man" (ἀνήρ). ... And he that has lived his appointed time well shall return again to his abode in his native star, and shall gain a life that is blessed and congenial; but whoso has failed therein shall be changed into woman's nature (γυναικὸς φύσιν) at the second birth....
>
> According to the probable account, all those creatures generated as men who proved themselves cowardly and spent their lives in wrong-doing were transformed, at their second incarnation, into women (γυναῖκες).

A similar characterization of the female as a defective male is found in Aristotle's *De Generatio Animalium*: "Females are weaker and colder in their nature; and we should look upon the female state as being as it were a deformity, though one which occurs in the ordinary course of nature" (IV, vi., 775a, LCL).

It is on sources such as these that Philo draws for his cosmology in general and his exposition of gender attributes in particular. That Philo's attitudes are quintessentially Greek there can be no doubt. Genevieve Lloyd, who devotes several pages to Philo in *The Man of Reason*, puts matters thus: "Philo ... used Greek philosophical models in interpreting Jewish Scriptures ... in a remarkable synthesis of the Genesis account of relations between the sexes with a Platonic treatment of Reason's corruption through the senses."[22] In particular, we have seen how Philo draws on Plato's notion of the divided soul, in which male reason contends with non-rational human qualities associated primarily with the female.

Philo's Gratuitous Depreciation of Women. When Philo turns from analyzing the "female" in the abstract to discussing the metaphorical significance of individual women mentioned in Scripture, two curious features emerge. First, he insults women beyond the needs of the context; second, when the context forces him to praise some desirable quality in a particular woman, he routinely maintains that the trait in question is really "male" rather than "female."

A typical disparagement of women appears in Philo's exposition of Gen 25:5-6, "And Abraham gave all that was his to Isaac his son, and to the sons of his concubines he gave gifts":

> So much superior was Isaac to (the sons) of the concubines as are possessions to gifts. Wherefore (Scripture) recently described Isaac as *motherless,* and it calls those born to the concubines *fatherless.* Accordingly, those who were harmonious in the father's family are of the male progeny, while (the sons) of the women and those of inferior descent are certainly to be called female and unvirile, for which reason they are little admired as great ones. (*Quæst. Gen.* 4:148, emphasis added)

The exegesis is clearly strained. Philo's comment that Scripture calls Isaac "motherless" presumably rests on the preceding statement "and Isaac was comforted for the death of his mother" (Gen 24:67). But to suggest that Isaac never had a mother is very strange; explication of Gen 25:5-6 calls for nothing of the kind. Similarly, Philo's depiction of the concubine's sons as "fatherless" seems to be based on their rejection by Abraham as his heirs. But Gen 25:6 makes clear that the gifts were in lieu of inheritance, for the text continues: "Abraham let them go while he was yet alive." This is a far cry from saying he rejected them as his sons.[23]

---

[22]Ibid., 22-23. Lloyd's discussion of Philo does not cite the earlier (1982) version of the present paper. Her discussion of Augustine and Aquinas likewise fails to cite the earlier exhaustive treatment by Børreson (n. 19, above). Both sources, no doubt, escaped her attention.

[23]The translator's note to the passage is misleading. The sons of the concubines were not "illegitimate" in biblical (Semitic) law. cf. Jephtha in Judg 11, whose half-brothers expel him *explicitly to prevent* his inheriting from their common father, as he normally would. Sons of concubines were not *ipso facto* barred from inheritance. They could, however, remain slaves unless emancipated by their father. The word *va-ye-shallehem* (וישלחם, lit., "he released

A similar denigration of women appears in the explanation of the promoting of Jacob over Esau, the elder (see Gen 25:25):

> But a distinction should be made between "first-born" and "first-begotten." For the one is (the offspring) of female and material matter, for the female gives birth; but the first-begotten is a male and (the offspring) of a more responsible power, for it is the property of the male to beget. (*Quæst. Gen.* 4:160)

Again we see Philo's greater dependence on his Hellenistic education than on his Jewish background; while this piece of biological nonsense lacks any scriptural basis, it draws on concepts of classical Greek biological science, which saw the father as the formative cause that begets, and the mother only as the matter that nourishes the begotten child until it is ready to be born.[24]

Another gratuitous insult appears in the discussion of the prescription of a male animal for the paschal sacrifice:

> Q. Why does [Moses] command [them] to take a "perfect male sheep of one year" (Exod 12:5)?
>
> A. [It is to be] perfect. ... For an imperfect [sacrifice] is not worthy to be brought to the altar of God. And it is to be male, first, because the male is more perfect than the female. Wherefore it is said by the naturalists that the female is nothing else than an imperfect male.
>
> Q. Why is a sheep chosen?
>
> A. Symbolically, as I have said, it indicates perfect progress and at the same time the male. For progress is indeed nothing else than the giving up of the female gender by changing into the male, since the female gender is material, passive, corporeal, and sense-perceptible (sc., "sense-perceptive"?), while the male is active, rational, incorporeal and more akin to mind and thought. (*Quæst. Exod.* 1:7)

Explicit here is Philo's indebtedness to classical Greek education. The reference to "the naturalists'" view of the female as an "imperfect male" recalls Aristotle's statements, while the list of dichotomies is basic Pythagoras.

Furthermore, the passage amplifies both answers beyond

---

them") in Gen 25:6 is a technical term for emancipation (the same term is used in the law of divorce, i.e., the "release" of the wife, in e.g., Deut 22:29). Thus Abraham here is *favoring* his concubine's sons, not releasing them or rendering them fatherless.

[24]Plato, *Timæus* 50d; Aristotle, *Metaphysics* I,6.998a.

anything biblically warranted. Very likely the practice of sacrificing male beasts originated in a purely pragmatic need to preserve potentially reproductive females — if anything, a *superior* valuation of the female. In Exod 12:5, however, the biblical writer linked the paschal offering (an ancient rite found in many Semitic cultures)[25] to the death of the firstborn Egyptian males and so made a male sacrifice more apposite. But instead of offering this plausible explanation, Philo chooses, as always, to extract from the verse his pound of female flesh.

There is likewise a sting in the tail of Philo's explanation of Exod 32: "The calf, you observe, is not made out of all the things with which women deck themselves, but only their earrings (Exod 32:2), for the lawgiver is teaching us that no manufactured god is a God for sight and in reality, but for the ear to hear of, and vogue and custom to proclaim, *and that too a woman's ear, not a man's, for to entertain such trash is the work of an effeminate and sinewless soul*" (*Post.* 166, emphasis added). Clearly the exegesis would have sufficed without the final comment.

Perhaps the ultimate insult to women appears in the discussion of the daughters of Zelophehad (Num 27:1-11). Here, Philo offers the following ingenious explanation of Zelophehad's producing daughters and not sons: "Do you not notice, that the five daughters of Zelophehad ... are of the tribe of Manasseh [whose name means] 'from forgetfulness' .... 'and he had no sons' (Num 27:3) but only daughters, for whereas the faculty of *memory*, being naturally wide awake, has *male* progeny, *forgetfulness* rapt in a slumber of reasoning power, has *female* offspring..." (*Mig.* 205-6, emphasis added). Daughters, then, are begotten in a fit of absentmindedness.[26]

Philo and the Anomaly of the Virtuous Woman. Philo's exegetical enterprise sometimes forces him to account for the excellence of certain women whose virtue is recorded in Scripture, and this poses

---

[25]Including pre-Islamic Arabic religion, as is clear from qur'anic reference to the *faskh* (Heb.: *pesah*, חספ). an animal sacrifice offered at the Ka'aba since time immemorial and assumed by Muhammed to be familiar to his audience, which included pagan Arabs.
[26]This is one of the many instances that led Wolfson to surmise that Philo knew Hebrew. But others have noted that wherever Philo refers to the Hebrew meaning of a biblical name, the meaning is generally supplied by the text itself (see, for Manasseh = "forgetting," Gen 41:51). In this case coincidentally the Hebrew consonantal roots for "male" and "memory" (z-k-r, רכז) happen to be identical. However, since the text of Num 27:3 provides Philo with a connection between Manasseh ("forgetting") and daughters, one cannot say that this example necessarily supports Wolfson's thesis.

a problem inherent in the very term *virtue*, whose basic meaning is "manliness" in both Latin and Greek.[27] Virtue, by definition, is any praiseworthy quality exhibited by a *man*. Let us see how Philo handles the anomaly of the virtuous *woman*.

The case of Sarah, wife of Abraham and founding mother of the Hebrew people, is prototypical. It is true that, for Philo, Sarah's main significance is metaphorical; she hypostatizes virtue (*Abr.* 206, *Ebr.* 59-61, and elsewhere). But in the mythic-historical context of Genesis, Sarah is a "real" woman; and, to Philo, the appearance of such excellence in a woman requires explanation. His solution is to prove from Scripture that Sarah is an exception to the rule of female inferiority. This he does by offering an extraordinary interpretation of Gen 18:11, "The way of women had ceased for Sarah."

> The literal meaning is clear. For [Scripture] by a euphemism calls the monthly purification of women "the way of women." But as for the deeper meaning, it is to be allegorized as follows. The soul has, as it were, a dwelling, partly men's quarters, partly women's quarters. Now for the men there is a place where properly dwell *the masculine thoughts (that are) wise, sound, just, prudent, pious, filled with freedom and boldness, and kin to wisdom.* And the women's quarters are a place where womanly opinions go about and dwell, being followers of the female sex. *And the female sex is irrational and akin to bestial passions, fear, sorrow, pleasure and desire, from which ensue incurable weaknesses and indescribable diseases.* He who is conquered by these is unhappy, while he who controls them is happy. And longing for and desiring this happiness, and seizing a certain time to be able to escape from terrible and unbearable sorrow, which is (what is meant by) "there ceased to be the ways of women" — this clearly belongs to minds full of Law, which resemble the male sex and overcome passions and rise above all sense-pleasure and desire.... (*Quæst. Gen.* 4:15, emphasis added).

Eventually, Philo removes Sarah completely from the world of women:

> For the customs of women still prevail among us, and we cannot as yet cleanse ourselves from them or flee to the dwelling-place where the men are quartered, as we are told that it was with the virtue-loving mind, named Sarah. For the oracles

---

[27]Latin *virtus*, abstract noun from *vir* = "man." The Greek ἀρετή may be similarly connected with ἄρρεν = "man."

> represent her as having left all the things of women. ... (Gen
> 18:11). (*Ebr.* 59-61)

To this, Philo adds the following extraordinary claim:

> She is declared, too, to be without a mother, and to have in-
> herited her kinship only on the father's side and not on the
> mother's, and thus to have no part in female parentage. For we
> find it said: "Indeed she is my sister, the daughter of my
> father, but not of my mother" [Gen 20:12]. (Ibid.)

Philo does not begin, as in *Quæst. Gen.* 4:15, by noting the literal
meaning of the cited verse, because here he is not systematically
expounding Scripture, while there he follows the traditional method
of giving both the literal and the figurative interpretation.[28]
However, while Gen 18:11 states that "the way of women had ceased
for Sarah" (and thus opens the way to allegorical interpretation),
Gen 20:12 does not declare Sarah to be "without a mother" but
merely points out that she was Abraham's half-sister from a
different mother.

With Miriam, another biblical woman whose excellence cannot
be ignored, Philo also feels constrained to explain that she was not a
typical female. To justify her leadership qualities described in Exod
15:20, sense-perception suddenly becomes a virtue rather than a
defect! Thus Miriam personifies "Sense perception *made pure and
clean.* For it is right with both mind and sense to render hymns and
sing blessings to the Godhead without delay..." (*Agr.* 80, emphasis
added). Though Philo does not cite Scripture here, his prooftext for
declaring Miriam "pure and clean" is presumably the story of her
healing from leprosy (Num 12:14-15).

So reluctant is Philo to concede any excellence whatever to the
female that he divests even the Sabbath of its traditional feminine
aura. While conceding that some call her virgin,[29] he claims that the
seventh day is motherless: "begotten by the father of the universe

---

[28]This emphasis on allegorical interpretation is precisely what recom-
mended his work to the Church fathers who preserved it. Early Christianity's
quest for Hebrew prooftexts for the messiahship and divinity of Jesus
depended on the figurative interpretation of the biblical materials — texts
whose literal meanings referred to clearly defined historical contexts — did not
mention the name of Jesus, and never suggested that the messiah would be
other than a human descendant of King David.

[29]In the Hebrew Scriptures, the word *Shabbat* (שבת, Sabbath) is, with few
exceptions, treated as masculine. Only in later Jewish tradition is the Sabbath
hypostatized as a female (e.g., the medieval mystical labels of "queen" and
"bride"). Philo's statement that "some call her virgin" may reflect such a perception among Alexandrian Jews at a much earlier time than is the case in
rabbinic thought.

alone, the ideal form of the male sex with nothing of the female" (*Spec. Leg.* 256). This comment even contradicts Philo's own description in *Mos.* 2:210 of the seventh day as female and virgin. But the latter passage is a rare deviation from his relegation of the female tc an inferior status. In general, as Lloyd points out, Philo's version of moral progress "calls on [women] to set aside those character traits which are supposed to characterize them as female."[30]

This attitude is, finally, not merely *Greek* as opposed to Jewish, it also becomes *Christian* rather than Jewish. John Chrysostom, for instance, makes similar statements; as Elizabeth Clark observes: "there was within patristic Christianity an elevation of status for celibate women, but not for married ones."[31]

Social Status Enshrined in Law?

Thus far, we have discussed Philo's stance on "male" and "female" attributes and his attitude to the image of "woman" in the abstract. The following section examines his view of women's status in society, as reflected in his exegesis of the Torah laws. Of course, here we cannot necessarily draw conclusions about the actual legal status of Jewish women in Philo's Alexandria from his analysis of a Scripture dating from several centuries before.

Where Philo had much to say about the allegorical female, especially as the personification of sense-perception, he says surprisingly little about women in the culture of his day. In line with his general preference for figurative exegesis over literal exposition, Philo did not find "real" women sufficiently important to discuss. The closest he comes is *Spec. Leg.* 3:8-84, where he subsumes under the general rubric of the Seventh Commandment all the Mosaic legislation on sexual morality: consanguinity laws and other prohibited sexual conduct (Lev 18), rape and seduction (Exod 22:16-17, Deut 22:23-29), the suspected adulteress (Num 5:11-31), and accusations of unchastity against new brides (Deut 22:13-21). The discussion, which follows the biblical text closely, aims primarily to endorse Mosaic morality as a model for Philo's own (Jewish) community, in contrast to the scriptural "abominations" (notably Greek homosexuality and Egyptian incest) practiced in the

---

[30]*Man of Reason*, 27.
[31]*Jerome, Chrysostom and Friends* (Lewiston, NY: Edwin Mellen, 1979), vi and *passim*. See also R. R. Ruether, "Misogynism and Virginal Feminism in the Fathers of the Church," in idem (ed.), *Religion and Sexism*, 150-83.

surrounding pagan cultures of his day.

Here too the treatment of women is incidental. Thus, Philo assumes the double standard for adultery in biblical law, which reflects a polygynous but not polyandrous culture: the offense occurs when a man has intercourse with another man's wife or betrothed wife (Deut 22:22ff), but not (contrary to the Christian view) when a married man has intercourse with an unmarried woman. He equally assumes that the biological function of a young marriageable girl virtually belongs to her father, who may without consulting her permit or deny her marriage to her seducer (*Spec. Leg.* 3:70). He even accepts the view, implicit in Deut 22:29, that the forced marriage of a rapist to his victim constitutes some "consolation" for the girl, secure in the knowledge that her violator has forfeited in perpetuity his right to divorce her (*Spec. Leg.* 3:71).

The general flavor of this section of Philo's writings is clearly not Hellenic but uncompromisingly Judaic. This is exactly as we might expect; in traditional cultures family law (which deals with the most basic of human activities) historically has always been closely bound up with religion, which tends to preserve rules governing sexual conduct even when members of minority groups become acculturated in all other respects to the law and customs of the dominant society.[32] Thus it is no surprise that Philo values the sexual morality of the Hebrew Bible above that of his Hellenistic environment, while he adopts the more sophisticated Greek culture in matters of philosophy and science.

In the *Special Laws*, Philo cites other scriptural injunctions pertaining to women. Thus, he finds it appropriate that the High Priest must marry a virgin (Lev 21:13):

> [By] mating with souls entirely innocent and unperverted [high priests] may find it easy to mould the characters and dispositions of their wives, for the minds of virgins are easily influenced and attracted to virtue and very ready to be taught. But she who has had experience of another husband is naturally far less amenable to instruction. (*Spec. Leg.* 1:105-6)

In the same document, Philo approves of the law (Num 30:2-17) permitting fathers and husbands to revoke religious vows of daughters and wives: "That is surely reasonable, for the former,

---

[32]As witness the surprisingly large proportion of modern Jews who adhere to Jewish marriage and divorce laws rather than avail themselves of the civil codes. Similarly, in the Middle East, while Israel and the more progressive Arab states have modelled their civil and criminal codes on those of modern Europe, family law remains the preserve of the religious authorities.

owing to their youth, do not know the value of oaths, so that they need others to judge for them, and the latter often, through want of sense, swear what would not be to their husbands' advantage..." (*Spec. Leg.* 2:24).

One place outside the *Special Laws* presents a catalogue of the biblical injunctions Philo considers most important. This is the *Hypothetica*, described in its subtitle as an "apology for the Jews," which does indeed look like an apology for Judaism to the Hellenistic, pagan world. The work is known to us only from its citation in Eusebius (*Præp. Evan.* 8, 5:11-7:20). Following an historical introduction, Philo lists the principal laws of the Torah. Naturally, he begins with capital crimes (murder, adultery, etc.). Then, among the other laws, he accords pride of place to the following: "Other rules again there are of various kinds: *wives must be in servitude to their husbands*, a servitude not imposed by violent ill-treatment but promoting obedience in all things" (7.3; emphasis added). Here Philo is thinking of Gen 3:16, "Thy desire shall be to thy husband, and he shall rule over thee." His selection of this rule to head the list of non-capital laws surely indicates the importance he assigned to it, as well as his views on the subordination of women.

The sociocultural perception of women that underpins their legal subordination is aptly reflected at *Spec. Leg.* 3:32-34, where Philo's view of women's status is expressed by metaphors for intercourse and childbearing. He speaks of "sowing wheat and barley" and calls the womb a "cornfield." Mating with a barren woman is described as "ploughing the hard and stony land." These metaphors are found in many cultures, including Semitic and Hellenistic. Thus, Plato speaks of "the ploughland of the womb" (*Timaeus* 91d), while the Mishnah formally compares the acquisition of a wife to the acquisition of a field,[33] and the Qur'an describes women as a man's "tilth, which may be ploughed as he pleases" (*sura* 2:228). The general sense underlying these metaphors is that a woman's sexual and reproductive function was perceived as a form of property belonging to men.[34]

Thus far, we have considered Philo's use of woman as allegory and his perception of women as the generic object of certain laws. In

---

[33]*M. Qidd.* 1:1: A wife may be acquired "by money, by deed, or by intercourse." Cf. *m. Qidd.* 1:5: Land may be acquired "by money, by deed, or by usucaption." Intercourse is a form of usucaption; it is specifically the form appropriate to marriage. See also *m. Ketub.* 2:6, where a betrothed woman who is subsequently raped by another man must tell her fiancé: "Thy field has been flooded."
[34]See Wegner, *Chattel or Person?*

one place, however, he mentions an historical woman. Recording Herod Agrippa's petition to rescind Caligula's decree requiring placement of the emperor's statue in the Jerusalem Temple, he fulsomely praises Julia Augusta, the emperor's great-grandmother:

> Under such an instructor in piety [sc., Augustus], your great-grandmother Julia Augusta adorned the temple with golden vials and libation bowls and a multitude of other sumptuous offerings. What made her do this, as there was no image there? *For the judgments of women as a rule are weaker* and do not apprehend any mental conception apart from what their senses perceive. *But she excelled herself in this as in everything else,* for the purity of the training she received supplementing nature and practice gave virility to her reasoning power, which gained such clearness of vision that it apprehended the things of the mind better than the things of sense.... (*Leg.* 319, emphasis added).

If the pen was the pen of Agrippa, the voice is the voice of Philo and his classical mentors. But here, as with biblical heroines, Philo emphasizes the unfeminine character of Julia's excellence by stressing the "virility" (ἀρρενωθεῖσα) of her reasoning power. This passage demonstrates that Philo was no mere philosopher with his head in the clouds but also a savvy politician with his feet on the ground, willing, for political gain, to praise a woman without resorting to scriptural prooftexts; moreover, it illustrates that in the last analysis Philo can distinguish *real* women from allegorical biblical figures.

Of Philo's *personal* feelings toward women, little can be deduced. Since he says nothing of wife or family, we cannot even tell if he was married. Some light may be shed by the following diatribe, found in another fragment of the *Hypothetica* cited by Eusebius. While it is not clear whether the opinion is Philo's own or one that he attributes to the Essenes, it is consistent with everything else he says about women:

> For no Essene takes a wife, because a wife is a selfish creature, excessively jealous and an adept at beguiling the morals of her husband and seducing him by her continued impostures. For by the fawning talk which she practises and the other ways in which she plays her part like an actress on the stage she first ensnares the sight and hearing, and when these subjects have as it were been duped she cajoles the sovereign mind. And if children come, filled with the spirit of arrogance and bold speaking, she gives utterance with more audacious hardihood

to things which before she hinted at covertly and under dis-
guise, and casting off all shame she compels him to commit
actions which are all hostile to the life of fellowship. For he who
is either fast bound in the love lures of his wife or under the
stress of nature makes his children his first care ceases to be
the same to others and unconsciously has become a different
man and has passed from freedom into slavery. (*Hyp.* 11:14-
17)

This diatribe sounds as though it came from the heart. In
Philo's defense (though not justification), we note that similar statements abound in other Jewish sources, especially in late writings
like Ben Sira — suggesting that their authors, too, were influenced
by the dominant surrounding Hellenism — as well as in many pagan
sources. Such views seem to have prevailed throughout antiquity,
and they may be universal in patriarchal culture.

Philo's View of Women: Hebraic or Hellenic?

Philo was heir to two cultures, Jewish and Greek. As *Philo
Alexandrinus*, the dominant influence on his work was certainly the
Hellenistic world of which Alexandria formed the epicenter. But he
was clearly *Philo Judæus* in fundamental ways: loyal to his ethnic
community, the Jewish people, and devoted to his ethnic heritage,
the Hebrew Scriptures, albeit in Greek translation. True, his exegesis
often wears a Greek guise (particularly in his emphasis of the
figurative over the literal); but at the same time, his Jewish self-
definition is total, as his use of the first person plural when speaking
of his people clearly demonstrates. This self-identification is particularly evident in those works directly concerned with presenting the
history of the people Israel and its obligation to observe the rules of
the Torah literally even while granting their allegorical significance.
One might even say that Philo's νοῦς ("cognitive faculty") is Greek,
while his αἴσθησις ("affective faculty") remains staunchly Jewish.

Until recently, this "Greek" aspect was downplayed by Jewish
scholars like H. A. Wolfson, who sought a nexus between Philo's
ideas (assumed to represent Alexandrian Jewish scholarship) and
the exegetical enterprise of his historical contemporaries, the Jerusalem sages in the last years of the Second Temple.[35] Conversely,
Philo's "Jewish" aspect was downplayed by Christian scholars like
E. R. Goodenough, eager to portray the discussion of *Logos* (which

---

[35]*Philo: Foundations of Religious Philosophy in Judaism, Christianity and
Islam* I, II (Cambridge: Harvard, 1947).

Church fathers like Clement, Origen and Ambrose somewhat anachronistically identified with the *Logos* of John) as more Christian than Jewish in spirit.[36] Today, the general opinion lies, with Samuel Sandmel, somewhere between these two extremes. In Sandmel's words: "Philo's basic religious ideas are Jewish, his intuitions are Jewish, and his loyalties Jewish, but his *explanations* of ideas, intuitions and loyalties are invariably Greek.[37] Philo's stance neither melded Greek and formative-Christian ideas nor contained strong elements of traditional rabbinism. Nothing in his writings suggests personal acquaintance with the Nazarenes or the rabbis of Jesus' time, or with the ideas of either group.[38] Conversely, neither Mishnah nor Talmud mentions Philo (or, for that matter, Socrates, Plato or Aristotle), even though classical rabbinic literature often exhibits Greek vocabulary and Hellenistic influence. Nor do we have clear evidence that Philo represented a whole school of Alexandrian Jewish scholarship. The survival of his work is a historical accident resulting from its usefulness for Christian *midrash*; Philo himself may have been *sui generis*, a unique phenomenon.

In assessing Philo's dependence on earlier epistemological systems, demonstration of the many parallels between his terminology and that of the Greek classics on which he draws is only half the enterprise. One must also consider whether Philo's views have any warrant, linguistic or conceptual, in the Hebrew Scriptures (or, more precisely, in the LXX). When we compare Philo's views on women with those expressed in Scripture, we find that the Bible paints a far more favorable picture.

---

[36]*An Introduction to Philo Judæus* (New Haven: Yale University Press, 1940); *By Light, Light: The Mystic Gospel of Hellenistic Judaism* (New Haven: Yale University Press, 1935).

[37]*Philo of Alexandria: An Introduction* (Oxford University, 1979), 15 (emphasis added). See also Naomi G. Cohen, "The Jewish Dimension of Philo's Judaism — An Elucidation of *de Spec. Leg.* IV 132-150," *JJS* 38 (1987): 165-86.

[38]This observation is all the more remarkable when we recall that Philo does seem to know of the Essenes — if his essay on the Therapeutae in fact describes the Essene sect rather than an otherwise unknown group. Marcus suggests in his "Introduction" to *Questions and Answers on Genesis and Exodus*, that "Philo's twofold method of interpretation is a forerunner of the fourfold method used by Rabbinic and Patristic commentators." This is not to say that the rabbis knew of Philo's work or even of his existence; nor need they have, since the Mishnaic and Talmudic editors lived long after Philo's time. But even his fellow sages in Judæa probably never heard of him. Though the rabbis clearly knew some Greek vocabulary, there is no convincing evidence that any of them spoke Greek with fluency. While Philo mentions taking part in a pilgrimage to Jerusalem, he does not mention any rabbis by name, even though he was engaged in a similar exegetical enterprise.

This is not to say that Scripture contains no pejorative statements on women; one thinks in particular of texts like Proverbs and Ecclesiastes, which depict the unattached woman as a sexual snare. But scriptural disparagement of women stems mostly from the later biblical and intertestamental books — precisely those subject to Hellenistic influence. Earlier traditions, including the Torah itself and sections of the historical books such as Judges and Kings, express quite different, "native Israelite" attitudes towards women. This is true even of the creation accounts. Genesis 1 (as interpreted in rabbinic and patristic literature) has both sexes created equally in the image of God. Even Genesis 2, which (read as myth of origins) aims to explain such social realities as the subordination of women, does not assert women's *intellectual* inferiority as do classical Greek sources. And rabbinic exegesis merely distinguishes two different types of intelligence assigned to the sexes: it claims that while *hokmah* (חכמה, in the sense of cognitive wisdom) was given to man (*b. Yoma* 66b), *binah* (בינה, intuitive understanding or common sense) was given to woman (*b. Nid.* 45b and elsewhere) — as shown by a talmudic pun on Gen 2:22, "and he built [the rib] into a woman." This distinction (resting on the anagram of *b-n-y* [ב-נ-י], to build, and *b-y-n* [ב-י-נ], to understand) is far less damaging to women than Philo's Hellenistic distinction between male νοῦς and female αἴσθησις.

When we look at the image of women in Genesis as a whole, we find Scripture far from portraying women in the Greek fashion as *bereft of intellect* or as primarily *passive*. To the contrary, the matriarchs are presented as cunning creatures who compensate for their lack of legal authority by their powers of deceit, cajolery, and manipulation. Scripture openly acknowledges women's cleverness and capacity to lead. One need only recall the resourcefulness of Sarah and Rebekah in helping younger sons supplant the firstborn (Gen 21:9ff.; 27:5ff.); Rachel's quickwitted deception of her father (Gen 31:19ff.); the leading roles of Miriam (Exod 15:20ff.), Deborah (Judg 4-5), and Huldah (II Kgs 22:11ff.); or the effective game plans of Naomi (Ruth 2:17ff) and Esther (Esth 4-5) to realize this. All these women are extremely savvy and well endowed with Philonic νοῦς. For Scripture, this was no problem; but it bothered Philo, who felt constrained to maintain that the wisdom of a Sarah or a Miriam was in essence a masculine attribute with which the woman was anomalously endowed.

As for Philo's strictures on women's *morality*, here too we note that Scripture makes no negative moral judgment of those women who fulfill their anatomical destiny and domestic duties as devoted wives and mothers (epitomized in Prov 31:10-31). Disparagement of women occurs only in the context of the "strange" woman (i.e., the outsider to the family), who is reviled as a potential source of sexual temptation (cf. Prov 6:20-7:27). Moreover, such strictures are found almost exclusively in the later wisdom literature or in post-biblical writings like Ben Sira. Yet these late sources — precisely those so prominently featured by Swidler[39] — are of late enough provenance to have been influenced by the Hellenistic ideas that prevailed in the Eastern Mediterranean after the conquests of Alexander the Great. Hence they may well reflect Hellenistic rather than Judaic culture.

In comparing Philo's thought with that of the rabbis of Judæa, we need to distinguish modes of thought from attitudes. Rabbinic literature, reduced to writing from about 200 C.E. onward, certainly exhibits the influence of the Greek *mode of dichotomous thought*. But when it comes to *judgments*, certain perceptions of women were common, perhaps universal, throughout the ancient world. All these societies were patriarchies. Yet as Ross Kraemer points out, we must be wary of equating the status or opportunities of all women in the public domain of all patriarchal cultures. Other factors, such as class, may have played a part as significant as that of gender.[40]

It is true that both Greek and Jewish literatures tend to polarize male and female attributes. A crucial theme for Philo is the distinction between the male as personification of νοῦς and the female as personification of αἴσθησις. The same dichotomous mode of thought generates the formally (though not conceptually) similar rabbinic exegesis in the Babylonian Talmud. The talmudic assertion that God had bestowed *hokmah* (חכמה, cognitive wisdom) on men and *binah* (בינה, intuitive understanding) on women explains R. Eliezer's statement that women have no *hokmah* but with the distaff[41] — a view which has its counterpart in Hector's telling

---

[39]See above, n. 7.

[40]See *Maenads* on women's opportunities to take part in various public religious rituals, which were denied to women in the Jewish tradition. Kraemer maintains that in those cultures, class was more significant than gender in determining who had access to the life of the mind and spirit. See also her "Jewish Women in the Diaspora World of Late Antiquity," in Baskin (ed.), *Jewish Women in Historical Perspective*. However, it is not clear to what extent women's religious rituals were treated with the same degree of respect or importance as rituals performed by men in the exercise of the official, "civil" religion of the Greek city-states or other Hellenistic cultures.

[41]*B. Yoma* 66b. This judgment rests on a wordplay about different meanings of *hokmah*. The noun rarely appears in the Torah outside of Exod 28-36, where it refers exclusively to the manual skills of making priestly accoutrements and

Andromache to return to her loom and leave the conduct of the Trojan war to men.[42] The Greek cultural distinction between men as rational "thinkers" and women as emotional "feelers" still persists in the western world largely because of the influence of Greek classics, the cornerstone of a "good" education until the second half of the twentieth century.

In sum, Philo's depiction of the female character owes far more to Greek ideas, mediated through Hellenistic culture, than to the Jewish Scripture he inherited from his ancestors.

Philo, Paul, and Christian Feminism

This conclusion is important in another context. The early Church identified Philo with an enlightened, progressive Hellenism more compatible than Jewish thought with Christian doctrine, and some Christian feminists have claimed Greco-Roman culture as the source of the alleged "improvement" in women's status achieved by the early Church. But here, the well-known Pauline strictures on women (e.g., I Cor 7:1-9; 11:2-16; 14:31-35; Col 3:18-22; Eph 5:22-33; I Tim 2:8-15; 5:3-16) present an exegetical quandary. Some simply dismiss the problem by ascribing Paul's misogynism to his Jewish heritage rather than his Hellenistic background.[43] Others observe that we cannot blame Paul for the strictures on women in I Timothy when critical opinion is not convinced that Paul wrote it.[44] One cannot have it both ways. If the views expressed in the Pastorals are not authentically Pauline, then *a fortiori* they cannot be blamed on his Jewish background! But even granting Paul's authorship of I Timothy, enough has been said here to suggest that his views on women (like Philo's) cannot be assumed to stem exclusively from Jewish heritage. It is also worth considering whether the statements in Timothy may represent the Church's response to the growing Gnostic heresy that, as Elaine Pagels has shown, assigned women an ecclesiastical role far closer to that of men.[45] In any case, as Elizabeth Clark puts it, "[t]he oft-repeated theory that early Christianity exalted women's status in general is not borne out by

---

decorations for the tabernacle. Eliezer meant that a woman's *hokmah* was only of the type required for spinning and weaving, and not of the cognitive type signified by the term as used in the Talmud. In both Mishnah and Talmud, the adjective *hakam* (חכם), "wise," used as a noun, specifically denotes a Jewish sage.

[42]*Iliad* 6: 490-93; cf. the discussion by Mary Lefkowitz in this volume.

[43]E.g., Constance Parvey; see above, n. 5.

[44]E.g., Bristow, *What Paul Really Said*, esp. 67-69.

[45]*The Gnostic Gospels* (New York: Vintage/Random House, 1981), 57-83.

the evidence."[46]

Some early Christian feminists based their assumptions about Paul's views on uncritical reliance on Swidler, whose work erroneously implied both that the Talmud (a voluminous and discursive compendium of traditions transmitted through six centuries) presented a monolithic view of the status of women in Jewish law, and that the rabbinic image of women was unrelievedly negative. His work reinforced the notion that evidence of suppression of women in the New Testament, or in the early Church, can be laid at the door of "retrograde" Jewish tradition while progressive elements must be credited to the influence of Greco-Roman culture.

Quite apart from its question-begging character, serious methodological errors of ahistoricism affect this hypothesis. First, it totally ignores one crucial fact: the Babylonian Talmud stems from quite another time and place (much later, against the backdrop of Zoroastrian Persia), so that its statements on women cannot arbitrarily be taken to reflect first-century Palestinian Judaism. Second, even the Mishnah, though created in Roman Palestine, was not edited until 200 C.E.; here too one must avoid anachronism. Third, no weight is assigned to evidence that classical Greek disparagement of women still prevailed in the Hellenistic culture of Philo's Alexandria, Paul's Asia Minor, and throughout the eastern Mediterranean of late antiquity. And fourth, Swidler and his followers ignore the prevalence of misogynistic attitudes in the writings of Church Fathers like Tertullian, who identified all women with Eve and called them "the devil's gateway"[47] (*On the Apparel of Women*). These errors of interpretation are happily corrected by the works of Rosemary Ruether, Elisabeth Schüssler Fiorenza, and others who have based their analysis on a more rigorous methodology.

Writers on women in the ancient world should try to steer between the Scylla of polemic and the Charybdis of apologetic. Here I have indicated the folly of making snap judgments about women's image or status in any culture of antiquity, considered in isolation, before all the evidence is in.

---

[46]*Jerome, Chrysostom, and Friends,* vi.
[47]"On the Apparel of Women," trans. S. Thelwell, *Ante-Nicene Fathers* (Grand Rapids: Eerdmans, 1982).

The "Woman with the Soul of Abraham"
Traditions about the Mother of the Maccabean Martyrs

Robin Darling Young

Her name is unknown in the earliest literary records of her heroic death in the persecution of Antiochus IV Epiphanes, yet the mother of the seven brother-martyrs achieved sufficient renown in Hellenistic Judaism to become a subject of celebration in two apocryphal books and, later, a paragon of self-sacrifice in both the Jewish and early Christian traditions. In the Jewish tradition she would become known as Hannah or Miriam bat Tanhum,[1] in the Greek Christian tradition, Solomone, and in the Syriac, Mart Simouni.[2]

---

[1] Aharon (Ronald E.) Agus, *The Binding of Isaac and Messiah. Law, Martyrdom and Deliverance in Early Rabbinic Religiosity* (Albany: SUNY, 1988), 11-32. See also Gerson D. Cohen, "The Story of Hannah and Her Seven Sons in Hebrew Literature," in *Mordecai M. Kaplan Jubilee Volume* (New York: Jewish Theological Seminary of America, 1953), 109-22. Finally, see J. Gutman, "The Mother and her Seven Sons in Aggadah and in II and IV Maccabees" (Hebrew) in M. Schwabe and J. Gutman (eds.), *Sefer Yohanan Levi [Commentationes Iudaico-Hellenisticae in Memoriam Iohannis Lewy]* (Jerusalem: 1949). General surveys of IV Maccabees may be found in Schürer-Vermes III.1, 588-93. See also H. Anderson, "Four Maccabees," in *OTP* II, 531-62. Still useful are A. Dupont-Sommer, *Le quatrième livre des Maccabées* (Paris: H. Champion, 1939) and F.-M. Abel, *Les livres des Maccabées* (Paris: Editions du Cerf, 1948). M. Hadas, *The Third and Fourth Books of Maccabees* (New York: Harper, 1953) is an older English translation. On dating, E. J. Bickermann, "The Date of Fourth Maccabees," *Louis Ginzberg Jubilee Volume* (New York: Jewish Theological Seminary of America, 1945), 105-12, is to be preferred despite the recent contention of Breitenstein that IV Maccabees was composed in the second century. See U. Breitenstein, *Beobachtungen zu Sprache, Stil und Gedankengut des vierten Makkabäerbuches* (Basel and Stuttgart: Schwabe, 1978). Most recently, see J. W. van Henten, "Einige Prolegomena zum Studium der jüdischen Martyrologie," *Bijdragen* 3 (1985).

[2] There is an extensive literature on the use of the Maccabean martyrs in later Christian literature. See, for example, O. Perler, "Das Vierte Makkabäerbuch, Ignatius von Antiochien und die Ältesten Martyrerberichte," *Rivista di Archeologia Christiana* 15 (1949): 47-72. Also cf. Abel, *Les livres*, 381-84: "Excursus VI, Les sept frères Maccabées dans la tradition"; M. Maas, "Die Maccabäer als christlicher Heilige," *MGWJ* 44 (1900): 145-56; J. Oberman, "The Sepulchre of the Maccabean Martyrs," *JBL* 50 (1931): 250-65; E. Bickermann, "Les Maccabées de Malalas," *Byzantion* 21 (1951): 73-83. Margaret Schatkin, "The Maccabean Martyrs," *VC* 28 (1974): 97-113, argues for an Antiochene location for the events, despite the Jerusalem setting of II Maccabees and the unclear setting of IV Maccabees. A mid-fourth century Syriac translation from a Greek martyrology is the first to call the mother Shimuni. See W. Wright, *Journal of Sacred Literature* 8 (1865/66): 45-57, 423-32. For further Syriac works on the martyrs, see R. L. Bensly and W. E. Barnes, *The Fourth Book of Maccabees and Kindred Documents in Syriac* (Cambridge: University Press, 1895). The foundations of the Greek tradition

Despite her popularity and the official devotion to her in ancient and medieval religious life, the depiction of the mother in the two earliest documents in which she appears — II and IV Maccabees — has not received a separate study. Although the apocryphal works themselves have been repeatedly and exhaustively discussed,[3] no study in English of their understanding of the faithful womanmartyr has yet appeared. Furthermore, since the role of women in Hellenistic Judaism has been subject recently to a thorough reexamination, a review of the figure of the mother in the Maccabean texts is timely if not overdue. This essay discusses, first, the narratives of the Maccabean martyrdoms and the mother's role in them; it examines next the terminology used to refer to the mother; finally it attempts to assess her inner life and her public role in persecuted Judaism as portrayed by each author.

There is no good reason to doubt that an actual mother of seven sons existed and was put to death publicly along with them; even the various tortures the family members endured are not implausible historical occurrences. Yet it does seem likely that each author exercised some interpretation of the subject matter in order to present the particular significance of the martyrdoms for Jewish audiences. Hence, details of the events, of the accompanying speeches, and of the character and location of the participants vary from the first composition to the second. These differences may indicate the sort of audience each author wished to address. Moreover, in each audience there were quite likely women for whom the mother, in her virtuous conduct and sacrifice, was meant to be a model to emulate.

The Events of the Martyrdom in II Maccabees

The story of the mother and her seven sons first appears in II Maccabees. Like the history by Jason of Cyrene, of which it is an abridgment, this first-century B.C.E. apocryphon both recounts the events of 180-161 in Seleucid-controlled Palestine and, further, interprets the events theologically.[4] Within this history, the author of II Maccabees has inserted several accounts of martyrdoms under

---

may be found in sermons on the subject of the martyrs and their contemporary cult by Gregory Nazianzen and John Chrysostom.

[3]General bibliographic information may be found in Anderson, *Four Maccabees*, and in Schürer-Vermes.

[4]For a good bibliographical survey of II Maccabees, see Schürer-Vermes III.1, 531-37. Especially helpful are A. Momigliano, "The Second Book of Maccabees," *CP* 70 (1975): 81-88; and R. Doran, *Temple Propaganda: The Purpose and Character of 2 Maccabees* (Washington, D.C.: CBQMS, 1981).

Antiochus IV Epiphanes, the Seleucid king, following the profanation of the Temple in Jerusalem.

The martyrology (6:7-7:42) constitutes a distinct literary unit which both emphasizes the evil of the Seleucid rulers and explains the success of Judas Maccabeus. Thus, it is both an independent narrative and an interpretation of the events of the war. The transition to the martyrology — the remark that "A man could neither keep the Sabbath, nor observe the feasts of his fathers, nor so much as confess himself to be a Jew" (6:6) — succinctly provides the catalyst for the action of the faithful. The martyrology proper begins and ends with the deaths of pious, observant Jewish mothers along with their children. This narrative section emphasizes the contrast between the highly public events of Hellenistic Palestine and the private, domestic life interrupted with the compromise of the Law. The rejection of this compromise by faithful Jews leads directly to persecution and death.

The martyrology of II Maccabees first describes (6:7-17) the compulsion of Jews to participate in pagan rites celebrating Antiochus's birthday and the public humiliations and executions of mothers who circumcised their sons; it adds that Jews had to meet secretly to observe the Sabbath. Next, II Mac 6:18-31 describes the martyrdom of the scribe Eleazer for refusing to eat pork. The trial, interrogations, tortures, and deaths of the sons and their mother occupy vss. 1-42 of the following chapter.

The author of II Maccabees explicitly states that these accounts of the Jerusalem martyrdoms are to "serve as a reminder (ἕως ὑπομνήσεως) to us" (6:17) and that those events were "punishments designed not to destroy but to discipline our people" (μὴ πρὸς ὄλεθρον, ἀλλὰ πρὸς παιδείαν τοῦ γένους ἡμῶν εἶναι; 6:12). Although the author does not explicitly make the point, there seems to be an implicit contrast between the propaedeutic punishments of the nation as a sacrificial offering and the impious sacrifices that the "Athenian senator" (6:1) as the delegate of Antiochus has forced upon the Jews of Jerusalem.

A further purpose of the martyrdom's literary account, as the author makes Eleazar say, is to "leave to the young a noble example (ὑπόδειγμα γενναῖον) of how to die a good death willingly and nobly for the revered and holy laws" (6:28). Eleazar declares that although he "might have been saved from death," he was "in my soul ... glad to suffer these things because I fear him" (6:30). The reported speech of Eleazar is emphasized by the author's comment that he was "leaving in his death an example of nobility and a memorial of courage, not only to the young but to the great body of his nation" (6:31).

Particularly interesting in this passage is the way in which the author not only heightens the impact of the narrative but also inserts an encapsulated description of Eleazar's emotional states: gladness and fear, moderated by the Stoic virtue of ἀνδρεία, manliness. These states, and the choice between temporary safety and that eternal reward yielded by keeping "the law of our fathers" (7:1), presage the climax of the martyrology, the deaths of the mother and her sons. The author has constructed the narrative to demonstrate how effective Eleazar's ὑπόδειγμα was, because the very example of manliness which he provided is immediately followed by the startling accounts of the "manliness" of children and of a woman.

The graduated construction of the first part of the martyrology consists of each son's examination by Antiochus, an attempt to persuade the child to break the Law by eating pork, the son's speech of refusal, and finally his torture and death. Throughout, the sons are encouraged by their mother to choose Torah instead of the proposals of the king. Her influence must be seen as essential, even though it is moderated by that of Eleazar. Further mitigating her role is the presentation of her discourse: she never speaks publicly; her remarks are confined to private exhortations, and these only to her younger sons. That the conflict occurs with Antiochus himself makes this contrast even more striking. Each son will give a short interpretation of the significance of his torture and death, but the spokesman for the group, probably the eldest son, states the general opposition: "We are ready to die rather than to transgress the laws of our fathers" (7:2).

The sons' deaths provided a rich opportunity for this, and also for the author's descriptive powers. The first son's tongue is extracted, he is scalped, his hands and feet are cut off, and even then "the king ordered them to take him to the fire, still breathing, and to fry him in a pan" (7:5). With the smoke from burning flesh surrounding them, the mother and her sons are portrayed as stating their confidence that the deity is "watching over us and in truth has compassion on us" (7:6). The author means to link the group to Moses' prediction in Deut 32:36 that "The Lord will vindicate his people and have compassion on his servants when he sees that their power is gone, and there is none remaining...." Israelite paganizing is thus associated with the Jewish Hellenizers under the Seleucids. The Deuteronomic notice that the deity "takes vengeance on his adversaries, and makes expiation for the land of his people" thus applies to the situation of the Maccabean martyrs. Such a typological reading on the part of the author of II Maccabees allows the casting of the family as a prediction of divine wrath. This wrath is in turn fulfilled in II Macc 8:5, where the author writes of Judas Maccabeus: "The Gentiles could not withstand him, for the wrath of the Lord had turned to mercy [on the people of Israel]."

The mother and her sons, along with the martyrs who preceded them, are both examples of observant Judaism and fulfillments of prophecy. This historical and typological viewpoint dominates the character depictions. However, the text's theological interests are also pronounced and, like the martyrdoms, they lead in ascending order to the exhortation of the mother. The sons each make a short speech to the king in which they contrast the royal power with heavenly power and emphasize their expected resurrection (e.g., 7:9). The fifth and sixth sons predict vengeance from God and, in addition, explain that their suffering comes about because of "our sins against our own God" (7:18). This explanation recalls once more the Mosaic prophecy.

The climax of the martyrology occurs at the last son's decision between transgression and death. Here the author introduces the narrative device of private speech: that of the mother, in her own language of Aramaic or, less likely, Hebrew (the author claims she speaks "in the paternal language"; the phrase is τῇ πατρίῳ φωνῇ). Two sections in chapter seven, 21-23 and 27-29, record her speeches to her sons. These can be characterized as hortatory and persuasive, but each is brief when compared with the lengthy exhortation of IV Maccabees.

In 7:21-23, the mother speaks to all seven of her sons. She is in possession of several virtues, again Stoic in origin but not unconnected to Jewish tradition. She has good courage, but this is due to her "hope in the Lord," i.e., her expectation of resurrection and immortality already pronounced by the six sons: εὐψύχως ἔφερεν διὰ τὰς ἐπὶ κύριον ἐλπίδας (7:21). She is said to encourage (παρακάλει) each son because he has a "noble spirit" (γενναίῳ ... φρονήματι) and to have "awakened the female (or, delicate) reasoning with masculine courage" (τὸν θῆλυν λογισμὸν ἄρσενι θυμῷ διεγείρασα). This is the author's understanding, based on a Stoic division between masculine and feminine attributes, of how a mother could have pronounced the following speech, which asserts the contemporary belief in the creatio ex nihilo and the resurrection to life as a reward for obedience to the Law.[5]

---

[5]For the general features of contemporary Stoicism, see J. M. Rist, *Stoic*

The mother's second speech is a reprise of the first, although in this instance it is a deception of Antiochus, who had urged her to dissuade the youngest boy from death. Again, the author contrasts the benefits of the temporal king with those of the "King of the Universe" (7:9). Antiochus promises to make the boy "rich and enviable ... he would have [him] as friend and entrust him with [public] services." To dissuade her son, the mother makes three statements. The first (7:27b) begins with a plea (Υιε, ἐλεησόν με) that the son be merciful and remember that she bore, suckled, and raised him. The second (7:28) begins with an instruction (ἀξιῶ σε, τέκνον) to observe that the cosmos takes its origin, as does mankind (ἄνθρωπος) itself, in God and not in preexistent matter.

The final statement of the mother's speech is hortatory: she commands the son not to fear "this public executioner" (μὴ φοβηθῆς τὸν δήμιον τοῦτον) but to follow his brothers' example and be restored to her, presumably in the general resurrection. The final son, of course, makes an even longer speech to Antiochus in which he expands on the points his mother had made. He recalls the Law of Moses, the covenant with Abraham and the promise of resurrection which by now it is understood to entail, and he casts the children's deaths in sacrificial terms. He has hopes that Antiochus will confess the one God, and that God will end the afflictions of Israel "and through me and my brothers to make stop the anger of the all-ruling [God] which justly has come upon our race together" (7:38). Nothing more is heard from the mother; the author notes only that after her youngest son's death, the mother died "last of all" (7:41). Perhaps the Greek verb, ἐτελεύτησεν, can be read as a tribute, connoting as it does "completion" or "fulfillment." The author then resumes the narrative of the Maccabean revolt.

Within two chapters, the author of II Maccabees has initiated a genre, the martyrology, which employs both Stoic terminology and religious ideas to portray a new set of heroes for Israel. These figures are set apart from the military heroes who occupy most of the Maccabean literature, but is it the opinion of the author that their sacrifice for the covenant, the Mosaic Law, and the more recent doctrines of *creatio ex nihilo* and the resurrection to life, familiar in the contemporary Wisdom tradition, makes possible the Jewish military victories which follow their deaths in Jerusalem.

Philosophy (London: Cambridge University Press, 1969). Philo also accepted an eclectic combination of Stoic moral philosophy and Middle Platonic metaphysics. An ancient philosophical commonplace claimed the feminine element in the human constitution to be weaker and more subject to the emotions than the manly, reasonable element.

The Mother in IV Maccabees

Written perhaps a century later, IV Maccabees is an interpretive expansion of the prior work. In this text, the narratives of the Maccabean military engagements are relatively unimportant. The theological interpretation, combined with an even more thoroughgoing use of Stoic ideas, provides the substance of the later treatment. From his predecessor he takes the notion of manly reason, hope in the resurrection (or at least in the certainty of life with God in heaven), and a speculation upon descent from Abraham in a now-spiritualized covenantal parentage. Where the author of II Maccabees had shown the coherence of the Jewish families in death, his later counterpart will show how the family, although important for training in religious devotion, will be transcended into a kind of spiritual parentage superior to that of the flesh.

The fourth apocryphal volume devoted to the subject of the Maccabean revolt is considerably longer than the account devoted to the martyrs in its predecessor. Fully eighteen chapters describe, in much greater detail, the deaths of Eleazar, the seven sons, and their mother. Furthermore, very little historical information is provided; instead, the author seems to assume that his audience commemorates the martyrs on the anniversary of their deaths. However, this last observation remains a point of controversy.[6] The account of the mother's actions, and the interpretation of them, is considerably more complex than in the previous volume. They are set at the end of the entire work, itself rather clear in structure, and function as its climax.

IV Maccabees has been described as a diatribe or discourse, and among forms of philosophical literature it most closely resembles that genre. It includes panegyrics, one of which is devoted to the mother of the sons. It also, however, verges on paraenesis, or the hortatory genre, and clearly is intended to persuade and move its readers to consider the virtuous Jews as models for their own attitudes toward unjust rulers (cf. 18:1-2). If it was composed in the mid-first century, then the increasing tensions with Rome, at least in Palestine, would have given the accounts contemporary relevance.

Although the book uses a philosophical form and employs the vocabulary of eclectic Stoicism and Middle Platonism, it places sacri-

---

[6]On the date of delivery and the setting of IV Maccabees, see most recently the discussion and summary in Anderson, *Fourth Maccabees*, 534-37. On its philosophical background, see R. Renehan, "The Greek Philosophic Background of Fourth Maccabees," *Rheinisches Museum für Philologie* 115 (1972): 223-38.

fice, a customary feature of Jewish religiosity, at the center of the events it describes. The author begins the work by labelling the work a φιλοσοφώτατον λόγον; in fact, it is debatable whether, by the end of the book, the author has been able to maintain the philosophical meaning of the vocabulary employed; perhaps this vocabulary has been conformed to the theological interpretation lying behind notions of sacrifice, spiritual parentage, devotion to the Law, and resurrection to eternal life.

This tension is evident right at the beginning of the work, which states that it is meant to be a demonstration that "devout reason (εὐσεβὴς λογισμός) is sovereign (αὐτοδέσποτός ἐστιν) over the emotions (τῶν παθῶν)" (1:1; cf. 1:13, 76). Although many examples would prove the point, the author states that it can best be shown by the "noble bravery of those who died for the sake of virtue, Eleazar and the seven brothers and their mother" (1:8b). Nine distinct parts can be counted within the book. The first of these is a prologue, an attempt to prove the point of 1:1.

As with II Maccabees, two types of kingship are contrasted: the temporal kind belonging to Antiochus, and the eternal kingship of God. Since reason is the human being's link to God, it too is a kind of king. Along with αὐτοδέσποτος it is, in this section, called αὐτοκράτωρ (absolute master). The prologue occupies 1:13-16. It equates following the Law (1:2, 8, 10) with a life of reason prompted by the cultivation of virtues. The next section, 2:17-3:18, lists testimoniae of reason's rule over Moses, Jacob, and David. In 3:19 the author makes a transition to the "present occasion" (perhaps the anniversary of the martyrs' deaths) to add names to the testimonia list by pointing out new heroes. He can also, of course reinterpret the significance of the old heroes through the schema of the "pious" or of "devout reason." The next section, 3:20-4:26, establishes the context by means of a recollection of events under Antiochus.

The next five sections alternate the narrative material of the martyrologies proper with interpretive panegyrics that address reason. The material in 5:1-6:30 records the speech and death of Eleazar, which are followed in 6:31-7:31 by an address to reason. The successive deaths of the sons are recounted in 8:1-14:1; again, the narrative is followed by a section of direct address to that reason which ruled in the sons. Finally, in 14:12-18, the story of reason operative in the mother occupies a narrative, a panegyric, and an final section which may be a kind of appendix. The author, then, has followed the basic structure of the martyrology of II Maccabees but has added the diatribe and panegyric forms. Further, IV Maccabees accords much greater space, proportionally, to the paradox of reason's triumph in the weakest of rational beings: a woman tied spiritually with the bonds of motherhood.

This paradox has been anticipated already at the end of the panegyric, where the brothers are recorded as exhorting each other to courage in the face of tortures by recalling examples of faith such as the three boys in the furnace (Dan 3). One however, states to the others: "Remember whence you came and at the hand of what father Isaac would have been sacrificed for the sake of piety (εὐσέβειαν)" (13:13). Later, the sons exclaim in unison: "If we die in such a way, Abraham and Isaac and Jacob will welcome us, and all the fathers will praise us" (13:18). This recollection of Abraham is echoed in 14:20; 15:29; and 17:26, where, as we shall see, the mother is compared to Abraham, who is himself more than a mere example of faith. As in the Wisdom tradition (e.g., Wis 10:5), the supposed willingness of Isaac to be slain and the willingness of Abraham to sacrifice him are supreme examples of self-sacrifice and obedience on the part of both parent and child.[7]

The text does not ignore the brothers' mutual affection but uses it to heighten the pathos of their death scene. Coming from the same womb, suckling the same milk, and enjoying the embraces of the same mother prepares them for training in the Law and discipline in the virtues. These virtues – righteousness (τῷ δικαίῳ βίῳ), the zeal for beauty and goodness (καλοκἀγαθία), and piety (εὐσέβειαν) – made them not only loving brothers but, through εὔνοια and ὁμόνοια (literally, being of one, good mind), able to disregard both their suffering and their brotherly love (φιλαδελφίαν).[8]

If the brothers' mutual love comes from their childhood and training, their mother is subject to the same emotions (πάθη) as her children, on the principle of likeness (15:4). More than fathers, mothers have a "deeper sympathy" with their children (15:4-5). The author informs his audience at the beginning of this section that the youths' fortitude paled beside that of their mother as she watched them dismembered and dying. "Do not be amazed that reason ruled these men in their tortures, since a womanly mind despised even more varied tortures [than those]" (14:11). The γυναικὸς νοῦς was weak by definition, and logically it would be more likely to be con-

---

[7]In his *Philo's Place in Judaism: A Study of Conceptions of Abraham in Jewish Literature* (New York: KTAV, 1971), S. Sandmel devotes only four pages (56-59) to the figure of Abraham in IV Maccabees.

[8]The interpretation of the Akedah or "Binding" of Isaac became popular in later tradition. See, for example, J. Daniélou, 'La Typologie d'Isaac dans le christianisme primitif," *Bib* 28 (1947): 363-93.

quered by the συμπάθεια which even irrational animals feel toward their offspring in the natural order. Since mothers are "weaker in being" than fathers, they also feel more love for their children, the more they bear (15:4).

Furthermore, maternal love (στοργή) was of a lower order; it was complex (πολύπλοκος) and connected to the bowels (πρὸς τὴν τῶν σπλάγχνων συμπάθειαν, 14:13); the author uses this to contrast it to the mother's λογισμός, trained in the law, which overcomes her natural love. This passage initiates a series of contrasts which forms the entire section and echoes the contrasts already established between self-sacrifice and safety, the Law and the temporal king, the eternal life enjoyed by the martyrs and the everlasting punishment of Antiochus (18:5), and the like.

The treatment of the mother may be divided into a series of separate rhetorical units which allow the reader to see how the author intends to move the audience. Since the text, like the prose style employed, is complex, it is possible to divide it in various ways. However, eleven major sections suggest themselves if the divisions follow rhetorical lines. They also serve to heighten the interest of the audience with a series of apostrophes, explanations, speeches, and a final exhortation.

The first section has been described above; 14:11-20 is a description of maternal love and an attempt to make the audience recognize that this mother's love alone surpassed that of all mothers, rational and irrational. Her status as ὁμόψυχος with Abraham may be seen as an echo of 13:12, and it emphasizes her high religious status through her bonds with the patriarch; just as her sons, nourished together physically and morally are ὁμόνοια with each other, she is ὁμόψυχος with Abraham. This will later be explained in 18:6-23, which treats the mother's training in virtue.

The next four sections, 15:1-10, 12-15, 16-28, and 29:6-16, are apostrophes. The first two address personified beings as if they were present to receive the praise, and likewise the second two address the mother herself as a preparation for her direct address later. Of the first set, the author makes the initial address to reason (λογισμέ) as "lord over the passions." This τύραννος is, again, meant to contrast with Antiochus the ruler, as is the εὐσέβεια meant to be set over against the sons as ποθεινοτέρα — dearer to her than they.

The author of IV Maccabees does not underestimate the strong passions of the mother at the level of the emotions, and a later passage (15:20) will not avoid a graphic description of her sons' fates and her own "tortures" at the sight. At this point, however, the diffi-culty is the choice between affection and piety or, in 15:2, between σωτηρία προσκαίρου, temporary safety or salvation at the word of Antiochus, and the εὐσέβεια which leads to "eternal life according to God" (εἰς αἰωνίαν Ζωὴν κατὰ θεόν). But the mother's choice is made more difficult because her natural love is increased by their own obedience and virtue (15:11).

The apostrophe to piety is balanced and completed by an apos-trophe to human affection, which in turn allows for the following section in praise of the mother. Human affection is here addressed as "sacred nature (ψύσις ἱερά), parental love, filial affection, nurture, and unconquerable maternal affections."

The two apostrophes to the mother herself each have a differ-ent object. The first describes her as she sees her children and offers an explanation for her refusal to weep, even though the family is surrounded by a group of spectators. First, devout reason, εὐσεβὴς λογισμός, gave her manliness (ἀνδρειώσας) in the midst of her pas-sions in order to transcend a temporary love of children (τὴν πρόσκαιρον φιλοτεκνίαν) understood as their material welfare. And second, "in the council-chamber of her heart" she could cast the correct ballot (15:29) because of her faith in God. The second apos-trophe promotes the mother to a special status by comparing her to other heroes of the faith. She is now explicitly equated with Abraham in her willingness to sacrifice her sons for the Law; this is seen as a greater good than their temporary presence on earth. "The daughter remembered," writes the author, "the bravery (καρτερία) of God-fearing (i.e., religious) Abraham." Since she has behaved like Abra-ham, she occupies a similar place in the spiritual history of Israel, as the titles the author accords her make clear. She is addressed as μήτηρ ἔθνους (mother of the nation), ἔκδικε τοῦ νόμου (vindicator of the Law), ὑπερασπίστρια τῆς εὐσεβείας (defender of piety), and τοῦ διὰ σπλάγχνων ἀγῶνος ἀθλοφόρε (prize-winner in the contest of the heart [or, innards]). She is "nobler than men in fortitude and stronger than heroes in endurance" (πρὸς καρτερίαν ... πρὸς ὑπομονήν). She is compared to the Ark of Noah because she was "buffeted on every side in the flood of passions and is, furthermore, the guardian of the law."

If these four successive addresses to the mother's piety and affection, and to her person itself, serve to move the audience to sympathy and perhaps even ὁμόνοια with the heroes being de-scribed, the author makes them in 16:1 appear to be a "proof" (ὁμολογουμένως, we must confess) of his original proposition: that αὐτοδέσποτός ἐστιν τῶν παθῶν ὁ εὐσεβὴς λογισμός, pious reason is the sole ruler of the passions.

Having established this point, the author continues to heighten the contrast between life ruled by the passions and that ruled by piety. He does this by recording in 16:5-11 a speech which might have been given by the mother had she been "weak in spirit" (δειλόψυχος). The false speech is a lament over her fate: she is deprived of children and grandchildren and she lacks an heir to bury her. By contrast, the next section heightens the mother's honor by calling her "holy and God-fearing" (16:12) in that she refuses to lament her sons at all. In verse 14 she is given explicitly masculine titles to match the ἀνδρεία of her soul: ὦ μῆτερ δι' εὐσέβειαν θεοῦ στρατιῶτι πρεσβῦτι καὶ γύναι – "Mother, through piety [you are at the same time] soldier, elder (a religious title; here perhaps signifying an official of the synagogue) and woman." Again, there is an implicit comparison with Abraham, for she is said to have encouraged her sons as if with hardened mind she "were this time bringing her sons to birth into immortal life..." (16:13). She has substituted, apparently, her natural parentage with one resembling that of Abraham through her devout reason and willingness to sacrifice her sons.

From the foregoing it is clear that that author of IV Maccabees has paid considerably more attention to the moral character of the mother than did the author of II Maccabees. The series of contrasts being described is not present, or is present only in a milder form, in the earlier work. Given the expanded treatment of the martyrs in IV Maccabees, a lengthier and more theological speech might have been expected for the mother. However, in the two speeches put into her mouth – 16:15-23 and 18:6-23 – the mother says nothing about the religious beliefs such as the *creatio ex nihilo* so important in the earlier work. Rather, in the first she exhorts her sons to "endure all hardship for God's sake," since for that reason they came into the world. She recalls the series of heroes, including Abraham and Isaac, Daniel, and the three boys in the furnace. The author explains that the mother had thereby persuaded the sons to accept death, indeed to prefer it to breaking the Law, and that the sons already knew that "those who die for the sake of God live to God" (16:25), an apparent reference to their speedy journey to heaven (17:8; 18:23) after their martyrdoms.

The mother's second speech is out of place in IV Maccabees; it occurs at the end of the book, after the narrative conclusion. It appears to be an afterthought or an addendum, as the first line implies: "The mother of the seven sons also addressed these righteous sayings to her children..." (18:6). In this speech, the mother emphasizes that she had remained chaste before her marriage, was not sexually corrupted ("no seducer of the desert nor deceiver in the field corrupted me" seems to refer back to the chastity of 16:7), and was a faithful wife. Perhaps this text is an attempt to connect her death in 17:1 with her own prior training in virtue: "Some of the guards declared that when she was about to be seized and put to death, she threw herself into the fire so that no one would touch her body."

This final speech represents the deceased father as being the teacher of the sons, especially concerning the Law and the Prophets and the earlier martyrs Abel, Isaac, Joseph, Phineas, the boys in the furnace, and Daniel. It is the father who provides a chain of texts predicting afflictions followed by resurrection, or at least restored life; here the mother appears merely to be transmitting her husband's teaching. It is odd that no mention of the father occurred earlier in the text. The speech may be, then, the author's attempt to justify the mother by including her in a pious, domestic setting.

The real conclusion of the book, 17:7-18:5, has two parts. The first summarizes the entire work and interprets the death of the martyrs. They enjoyed "the prize for victory ... incorruption in the long-lasting life" (ἀφθαρσία ἐν Ζωῇ πολυχρονίῳ; 17:13). They stand by God's throne, alive; they receive honor on earth (cf. 17:7-10). Furthermore, through their death for "the nation," the enemies were repulsed, Antiochus punished, and the land (i.e. of Israel) purified. This was because all the martyrs served as a ransom, as a propitiation for divine wrath. The concluding exhortation occurs at 18:1-2: "O offspring of the seed of Abraham, children of Israel, obey the Law and be pious in every way, knowing that pious reason is despot over the passions, interior and exterior pains."

ὁμόψυχος τοῦ Ἀβρααμ

If the later tradition and the cult of the Maccabean martyrs is any indication, the authors of the martyrologies in the two apocryphal books were successful in recommending to their audiences respect for Eleazar, the seven boys, and their mother. Of special importance, then, is the epithet ὁμόψυχος τοῦ Ἀβρααμ, "Having Abraham's soul," in understanding the status of the mother.

It seems clear from 18:1 that "the children of Abraham's seed," the Jews, are truly his children only if they follow the Law and obey the devout reason. The author of IV Maccabees especially wants to draw a line between physical or ethnic descent from Abraham and the observant Jew who is truly his son or daughter. This is the reason for his emphasis upon the mother's transcendence of familial relationships, the συμπάθεια which in peaceable times would have been essential to national and religious ties. Both works, however, mention the sins of Israel, for which these martyrs are the expiation. Thus simply being a Jew guarantees neither Abrahamic descent nor, just as important, ascent to his side at the throne of God ("gathered together in the choir of their fathers, having received pure and deathless souls from God," 18:23).

Another chance for this restoration to life comes with the martyrdoms of the family. With πρόσκαιρον safely transcended, they are reunited in heaven, once they have been "born" to life from Abraham — or, in this case, from his ὁμόψυχος, their own "manly" mother. One passage well summarizes the theological interpretation which the author of IV Maccabees attaches to the martyrdoms:

O mother with the seven sons, who destroyed the tyrant's violence and foiled his evil ideas (κακάς ἐπινοίας) and showed forth the nobility (γενναιότητα) of faith. Nobly (γενναίως) placed like a roof on the pillars of your children you withstood unyielding the earthquake (σεισμόν) of the tortures. Be happy, therefore, mother of the holy soul (ἱερόψυχε) since you have a secure hope, in God, of endurance. The moon in heaven does not stand as revered as you, lighting the way according to devotion for your seven sons equal to the stars (ἰσαστέρους), honored by God and placed firmly with them in heaven. Because your procreation of children was from father Abraham. (17:2-6)

More clearly, perhaps, than in previous passages it can be seen here that the mother is directly comparable to Abraham because she has born children "through faith." The passage combines two emphases of Genesis 22. The first is that, like Abraham, her children are numbered among the stars (clearly a modification of the biblical text, in which Abraham's descendants will be as numerous as the stars). The second is that, like Abraham, the mother was willing to obey a commandment which entailed the sacrifice of her children because she knew of this generation into heaven.

Certainly the text does not mean that the mother has inherited Abraham's soul. However, since she has been trained in virtues, chosen obedience and piety over temporal satisfaction, and encouraged her children to do the same, she has gained a "holy soul" and has become a progenitrix of the same order as he. Thus, her child-bearing was *of the same sort* as his. As several texts suggest, she is a second parent to those who are, by piety and the Law and not by physical descent or ethnicity, Jews.

Because the author of IV Maccabees has adopted a philosophical form for his hortatory address, it is impossible to determine what audience would have found it most congenial. The prominence of the mother might prompt a modern interpreter to speculate that the work was produced with an audience of women in mind. However, it might also be the case that the author wrote to justify the beginnings of the cult in Antioch or elsewhere. During the Hellenistic period, when the cult of Abraham included visits by Jews to his tomb in Hebron,[9] it may have been that the devotion to these martyrs and their supposed tomb in Antioch both required and made possible the interpretations seen above. Nevertheless, the author certainly wished to point beyond both cult and ethnic group to encourage imitation by those whose obedience to the Law might endanger their lives.

---

[9]Josephus attests to the importance of this site in *BJ* IV, 530-32, 554. See A. Pelletier, ed. and trans., *Guerre des Juifs* (Paris: Budé, 1982), III, 82 and nn. 231-32. Sozomen, a Palestinian Christian, also describes the site. See *Historia Ecclesiastica* II, 4, 1-6, trans. P. Festugière in *Sources Chrétiennes* 306 (Paris: Editions du Cerf, 1983), 244-48.

Portraits of Women in
Pseudo-Philo's *Biblical Antiquities*

Betsy Halpern-Amaru

Although Pseudo-Philo's attention to biblical women has been noted,[1] studies devoted either to his portrayal of individual women or to his treatment of female characters in general are notably lacking. To some extent this lacuna reflects the relatively recent nature of interest in representations of women in classical Jewish literature. However, to a significant degree it must also be attributed to the many unresolved questions regarding Pseudo-Philo's *Biblical Antiquities*. One is naturally hesitant to undertake analysis of a single topic in a work for which there is no consensus regarding its date of composition, sources, and even the concerns and purposes which motivated its author.[2] Yet, in spite of the many questions which surround the work, it is possible to delineate certain patterns and to draw some general conclusions about Pseudo-Philo's portrayal of biblical women. This essay is offered as a prolegomenon for the greatly needed close analyses of the pseudepigraphon's diverse narratives and characterizations, which may or may not substantiate the conclusions drawn here.

Unlike Josephus, Pseudo-Philo makes no claim to presenting the holy books of the Jews. Not only is his account limited to the period from Adam to the death of King Saul,[3] it is also notably uneven in its treatment of the various biblical stories. The work contains sixty-five short chapters; nineteen are devoted to the pentateuchal narratives, four to the Book of Joshua, and the remaining forty-two to Judges and I Samuel. Moreover, there is a

---

[1]D. J. Harrington, "Pseudo-Philo. A New Translation and Introduction," in *OTP* II, 310.

[2]On the date of the *Biblical Antiquities*, see the discussion in ibid., 299. On Pseudo-Philo's awareness of and interest in *Jubilees*, see M. R. James, *The Biblical Antiquities of Philo*, 2d ed. (New York: KTAV, 1971), 45; John Strugnell, "Philo (Pseudo) or *Liber Antiquitatum Biblicarum*," in *EJ* XIII, 408-9; and Louis Feldman's contrasting view in his "Prolegomenon" to James's work, liii. For a review of the theories concerning the purpose of the work, consult the discussions in Feldman's "Prolegomenon" and the introductory essays of D. J. Harrington, Charles Perrot, and P. M. Bogaert in *Pseudo-Philon: Les Antiquités Bibliques*, II (Paris: Cerf, 1976).

[3]In its most complete form the narrative ends in the midst of Saul's final speech. Many scholars have argued that the text as we have it is incomplete. However, Harrington, Perrot, and Bogaert maintain that the received version is complete. On the various manuscripts and translations see James, *Biblical*

distinct difference in the manner and style with which the author
deals with the pentateuchal as opposed to the later material. For the
period from Adam to the conquest of Canaan, he adopts a chronicler's style: a rapid and highly selective review of biblical history into
which are inserted a few narratives not found in Hebrew Scriptures.[4]
In contrast, the early prophetic material, particularly that of Judges
and I Samuel, is retold and expanded in a manner comparable to
that of *Jubilees* and Josephus's *Antiquities*. Given this approach,
one does not find well-developed portraits of male, let alone female,
characters in the chapters devoted to the Genesis narratives. Nevertheless, the treatment of women in the first part of Pseudo-Philo
highlights the author's major interests and introduces the themes
around which he develops his full characterizations of women in the
later chapters of the work.

Female Characters in the Pentateuch

Pseudo-Philo begins not with a creation story, but like the
Chronicler, with genealogies. He has no narrative about the creation
of the female being in general, or of Eve in particular. His sole comment about the first woman occupies a single sentence: deceived by
the snake, Eve persuaded Adam to sin (13:8).[5] Nonetheless, the
genealogies do contain material that is relevant to an examination of
the treatment of women. Following the format of Genesis, Pseudo-
Philo provides the names of the non-firstborn male and female
children which are omitted in the biblical genealogies.[6]

The additions supplement not only Genesis, but also *Jubilees*,
an earlier work which focuses a similar interest in "naming" on the
wives of each generation of firstborn males.[7] Indeed, where *Jubilees*

Antiquities, and Harrington's introduction in *OTP* II, 298-99.

[4]The nature of the omissions and insertions in this section of the work led
James to conclude that Pseudo-Philo was supplementing and at times cor-
recting *Jubilees*. Pseudo-Philo's treatment of women generally supports
James's conclusion.

[5]The summary of the Eden story as an example of what "men have lost" by
disobedience is interjected into a limited rehearsal of the laws given to
Moses.

[6]Genesis simply reads "sons and daughters." Citing *b. B. Bat.* 91a, L. H.
Feldman characterizes Pseudo-Philo's interest in naming women in the
Genesis genealogies as an apologetic response to heretics who were pointing
to lacunae in the Scriptures. See his "Prolegomenon," xlvi. Interestingly, his
Talmudic citation refers specifically to the names of mothers, a lacuna filled
by *Jubilees* rather than by Pseudo-Philo.

[7]On the concern for naming anonymous biblical characters, see Bernhard
Heller, "Die Scheu von Unbekanntem, Unbenanntem in Agada und Apokry-
phen," in *MGWJ* (1939): 170-84.

fails to provide the identity of wives, Pseudo-Philo, who generally is
not interested in wives, identifies the missing female characters
either by their relationship to the husband's family or by name.[8]
More striking, on a number of occasions Pseudo-Philo's genealogies
do more than supplement Genesis and *Jubilees*; they provide alternative traditions. In terms of the portrayal of women, the most
significant of such changes involve the identity of Cain's wife and
the genealogical backgrounds of Serug and Sarah. In the biblical text,
Cain's wife is not named, but *Jub.* 4:9 specifically identifies her as
"'Awan, his [Cain's] sister."[9] Contrary to its usual lack of interest in
non-firstborn children, *Jubilees* also mentions a second daughter,
Azura, who was born to Adam and Eve after the fratricide and who
becomes the wife of Seth (4:8, 11). In fact, according to *Jubilees* (4:11,
13, 14), the subsequent three generations of Seth's firstborn male
descendants entered into marriages with their sisters. Although
these marriages, like those of Cain and Seth to their sisters, logically
account for a spousal source left unexplained in Genesis, none of the
sibling marriages is supported by the genealogies of named sons
and daughters in Pseudo-Philo. Adam and Eve's first daughter is
Noaba; among the seven named daughters born after Seth, one finds
no Azura;[10] and the names given in Jubilees for the sister/wives of
Enosh, Kenan, and Mahalalel do not appear in Pseudo-Philo's lists
of daughters.[11] While the discrepancies may simply reflect a
different tradition of names, Pseudo-Philo's statement that the
name of Cain's wife was Themech (2:1) so clearly contradicts the
information in *Jubilees* that it is very likely that the author had a
special point to make: opposition to sibling matches.[12] Themech, for

---

[8]*Jub.* 4:9 limits the genealogy of Cain to one generation; *Bib. Ant.* 2:5 carries it
through to Lamech, identifying Enoch's wife as "from the daughters of Seth."
Whereas *Jubilees* breaks up the genealogy of Shem's descendants (8:1-9;
11:1, 7-8) with a series of narratives and fails to provide full information on
the brothers Peleg and Joktan, *Bib. Ant.* 4:10 names Peleg's sons and notes
that "they took wives for themselves from the daughters of Joktan."
[9]The sibling relationship is confirmed and reinforced by the naming of 'Awan
in an earlier listing of the children of Adam and Eve.
[10]The text mentions Adam having eight daughters after becoming father of
Seth, but gives the names of only seven of them. Given the overall lack of confirmation of the wives named in Jubilees, it is unlikely that the missing name
is that of Azura.
[11]The names of the daughters in Pseudo-Philo's genealogies also do not coincide with the multiple instances of marriage to "the daughter of his father's
brother" in *Jubilees*, e.g., the lines from Enoch to Noah and from Shem to
Reu (cf. *Jub.* 4:16, 20, 27-28; 8:5-7; and *Bib. Ant.* 1:13-21; 4:9-10). The discrepancies in these cases cannot be attributed to some form of opposition to
marriage between cousins, for in expanding the genealogical information on
Peleg's descendants, Pseudo-Philo describes such unions (4:10).
[12]Similarly, Pseudo-Philo offers no genealogical support for the statement in

whom no family background is provided, bears a name meaning "she shall [or should] be wiped out." Her name, like that of another Themech in Pseudo-Philo, Sisera's mother, may be derived from her maternity to corruption, in this case as ancestress of the children of Lamech. Describing these children, Pseudo-Philo is far more judgmental than Gen 4. Jobal taught men to play musical instruments and "to corrupt the earth"; Tubal taught the arts using various metals from which developed the worship of idols (2:9).

In only three other instances in these early genealogies does Pseudo-Philo identify female spouses, be it by name or by their relationship to the husband's family: the wives of the generations descended from Cain, the sons of Peleg, and the wife of Reu. In the first two cases, the women's names are lacking in *Jubilees* as well as in Genesis. In the case of Reu's wife, Pseudo-Philo not only gives her a different name, but also develops a genealogical background that stands in direct contrast to the one set forth in *Jubilees*. *Jub.* 11:1 identifies her as Ora, daughter of 'Ur, son of Kesed. Her father is the founder of Ur of Chaldees, where men "begin making graven images and polluted likenesses"; her son, Serug, grows up in Ur, worships idols, and teaches his own son, Nahor the father of Terah, divination and astrology.[13] Thus she functions as a link between the pre-patriarchal history and the stories of Terah and Abraham in idolatrous Chaldea.

In spite of its assets as a transitional narrative to the Ur stories, this description of Abraham's idolatrous ancestors is clearly not acceptable to Pseudo-Philo. Starting with the identity of Reu's wife, he develops a story line completely different from that of *Jubilees*. Reu's wife is named Melcha, not Ora; her father is not named. She is simply called the daughter of an otherwise unidentified Ruth, whose name evokes that of the righteous Moabitess in David's genealogy. Melcha becomes the mother of Serug, the grandmother of Nahor, Abraham's ancestors who — in direct contradiction to *Jubilees* — did not join the rest of "those who inhabited the earth" in reckoning by the stars and having "their sons and daughters pass through the fire" (4:16). This transformation of Melcha's progeny from idolators to the righteous of their generation is but one aspect of Pseudo-Philo's rehabilitation of Reu's wife. Interrupting his recital of the genealogy of the descendants of Shem, he has Melcha predict the time of the delivery of Serug, and the

---

Jub. 12:9 that Abraham married the "daughter of his father." Pseudo-Philo's general opposition to sibling marriages is likely rooted in Lev 18:9.
[13]See *Jub.* 11:2-8 on Serug and 11:9-12:14 for Terah and Abraham in Ur.

eventual birth and covenant with Abraham: "From him there will be born in the fourth generation one who will set his dwelling on high and will be called perfect and blameless; and he will be the father of nations, and his covenant will not be broken, and his seed will be multiplied forever" (4:11). The prediction makes a prophetess of Melcha, and at the same time, creates the annunciation scene lacking in Genesis for the first patriarch. Moreover, in several regards Pseudo-Philo's treatment of Melcha anticipates his portrayal of the matriarchs: she appears in a genealogical context, but her background is notably vague; and her major significance lies in the miracle story that her prediction makes of the birth of Abraham.

Sarah is introduced as Abraham's wife in the quasi-genealogical context of a rapid review of patriarchal history from the first patriarch's entry into Canaan to Jacob's descent to Egypt. No information is given about her lineage. Her name is not among the various daughters listed as descendants of the line of Serug (4:13-15). And neither the tradition in *Jubilees* that Sarah is Abraham's half-sister nor the rabbinic identification of Sarah with Iscah, daughter of Haran, is supported by Pseudo-Philo's genealogies.[14] The only hint of a blood relationship between Abraham and Sarah (as well as between Nahor and Melcha) appears in Joshua's final address. In *Bib. Ant.* 23:4, Sarah and Melcha are described as having been born from the chiseling of the "one rock" from which God "quarried out" Abraham and Nahor. By making Sarah and Melcha sisters, this passage is consistent with the identification of Sarah with Iscah. However, given Pseudo-Philo's interest in genealogy and the absence of any reference to Haran's daughters in the list of Shem's descendants, the poetic description would seem to apply to a spiritual rather than a blood relationship among the four characters.[15]

There are three other short references to Sarah, all dealing with her inability to conceive. The problem is first presented as the

---

[14]In *Jub.* 12:9, Sarah is described as the daughter of Abraham's father, cf. Abraham's words to Abimelech of Gerar in Gen 20:12. In Josephus (*Ant.* I, 150) and the midrash in *b. Sanh.* 69b (cf. Gen 11:29), she is identified with Iscah the daughter of Haran. In *Bib. Ant.* 4:14 Iscah (Esca) is listed as Terah's sister, one of the five daughters of Nahor, Abraham's grandfather. The genealogy provides no information regarding the children of Abraham's brother Nahor. Pseudo-Philo has Haran as the father of Lot (4:15), but contrary to Gen 11:29 makes no reference to Haran's daughters.

[15]Feldman ("Prolegomenon," lxi) suggests the passage identifies Sarah with Iscah, and hence is evidence of agreement among Pseudo-Philo, Josephus, and the rabbis.

reason for Abraham's taking Hagar (8:1).[16] Nothing is said of Sarah's concern regarding her infertility or her initiative in urging the gift of Hagar on her husband. Sarah is unable to conceive, so Abraham simply "takes" her handmaid.[17] Second, in a dialogue created to describe the encounter between God and Abraham at Mamre, Pseudo-Philo has Abraham, not Sarah, demonstrate concern over her barrenness (23:5-7). In direct contrast to Gen 15:6, the patriarch responds to the promise of seed by expressing his disbelief: "Behold now you have given me a wife, and she is sterile. And how will I have offspring from that rock of mine that is closed up?" (23:5). God's response is to direct him to bring various sacrificial items, each of which is then metaphorically associated with fertility (23:5-7).[18] The dove is likened to Abraham and his sons, who will build before God; the turtledove to the prophets who will be born from him; the ram to the wise men who will descend from him; the calf to the multitude of peoples who will come from his seed; and the she-goat represents the women whose wombs God will open (23:7).[19]

The third passage utilizes Sarah's infertility to place Isaac's birth in the context of a double wonder story. Not only does Sarah conceive "out of a sterile womb" (32:1), she also gives birth in the seventh month of her pregnancy.[20] The passage is worth citing for it conveys the extraordinarily narrow nature of the author's interest in Sarah:

> And I gave him Isaac and formed him in the womb of her who gave birth to him and commanded it to restore him quickly and to give him back to me in the seventh month. And there- fore every woman who gives birth in the seventh month, her son will live, because upon him I have brought my glory and

---

[16]In the Abraham and Sarah narratives, Hagar is the only other woman men- tioned. Pseudo-Philo ignores Lot's daughters as well as Abraham's wife Keturah and her children.

[17]See the contrasting descriptions in Gen 16:1-3 and *Jub.* 14:22-23.

[18]As opposed to Genesis 15:6, Pseudo-Philo has Abraham say to God: "Behold now you have given me a wife, and she is sterile. And how will I have offspring from that rock of mine that is closed up?" (23:5). God responds by directing him to bring the various sacrificial items which are to serve as a witness that he will give Abraham "offspring from one who is closed up." In contrast, the version in *Jubilees* of the Mamre scene (*Jub.* 14:21-23) is essentially faithful to the description in Genesis.

[19]There is a similar midrash on the sacrifice at Mamre in *Gen. Rab.* 44, but the animals are not presented as symbols of fertility.

[20]The birth of Isaac in the seventh month also appears in *b. Ros Has.* 10b-11a; conversely, *Jub.* 15:21; 16:13, 16 stresses the full-term date of Isaac's birth. Sarah's infertility, so stressed by Pseudo-Philo, is underplayed in *Jubilees.*

revealed the new age. (23:8)

Pseudo-Philo's interest in Sarah is single-focussed. He omits the sojourns in Egypt and Gerar, the troubled relationship with Hagar and Ishmael, and the visit of the angels to announce the conception of Isaac. The primary motivation behind these deletions does not appear to be a desire to rehabilitate Sarah's character, for even the description of the change of her name is truncated such that she is the recipient of neither the blessing nor the prophecy of Gen 17:16.[21] Sarah is significant to Pseudo-Philo solely in terms of her role as the vehicle for the miraculous birth of a son to Abraham.

Rebekah receives similarly cursory treatment. Never mentioned by name, she is described in the chapter summarizing patriarchal history simply as the "daughter of Bethuel" who becomes the wife of Isaac and bears him Esau and Jacob. The only mention of her appears in Deborah's hymn where Pseudo-Philo again introduces a doubly miraculous birth. Like their father, Esau and Jacob are born "from a womb that was closed up" (32:5). To this initial wonder the author adds that the infertile mother had been married for three years before the twins were conceived, a miraculous conception that "will not happen in this way to any woman" (32:5). Rebekah's infertility is biblical in origin; the description of when she conceived is not.[22] Pseudo-Philo's circumscribed interest in Rebekah's maternal function is brought into even greater prominence when it is compared with the information presented in *Jubilees*. Despite its development of an extensive series of Rebekah stories,[23] the earlier text mentions neither Rebekah's initial barren-

[21]In the MT of Gen 17:15-16 the change of Sarah's name is accompanied by a blessing and a prophecy stressing her role as matriarch: "I will bless her and she shall be a mother of nations, kings of peoples shall be of her." *Jubilees* parallels the LXX by having the deity bless Sarah but direct the prophecy toward Isaac: "And I will bless her and I will give her you a son from her. And I will bless him. And he will become a people. And kings of nations will come from him" (*Jub.* 15:16). Pseudo-Philo omits the blessing and the prophecy, and treats Sarah solely as the woman from whom God will give Abraham the promised offspring: "To your seed I will give this land, and your name will be called Abraham, and Sarai, your wife, will be called Sarah. And I will give to you from her an everlasting seed and I will establish my covenant with you" (8:3).

[22]Gen 25:21 describes Rebekah as initially infertile. However, according to Gen 25:20, 26, she conceived in the fortieth, not the third, year of her marriage to Isaac. Rabbinic midrash tends to follow the biblical text in regard to the number of years. Oddly, the miracle Pseudo-Philo associates with the timing of the conception clearly fits the biblical and rabbinic data better than his own.

[23]On the development of the character Rebekah in *Jubilees*, see John C. Endres, *Biblical Interpretation in the Book of Jubilees* (Washington, D. C.: Catholic Biblical Association, 1987); and the article by R. Chesnutt in this

ness nor any miracle associated with the birth of her children.

Pseudo-Philo names Rachel and Leah as Laban's daughters, whom Jacob took as wives together with two concubines, Bilhah and Zilpah. Save for the clear distinction made in the marital status of the two sets of women, he demonstrates no interest in them either as individuals or as Jacob's wives. However, in describing Bilhah and Zilpah as concubines, Pseudo-Philo diverges from both biblical and midrashic tradition. In the MT, the women are called "handmaids" (שפחות), not concubines (פלגשים); in the LXX the term is παιδίσκη.[24] In his midrash about the reactions of the Hebrews trapped by the Red Sea and the pursuing Egyptians, Pseudo-Philo describes the tribes descended from Leah (except for Judah and Levi) as discouraged and ready to drown, the tribes descended from the concubines as favoring a return to slavery, and only Judah (representing the future monarchy), Levi (representing the priesthood), and tribes descended from Rachel as confident of divine assistance and prepared to fight the Egyptians (10:3). The midrash subtly conveys a value judgment of the character of each of Jacob's wives,[25] but nowhere in the text are those implications developed.

In contrast to Sarah and Rebekah, Rachel's initial difficulty in conceiving children receives no attention. The treatment of the matter in Gen 29:31 and *Jub.* 28:12 is perhaps sufficient,[26] for although he pays tribute to Joseph's steadfast unwillingness to "afflict his seed" by cohabiting with a foreign woman,[27] Pseudo-Philo does not develop a hero story around him or any of Jacob's sons.[28] Indeed,

---

volume.

[24]The exact nature of their status is a matter of some concern in midrashic literature. In *Jub.* 28:3, 9 and *T. Naph.* 1:9-12), they are described as sisters and handmaids. *Gen. Rab.* 74:13 and *Tg. Yer.* Gen 29:24, 29 portray them as the daughters of Laban and a concubine. Josephus, *Ant.* I.303, makes a point of their non-slave status.

[25]See S. Hartom's commentary on *Bib. Ant.* 10:3 (Tel Aviv: Javneh, 1967). A rabbinic midrash on the division among the tribes of Israel at the Red Sea is found in *Mek. Beshallah* 2.29a; *y. Ta'an.* 2, 65d; *Tg. Yer. Ex* 14:13; and *Pesiq. Rab Kah.* 43. However, it is only in the *Biblical Antiquities* that the division of counsel is determined by descent from the wives of Jacob.

[26]In neither narrative is Rachel's barren condition the basis for a "wonder" story; both sources view it as divine compensation for the fact that "Leah was hated."

[27]*Bib. Ant.* 43:5. In condemning Samson's marriage to a Philistine woman, God presents Joseph as a model to which Samson had "not paid attention." On Pseudo-Philo's polemics against union with a gentile, see further, below.

[28]In his concise summary of the biblical narratives concerning Joseph (8:9-10), he omits the incident of Potiphar's wife so highly developed elsewhere. *Jub.* 39:1-10 describes Joseph as adhering to the teachings of his father and great-grandfather concerning the prohibition not to "fornicate with a woman who has a husband"; *Ant.* II.40ff. contrasts Joseph's chastity with the uncon-

the children of Rachel, Leah, and the handmaids are listed in the same neutral tone as the immediately preceding reference to Esau's wives and their children.[29]

Of Jacob's children, only Dinah and Judah's daughter-in-law, Tamar, receive particular attention. In the case of Dinah, in 8:7 Pseudo-Philo rapidly summarizes the Shechem narrative[30] and focusses on her subsequent marriage to Job, to whom she twice bears seven sons and three daughters: one set preceding his test; the other following his healing (cf. 8:8). In contrast to the Book of Job, Pseudo-Philo provides the names of each son and daughter.[31] Consistent with his emphasis on maternal roles, Pseudo-Philo diverges substantially from Genesis, in which no record of Dinah's having children appears. Further, although Gen 46:8ff. does not record that Dinah accompanied Jacob to Egypt (Gen 46:8ff.), Pseudo-Philo notes that her household was among those who made the descent. The motivation behind the story of Dinah's marriage to Job is unclear.[32] Given a similar tradition in the targumim and in rabbinic midrash[33] as well as Pseudo-Philo's interest in genealogy, it is possible that the author simply used it to fill in lacunae regarding Dinah and her descendants.[34]

---

trollable passion of the villainous woman. Neither Pseudo-Philo nor *Jubilees* mentions Joseph's marriage to Aseneth, the daughter of an Egyptian priest.

[29]*Bib. Ant.* 8:5. The listing of Esau's wives and children may be attributed to their absence in *Jubilees*. The wives correspond to those enumerated in Genesis. However, Pseudo-Philo also adds the children of Judith and Mahalath to those listed in Gen 36.

[30]The narrative is reduced to two statements: Dinah is raped and the city of Shechem is destroyed by her brothers Simeon and Levi. Unlike *Jub.* 30 and *Ant.* I.337-41, Pseudo-Philo develops no characterization of Dinah, ignores her marriage to Shechem, and offers no moral or theological judgments.

[31]In the Bible, only the daughters are named. The names given by Pseudo-Philo coincide neither with those nor with the ones listed in *T. Job*.

[32]Louis Feldman views the marriage of Dinah and Job as indicative of the author's universalistic orientation since Job was not Jewish ("Prolegomenon," x). Given Pseudo-Philo's hostile polemic against intermarriage with gentiles, it is strange that he should hold such a universalistic perspective.

[33]The *Tg.* on Job 2:9, *b. B. Bat.* 15b, and *Gen. Rab.* 72:4, associate the description of Job's first wife as one of the נבלה (Job 2:10) with the rape of Dinah (Gen 34:7). In *Gen. Rab.* 80:4, Dinah's marriage to Job is described as a punishment for Jacob's refusal to have her marry Esau. In *T. Job* (1:6) the marriage legitimates the text by presenting its author not only as a descendant of Esau but also as related by marriage to Jacob and the twelve patriarchs. In these sources, Dinah appears as Job's second wife whereas Pseudo-Philo makes a point of describing her as his only wife and the mother of all his children.

[34]Perhaps on the basis of the same lacunae, the author of *Jubilees* has Dinah die of grief over the suspected death of Joseph (34:15-16). Assuming Pseudo-Philo's awareness of this tradition, he obviously found such an ending to Dinah's story unsatisfactory.

The depiction of Tamar is presented as an aside in the retelling of the birth of Moses. Encouraging his fellow Hebrews to have faith in God's promises and cohabit with their wives in spite of the decree that all male infants will be killed at birth and all females given as wives for Egyptian slaves,[35] Amram describes how Tamar's pregnancy remained hidden for three months because "our mother" determined "it is better for me to die for having intercourse with my father-in-law than to have intercourse with gentiles" (9:5). The speech is both polemical and apologetic.[36] Tamar is the first of a number of women around whom Pseudo-Philo develops a diatribe against union with gentiles.[37] Frequently, the polemical construction, like this one, is Pseudo-Philo's own creation, and it involves a certain manipulation of the biblical story line. The characterization is striking. The presentation of Tamar is reflexive; she is a point of reference, a model, not a live character in the narrative. Yet, she is the only female character in Pseudo-Philo's chronicle who is given, albeit through Amram, direct speech. Her femininity is expressed maternally: she is referred to as "our mother" (9:5); her thoughts and the dilemma which they resolve concern contextually maternal issues. Yet there is something untraditional in the depiction. Tamar is given the role of a male hero. She assumes and asserts full responsibility for the nature of the seed which she will produce. In so doing, she becomes, like Abraham and like her spokesman, Amram, a model of fidelity to the covenant. Her story is offered as evidence of

---

[35]According to *Ex. Rab.* 1:19 and *b. Sota* 12a, the plan is to marry Hebrew women to Egyptians. Amram advises the Israelites to divorce their wives, but Miriam convinces to the contrary.

[36]Within the focus of the Tamar story, *Jubilees* also presents a polemic against intermarriage as well as an apology; but the focus is not on Tamar as it is here. *Jub.* 41:2 has Er punished with death for desiring a wife from the daughters of Canaan, his mother's people, and consequently refusing to have intercourse with Tamar. Judah's reservation "lest he die like his brethren" (Gen 38:11) is deleted, and the withholding of Tamar is attributed fully to Judah's Canaanite wife (41:6-7). Moreover, since neither Er nor Onan had relations with Tamar, Judah technically did not have intercourse with the wife of his sons (41:27).

[37]A similar polemic appears in the description of Egyptian oppression (9:1); the introduction to the Deborah narrative (30:1); and the stories of Samson and the Philistine women (43:5), of Micah (44:7), and of the Levite's concubine (45:3). See also God's speech to Joshua in 21:1ff. The polemic attached to the Tamar narrative is unique to Pseudo-Philo, but the motif of the hidden pregnancy also appears in *t. Nid.* 1:7; *b. Nid.* 8:2; and *Gen. Rab.* 85:10. For the rabbinic apology for Tamar, see *Gen. Rab.* 85:6-9 and *b. Sota* 10a-b. *Jubilees* tends to insert polemic against union with gentiles more naturally into the flow of the biblical narrative. In Tamar's story, opportunity is provided by the reference to Judah's Canaanite wife in Gen 38:2. Other examples in *Jubilees* include the story of Dinah and Shechem (30:7-23), Isaac's reflections on Esau's marriages with Canaanite women (35:14), and the various blessing and

the surety of God's assistance.

Still, the context for Pseudo-Philo's Tamar, as for his matriarchs, is primarily a birth story. Given his interest in depicting miraculous births, it is not surprising that Pseudo-Philo is particularly attentive to Moses' nativity. Using the basic outline of the
biblical account, he develops a tale of a series of divinely effected
miracles, each associated with a female character. Miriam, like
Melcha in the Abraham story, is the annunciator. On this occasion,
the divine source of the prophecy which comes in a dream is made
explicit: "And the spirit of God came upon Miriam one night, and she
saw a dream..." (9:10). Moreover, in spite of the portrait of Amram as
a faithful believer in God's promises, a point is made of the fact that
Miriam's parents do not believe her prediction that their unborn
child will save his people and "exercise leadership always" (9:10).
Their disbelief thus parallel Abraham's response to the prediction of
Isaac's birth (23:5) and anticipate the disbelief associated with the
birth stories of Samson and Samuel. There are no Egyptian
midwives in Pseudo-Philo's story. Instead, Jochebed, like Tamar,
hides the infant within her womb for three months. When conceal-
ment is no longer possible, the prenatally circumcised newborn is
placed on the river bank in an ark constructed by his mother. Moved
by her dreams, Pharaoh's daughter comes to bathe in the river,
finds the baby, recognizes him as a Hebrew, and immediately begins
to nurse him (9:11-16).[38]

In Pseudo-Philo's reconstruction of the story of Moses' birth
female characters are significant; at each stage women act. Yet they
never demonstrate independence of will or heroic qualities comparable to those of Amram or even of Tamar.[39] Their actions are always
circumscribed by their limited function. Like Pseudo-Philo's first
matriarchs, these women have a single role: they serve as facilita-

---

testament scenes created for Jacob (22:16; 25:1-10; 27:8, 46).

[38]According to *Ex. Rab.* 1:22, Miriam also has a vision, but her dreaming is
unique to Pseudo-Philo. *Jubilees* (cf. 47:1-8) contains no annunciation, and according to *Ant.* II.212-17, Amram has a dream foretelling his son's redemp-
tory role. Jochebed's hidden pregnancy is found in *Ex. Rab.* 1:20; *b. Sota* 12a,
and *Tg. Yer.* Ex 2:2. Moses' being born circumcised appears in *Ex. Rab.* as well
as in *Deut. Rab.* 2:9. Pharaoh's daughter being directed to the river by her
dreams is unique to Pseudo-Philo, as is the story that she nursed the infant.
In *Ex. Rab.* 1:25 and *Ant.* II.226, Moses spurns the breasts of the Egyptian
nurses.

[39]In spite of the absence of additional narratives concerning her, Miriam's
significance to the wilderness generation is acknowledged. In relating how
the manna ceased at the time of Moses' death, Pseudo-Philo notes that God
gave the Israelites the well of the water of Marah on account of Miriam, the
pillar of cloud for Aaron, and the manna on account of Moses. The same

tors, God's agents in the wonder birth of an Israelite hero.

As a chronicler, Pseudo-Philo is not very interested in the portrayal of villainesses. The closest he comes is with two instances in which he describes inappropriate sexual unions. The "daughters of men" with whom the "sons of God" intermarry are "beautiful"; they are not simply fair but "exceedingly" so (3:1; cf. Gen 6:2). Similarly, the "daughters of Moab" sent to seduce the Israelites are described as "beautiful ... naked and adorned with gold and precious stones" (18:13). However, the narrative of the seduction of the Israelites in the wilderness is notably underdeveloped.[40]

Female Characters in the Early Prophets

As limited as the development of female characterization is in the first nineteen chapters, the themes that appear therein are the very ones which dominate the fuller characterizations of women in the second part of the *Biblical Antiquities*. Pseudo-Philo maintains his interest in naming anonymous women and in lineage in general. He continues to exalt motherhood and to focus on women in maternal roles. Even when the biblical basis provides opportunity, such as in the case of the Midianite seduction, he demonstrates minimal interest in the development of the characters of gentile women. Finally, when he does develop a female protagonist, he makes a point of her femininity even as he overtly or covertly associates her actions with a male role or role model.

Pseudo-Philo assigns names to five female characters unnamed in Judges and I Samuel: the mothers of Sisera (31:8), Samson (42:1), and Micah (44:2); Jephthah's daughter (40:1); and the Witch of Endor (64:3).[41] In three instances the names are linked to the character portraits. Sisera's mother, like Cain's wife, is called Themech, "she shall (or should) be wiped out."[42] The name of

---

midrash appears in *b. Ta'an.* 9a.

[40]Like Josephus and the rabbinic midrash, Pseudo-Philo builds on Num 31:16 in attributing the seduction plan to Balaam. Feldman ("Prolegomenon," xlvi) and Harrington ("Pseudo-Philo," 301) both include the description of the Midianite women as an example of Pseudo-Philo's polemic against the union with foreign women. However, unlike Josephus, Pseudo-Philo does not use the opportunity to develop such a polemic, nor does he make any reference to the idolatry which follows from the union (cf. Num 25:2). His comments are limited to a description of the women and the success of the seduction.

[41]He also names male characters, such as the Levite and his host of Judg 19. Conversely, he does not assign names to the woman of Timnah (41:1-2), the Levite's concubine (43:3), or the wife of Agag (58:3; 65:4).

[42]Pseudo-Philo (31:8) does not explain the derivation of the name "Themech" ("she shall/should be wiped out"). Harrington, "Pseudo-Philo," 345 n. d.,

Jephthah's daughter, Seila, "the one asked for" (40:1), is explicitly associated with her fate. And the name given to Micah's mother, Dedila, is either a misreading for, or purposely suggestive of, Delilah.[43] In addition, the author names the three daughters whom he attributes to Kenaz. The latter women do not appear in Judges, but their presence here is consistent with the Pseudo-Philo's deletion of Othniel ben Kenaz and his identification of Kenaz as the son of Caleb and as supreme among the leaders in Israel.[44]

The maternal lineage of male characters continues to be a matter of some significance to Pseudo-Philo. Goliath's death at the hand of David is related to the combatants' descent from two "sisters," Orpah, who chose the gods of the Philistines, and Ruth, who became an Israelite (61:6).[45] Similarly, the mother of the soldier who slays King Saul is Agag's wife, who is permitted to live long enough to bear a son for just that purpose (65:4).[46] It is from the perspective of such characterizations that one can understand the earlier concern with Melcha. For Pseudo-Philo the connection between mothers and destiny is direct evidence of the hand of God.

The biblical narratives of Samson, Samuel, Sisera, and Micah provide the framework for Pseudo-Philo's fuller portraits of mothers. The first two involve miraculous births; the latter, tales of villainous adult sons. Pseudo-Philo alters and/or expands the roles of the mothers in both story types. The nativity accounts retain all

---

suggests the name may have originally been Tanaach or may have been derived from חיבב or חבט in Judg 5:28. However, given the context and the parallel with Lamech's mother, the name appears more likely derived from her support of her son.

[43]All of the names with the possible exception of Dedila are unique to Pseudo-Philo. Noting that the amount of silver taken from Micah's mother (Judg 17:2) is equal to the bribe paid to Delilah (Judg 16:5), one midrash equates the two characters (*t. Tg.* on Judg 17:2, cited in *Legends* VI, 209 n. 125). Ginzberg argues that for Pseudo-Philo "we ought to read Delilah instead of Dedilah."

[44]The daughters' inheritance replaces the story of Caleb's daughter Aschah (Josh 15:17ff.; Judg 1:13ff.), which identifies Kenaz either as the father (MT) or as the younger brother (LXX) of Caleb. Pseudo-Philo makes Kenaz the son of Caleb and uses the story of the daughters to indicate the great success of his leadership: had he had sons, they would have succeeded him. The account suggests the potential of establishing a hereditary monarchy (29:1-2).

[45]The relationship between Goliath and Orpah is also found in *b. Sota* 42b; *Ruth Rab.* 1:14; and the *t. Tg.* on I Sam 17:4.

[46]God informs Samuel: "He has let the King of Amalek and his wife live. And now let them be, so that Agag may come together with his wife tonight and you will kill him tomorrow. But his wife they will keep safe until she bears a male child, and then she also will die. And he who will be born from her will become a stumbling block for Saul" (58:3). A similar rabbinic legend has the ancestor of Haman conceived in the interval between Agag's capture and execution (*Tg. Sheni* 4:13; *Esth. Rab.*, Introduction 7; and *Seder Eliyahu Rab.* 20:115; 21:117).

the elements developed in the descriptions of the births of Isaac and
Moses: a stress on maternal infertility, an annunciation scene predicting a great future for the unborn child, temporary doubt of the
prediction, and general enhancement of the roles of women as
maternal agents of God.[47]

Whereas a simple statement acknowledging the woman's
inability to conceive precedes the appearance of the angel in the
biblical account of Samson's birth (13:2-3), Pseudo-Philo develops a
full narrative of marital friction around the infertility of Eluma,
Manoah's wife (42:1-3).[48] Similarly, a preface stressing infertility
(49:1-8) is added to the tale of Hannah. Faced with a crisis of
leadership, the Israelites cast lots which, after several unsuccessful
attempts, fall on Elkanah. When he refuses their appeal, the people
turn in despair to God, who tells them that their leader is not to be
Elkanah, but his son. Asked which of the ten sons of Peninnah is
designated, God responds: "None of the sons of Peninnah can rule
the people, but the one who is born from the sterile woman whom I
have given to him as a wife...." And, lest there be any doubt as to the
nature of this wondrous birth, God adds: "And I will love him as I
have loved Isaac, and his name will be before me always" (49:8).[49]

The annunciation scene for Samson is already present in Judg
13:7. Pseudo-Philo simply enhances the biblical prediction that the
child "will free Israel from the hand of the Philistines" by attributing
it directly to God: the angel messenger prefaces the prophecy with
the words "As he himself has said..." (42:3). Samuel's story involves
greater restructuring, for the biblical birth story does not contain a
full annunciation scene. In I Sam 1:17, Eli tells Hannah she will
conceive and bear a son. The future of the child, however, is neither
foreordained nor revealed. Only after he has come to live in Shiloh in
fulfillment of his mother's vow is Samuel called to divine service.
Pseudo-Philo "repairs" all this by inserting the appointment of the
yet-unconceived Samuel as a prophet into the divine forecast with
which the story begins (49:8, cf. 9:7-8). Significantly, he also omits
Hannah's vow and so removes the female initiative in dedicating
Samuel to God. At the initial prayer scene in Shilo only Eli (like the

---

[47]C. Perrot, "Les récits d'enfance dans la Haggada," *RSR* 55 (1967): 481-518,
compares the aggadic descriptions of the births of Moses, Samson, and
Samuel.
[48]*Gen. Rab.* 10:5, 11 and *Lev. Rab.* 9:9 also portray a quarrel over who is
responsible for their childlessness. *Ant.* V.276-81 describes marital friction,
but this is caused by Manoah's inordinate jealousy rather than by the couple's
childless state.
[49]Cf. the parallel description of Isaac as having been born "out of a sterile
womb" (32:1).

reader) is aware that the boy's future as "a prophet had been foreordained" (50:8). He does not reveal it to Hannah until some two years later when, quite innocently, she comes with her son to show that her prayer had been fulfilled. And only later do Samuel's parents bring him to Shiloh for permanent service (51:7).

Pseudo-Philo inserts a faithful doubter comparable to Abraham and Moses' parents into both of these narratives. In the case of Samson, the role is assigned to the father. Manoah does "not believe his wife," yet he retires to the upper chamber to pray (42:5). The role of doubter in the second story is assumed by characters in Hannah's own mind. She prays in silence, for should Peninnah hear of the prayer for a child, she would taunt Hannah even more for trusting in God. Moreover, should others learn that her prayer was not answered, they would be led to blaspheme (50:5). Both rationales presuppose that her request will not be answered, and both reflect Hannah's doubt even as she prays.

Pseudo-Philo's enhancement of these two women focusses ultimately on their piety. Eluma retires in despair to "the upper chamber" and entreats God to reveal who is responsible for her childless state: she, her husband, or both.[50] In response to her acknowledgment of the relationship between childlessness and sinfulness (42:2), the angel appears and tells her that in fact she has been the infertile one. But now she will bear a child whom she is to nurture in accord with specific directions so that he will be prepared to assume his foreordained leadership role. In the Book of Judges, the angel directs her to abstain from alcohol and forbidden food, for the child is to be a nazir from the time of his conception (13:7). According to Pseudo-Philo, however, Eluma is directed to see to it that he does not eat "from any fruit of the vine" or "eat any unclean thing, because ... he will free Israel from the hand of the Philistines" (42:3). The piety ascribed to her is in no way diminished when she, unlike her biblical counterpart, joins her husband in expressing concern over having "seen the Lord face to face" (42:10). Pseudo-Philo has no need to emphasize a reassuring wife or a foolish husband (cf. Judg 13:23), for such would only distract from his portrait of a woman whose raison d'être is her maternity.

In the prayer scene at Shiloh, Pseudo-Philo's Hannah — taunted and tormented by Peninnah well beyond the biblical account (I Sam 50:1-2) — piously acknowledges that the open or

---

[50]In *Ant.* VI.276, the wife prays for a child. Unlike Judges and Pseudo-Philo, Josephus presents the wife, not Manoah, praying that the angel appear a second time (*Ant.* VI.280).

closed nature of a woman's womb reflects divine will (50:5). When her
son's future is revealed to her two years later, stress is again placed
on maternal nurturance: "And through this boy your womb has
been justified so that you might provide advantage for the peoples
and set up the milk of your breasts as a fountain for the twelve
tribes" (51:2).[51] This theme is then developed in Hannah's song,
which Pseudo-Philo rewrites to celebrate her maternity and role as
God's wondrous instrument. The personal exaltation of
motherhood, a departure from the biblical text, is striking:

> Drip, my breasts, and tell your testimonies, because you have
> been commanded to give milk. For he who is milked from you
> will be raised up and the people will be enlightened by his words
> and he will show to the nations the statutes and his horn will
> be exalted very high. And so I will speak my words openly, be-
> cause from me will arise the ordinance of the Lord, and all men
> will find the truth. (51:3-4)

The mother as mentor, as spiritual rather than physical nur-
turer, is the centerpiece of Pseudo-Philo's negative portraits of the
mothers of Sisera and Micah. Unlike the preceding set of mothers, in
neither of these instances does the biblical narrative provide a rich
character outline. The mother of Sisera is described in Deborah's
song (Judg 5:29-30) as anxiously awaiting her son's return and
imagining him busily involved in dividing the spoils of victory. Our
author does not so much alter this portrait as build upon it. First, he
gives the mother the meaningful name of Themech. Second, he
transforms the anxious woman of Deborah's song into an overtly
confident one: she does not peer through the lattice and wonder why
he is so long in returning (cf. Judg 5:28). Rather, she summons her
ladies to meet her son and see his Hebrew concubines (31:8). And
third, he makes a point of the close relationship between mother
and son. The fleeing Sisera thinks about returning to his mother
with Jael as his wife (31:3); awaiting him, the unknowing Themech
expresses pride in her son's scheme to capture the Hebrew women
(31:8), a plan not unlike that of the Egyptians which "seemed so
wicked before the Lord" (9:1). Indeed, Pseudo-Philo reinforces the
link between mother and son by having Barak cut off Sisera's head
and sent it to his mother with the message: "Receive your son whom
you hoped to see coming back with spoils" (31:9).

Less is left to the imagination in the more developed character-

---

[51]As opposed to the midrash in *b. Ber.* 31b, Pseudo-Philo does not include the
motif of nurturing in Hannah's prayer; it appears in Eli's revelation of the
child's future and is developed in Hannah's hymn of celebration.

ization of Micah's mother. In both Judg 17:3-4 and *Bib. Ant.* 44:2-3, she is portrayed as encouraging her son to worship idols. This encouragement is presented in direct voice in both texts, but Pseudo-Philo extends the mother's role far beyond the dedication of restored silver with which her son might construct an image. The account opens with the simple statement that Micah possesses a certain amount of gold and silver; no mention is made of his mother's prior connection to the wealth, and nothing is said of his theft and subsequent restoration of it. Micah's mother commands (45:3) him to melt the gold and make idols, instructs him in some detail on how to construct and profit from the establishment of an idolatrous sanctuary in his home, and entices him to comply with the assurance that he will make a name for himself as a priest and a "worshiper of the gods" (44:3). Thus she is presented as a negative version of Hannah, who also desired a leadership role for a son (cf. 51:4) who also was involved with a sanctuary. Micah responds with an ode to maternal instruction which leaves no doubt as to the extent of her culpability: "You have advised me well, Mother, on how to live. And now your name will be even greater than mine, and in the last days all kinds of things will be requested of you" (44:4).

The characterization of the mother is intriguing. Assigned the name Dedila, she recollects the biblical Delilah whose story immediately precedes. Given the markedly similar structure and substance of the biblical narrative of Delilah and that of Dedila here, Pseudo-Philo appears to have substituted characterization of the perversion of motherhood for that of the perversion of a proper wife. In the Book of Judges, Delilah is a fully developed character whereas Micah's mother is not. In the *Biblical Antiquities*, the situation is reversed: Dedila's seduction of her son into idolatry is expanded; Delilah's seduction of her spouse into revealing the secret of his strength is abbreviated. Moreover, immediately following his description of Dedila's successful enticement of her son, our author inserts a monologue in which God details how the children of Israel had departed from his commandments. The enumeration ends with "and they lusted after foreign women" (44:7), a sin that has nothing to do with the story of Dedila, but one which is quite pertinent to the story of Delilah.[52]

---

[52]Feldman's view that the "lusting..." is to be understood as a consequence of Micah's idolatry ("Prolegomenon," xlvii) is problematic. In earlier passages where the connection between foreign women and idolatry is made explicit (21:1; 30:1), the association is the catalyst for the idolatry. Here, because the sequence is inverted, it is more likely that the reference to foreign women reflects the extent to which Delilah and Dedila are joined in the author's

Prominent here are two themes that recur throughout the work: God directs Israel's history, and within that history obedience is rewarded and disobedience is punished. In relation to these themes female characters are cast as either the objects of divine punishment, as the instruments of divine retribution, or as agents/partners in God's governance of Israel's destiny. Micah's mother epitomizes the first role. Pseudo-Philo's additions not only enrich the characterizations in the story, they also provide the just punishment lacking in the biblical version. The deaths of Micah and his mother are predicted in a divine forecast constructed in direct counterpoint to the instruction scene opening the narrative. Eaten alive by worms, Dedila will finally chastise her son "as a mother," and the tortured, dying Micah will respond "as a son heeding his mother and acting cleverly, 'And you have done even greater wickedness'" (44:9).

Pseudo-Philo treats the story of the Levite's concubine in a similar fashion. Just as divine justice requires a punishment to end the Micah story, so the rape and violent death of the concubine require a basis not provided by Judges 19. Accordingly, the concubine is described here (45:3) as having "committed sin with the Amalekites; and on account of this the Lord God delivered her into the hands of sinners." In this version, the concubine is not named, although the Levite is identified as Beel and his host in Gibeah, here another Levite, is called Bethac.

The role of instrument of divine punishment is reserved for gentile women. When these women function to facilitate the punishment of Israel's sinful leaders, they are portrayed as villainesses who passively fulfill their ordained role. They acquire awareness neither of God nor of their own significance in salvation history. Agag's wife, Delilah, and the Witch of Endor are cast as such villainesses, and all three characterizations are brief and colorless. Agag's wife is introduced solely for the purpose of connecting Saul's death to his sin. Delilah is a Philistine harlot whom Samson, in violation of divine ordinance, takes as a wife. Her beauty, not directly mentioned, is merely implied in God's statement that "Samson had been led astray through his eyes" (43:4). His attraction, in turn, is presented as a matter of lust, not love (cf. Judg 16:4). Delilah pressures her husband until he reveals the secret of his strength, gets him drunk,

---

imagination. Pseudo-Philo's characterization of Dedila may have been influenced by the midrashic equation of Micah's mother and Delilah. However, the midrash is based on the silver Delilah received from the Philistines (Judg 16:5) and the silver taken from Micah's mother (Judg 17:1). Pseudo-Philo deletes both accounts.

cuts his hair, and calls in her countrymen who blind him (43:5-6). No reference is made to the eleven hundred pieces of silver offered by the Philistines; the act of betrayal is gratuitous, without motivation or explanation. Delilah's deed thus presented is simply a function of her sole purpose: unknowingly to facilitate the divine justice forecast when Samson married her (43:5).[53]

Pseudo-Philo identifies the Witch of Endor as Sedecla, daughter of a Midianite "who had led Israel astray with sorceries" (64:3).[54] Having made her a gentile and a villainess, the author proceeds to define and limit her role. No reference is made to the hospitality and tender care (i.e., maternal nurturing) she offers the forlorn king (I Sam 28:21-25). Instead, Sedecla causes Saul additional despair by not recognizing him (64:4). The insertion of this scene is awkward, for Pseudo-Philo never explains how she knew it was Saul standing by the risen Samuel (64:5). However, it does provide occasion to delineate her purpose, i.e., further to trouble the deservedly distressed monarch. Sedecla, however, is never made aware of her real significance, and her scene closes with Samuel's denial of the powers she presumes to have: "And so do not boast, king, nor you, woman, for you have not brought me forth, but that order that God spoke to me while I was still alive, that I should come and tell you that you have sinned now a second time in neglecting God" (64:7).

In contrast, Jael the Kenite, the gentile woman who wrecks vengeance on Israel's enemies, is portrayed as aware of being guided by an external force. The story opens with Deborah telling Barak of Sisera's plan to attack Israel and take beautiful women as his concubines. It is this plan, not Barak's insistence that Deborah accompany him to do battle (Judg 4:9), that prompts the forecast, here attributed to God, that Sisera would "fall into the hands of a woman" (31:1). The shift of responsibility from Barak directly to Sisera and the attribution of the prediction to God rather than to Deborah clearly reflect Pseudo-Philo's theology of divine retribution, as does the language of the forecast itself: "The arm of a weak woman would attack him and maidens would take his spoils and even he would fall into the hands of a woman."

---

[53]According to Judg 16:5, she is bribed by the Philistine lords. Unlike Josephus, who attempts to exonerate Samson to some extent at the expense of Delilah (*Ant.* V.308ff.), Pseudo-Philo attributes the downfall fully to Samson's sinful unions with "the daughters of the Philistines" (43:5). The description of Samson's marriage to the woman of Timnah is extremely brief (41:1-2), but she is clearly included in God's condemnation of Samson when he undertakes a second such alliance.

[54]In I Samuel, she is presumably an Israelite; *Pirqe R. El.* 33 identifies her as Abner's mother.

Introduced as "very beautiful in appearance," Jael cleverly supplements her natural resources by scattering suggestive roses upon the bed she offers the fleeing commander.[55] Sisera so succumbs to the enticement that he thinks of marrying Jael and taking her — instead of the Israelite women he had originally sought — home to his mother (31:1). Having drawn attention to her ingenuity, Pseudo-Philo next portrays Jael as hesitant and in constant need of reassurance. Every step of the way she seeks assurance that her acts will be divinely assisted. When she goes to the flock to get milk, and when, spike in hand, she approaches the sleeping Sisera, whom she had drugged by mixing wine with his milk, she seeks (and receives) signs to indicate that God is acting with her. Even as she hammers the stake into the general's temple, she appeals to God to strengthen her arm (31:5-7).[56] The scene closes with a statement of true vengeance achieved. In great pain Sisera mourns that he is dying "like a woman," to which Jael responds unsympathetically by repeating the phrase that predicted his death at the beginning of the story: "Go, boast before your father in hell and tell him that you have fallen into the hands of a woman" (31:8). Her taunt is not unlike David's words to Goliath before he kills him: "Then you will say to your mother, 'He who was born from your sister has not spared us'" (61:6).

The overall impact of the creatively reconstructed narrative is the transformation of the independent biblical heroine into a clever, but less autonomous, instrument of divine vengeance. The reconstruction places Jael at the center of a tale of divinely orchestrated retribution. Sisera, who had planned to take beautiful Israelite women as concubines, is slain by a beautiful gentile whom he would have as his wife. Moreover, unlike Delilah and Sedecla, who serve as instruments to punish Israel's fallen heroes, Jael is fully aware of the significance of her act. However, clever as she is in enticing the commander, each of her subsequent actions is portrayed as directly guided by God, who thus, albeit subtly, remains the chief actor in the narrative.

---

[55]Judg 4:17 simply states that Jael adorned herself and went out to meet him. In rabbinic midrash, she is portrayed as both beautiful and actively seductive (b. Meg. 15a; b. Yebam. 103a; and b. Nazir 23b). Josephus, however, lacks any suggestion of the seductive (Ant. V.207). For a comparison of the treatments of Jael and Deborah by Josephus and Pseudo-Philo, see L. H. Feldman, "Josephus' Portrait of Deborah," in A. Caquot, M. Hadas-Lebel, and J. Riaud (eds.), Hellenica et Judaica (Leuven and Paris: Peeters, 1986), 115-28.
[56]The scene is reminiscent of Judith's decapitation of Holofernes, but in character Judith and this Jael are very different. Judith seeks God's assistance; Jael prays for signs and reassurance.

Pseudo-Philo reserves the role of female protagonist for Israelite women who serve as God's agents/partners. These women confidently act out their parts, fully aware of their significance in the divine plan for Israel. Heroic mothers acquire their awareness in the contexts of the wonder births of their sons. For Deborah and Jephthah's daughter, women who are not mothers of Israelite leaders, the awareness is intuitive; it is a natural function of their heroic roles.

Again, there is a structural pattern to the stories of these two women. Their appointments are predicted by God before either appears, and each appointment is justified in terms of divine retribution. The forecasts, which permit the reader entry into God's mind, are similar to the predictions concerning the appointments of Abraham (7:4) and Moses (9:7-8). Deborah "will rule" and "enlighten" the Israelites because they have been led astray after the daughters of the Amorites and have served their gods (30:2).[57] And Seila will be sacrificed because of the carelessness with which Jephthah made his vow.[58]

Although their roles have been divinely designated in the prefaces to their stories, the women act as if no forecast had been presented. In both accounts there is divine action (the stars are commanded to immolate Sisera's army; "the tongues" of the wise men are shut so they cannot respond to Seila). But, in contrast to Jael, Deborah and Seila are self-directed heroines. Divine action supplements rather than assists their activities.

The biblical characterizations of both women (the heroic judge in war and the piously obedient daughter) are played down in favor of portraits of heroines far wiser than those whom they confront.[59] Deborah's leadership is depicted in notably verbal terms. Her ability to "enlighten" Israel is demonstrated through three extensive monologues in which she chastens God's flock (30:5-6), recalls God's wonders on their behalf (32), teaches them (33:2-3, 5), and prophe-

---

[57]Although the seductresses here are the "daughters of the Amorites," the comment that the Israelites "were led astray after the daughters ... and served their gods" is drawn from the description of the Midianite women in Num 25:1-2.

[58]God's anger is aroused by the lack of proper consideration preceding such a vow: "If a dog should meet Jephthah first, will the dog be offered to me?" (39:11). The same concern is expressed by God in *Gen. Rab.* 60:3; *Lev. Rab.* 37:4.

[59]The contrast is one of the means by which Pseudo-Philo portrays leadership ability. See G. W. E. Nickelsburg's "Good and Bad Leaders in Pseudo-Philo's *Liber Antiquitatum Biblicarum*," in idem and J. J. Collins (eds.), *Ideal Figures in Ancient Judaism: Profiles and Paradigms* (Chico, CA: Scholars

sies their future (30:7). Her role is thus comparable to that of Moses, Joshua, and Kenaz. The role of Seila is also expanded such that she is portrayed as the bearer of wisdom not shared by her father or even "the wise men" of her generation (40:4). The portrayal of Seila's wisdom is particularly complex. On the one hand, aware that the vow is invalid,[60] she goes to consult with the wise men, who are unable to respond. On the other hand, intuiting her place in the divine plan, she likens herself to Isaac and assures her father of her readiness to emulate him in being a willing, proper sacrifice (40:2-3).[61] Both aspects of her wisdom are praised by God, who finds her "wise in contrast to her father ... perceptive in contrast to all the wise men"; he finds her sacrificial death "precious" (40:4).

Like Tamar, both women assume roles associated with men, but each is portrayed in a manner which bespeaks her femininity. By connecting Deborah's appointment to the seduction of Israelite men by Amorite women, the forecast to her story clearly implies the impropriety of a female judge. Further, Deborah is quite purposely portrayed in terms that recollect the skills of all the great male leaders who preceded her. However, she does not assume a masculine or gender-neutral persona. To the contrary, she presents herself as "a woman of God ... as one from the female race" (33:1). Enhancing her maternal role, she includes the miraculous births of Isaac and Jacob in her review of Israel's history. Next, she chastises in maternal tones: she describes God as "sorrowful" over the need to punish Israel (30:5); she gently predicts Israel's future disobedience (30:7); and she explicitly urges her people "to obey" her "like a mother" (33:1). In return, she is perceived by the Israelites as "Mother" (33:4).

A similar duality characterizes Seila. As victim of her father's

Press, 1980), 49-65.

[60]The awareness is implied in her urging her father not to annul the vow (a strange response to her father's statement that he cannot call the vow back, cf. 40:1-2), and in her approaching the wise men before going to the mountain (40:4). According to Pesiq. Rab Kah. 5:7, she goes to the Sanhedrin to have the vow invalidated. In rabbinic midrash, the girl's death is attributed to the false pride of Jephthah and Phineas as well as to the fact that the sages of the day forgot that the vow was invalid. See Gen. Rab. 60:3; Lev. Rab. 37:4; Pesiq. Rab Kah. 5:7; and the citations in Legends VI, 203 n. 109.

[61]Other references to Isaac by Pseudo-Philo clarify the significance of Seila's comparison: the election of Abraham and his seed is attributed to Isaac's blood at the time of the Akedah (18:5), and Isaac is recalled by Deborah as saying: "... about me future generations will be instructed and through me the peoples will understand that the Lord has made the soul of a man worthy to be a sacrifice'" (32:2). The narrative is thus reminiscent of the rabbinic tradition that Isaac's willingness to be sacrificed had permanent atoning value for Israel (b. Yoma 5a and Mek. R. Shimon 4).

ill-conceived vow, she is strikingly feminine. A tragic case of unful-
fillment, she is given a poetic lament filled with imaginings of the
bride she will never become and the marriage chamber she will never
see. As heroine-martyr, however, she is cast as "the wise son," as an
Isaac who will atone for the sins of the people. Although Seila
assumes the martyr's role voluntarily, the model had already been
prescribed in the words by which God foretold the price of
Jephthah's vow: "his own firstborn ... the fruit of his own body ... his
only begotten" (39:11).[62]

In the stories of Seila and Deborah, as with all Pseudo-Philo's
narratives, there is no arbitrary event. Israel's history reflects the
hand of God rewarding those who are righteous, punishing those
who are not. Seila's death is no exception; she "will fall into the bosom
of her mothers" (40:4), a phrase that implies the company, if not the
status, of the matriarchs. There are a number of instances of such
maternal imagery. Amram holds up the model of Tamar, "our
mother" (9:5); at the sight of the golden calf, Moses becomes "like a
woman bearing her firstborn who, when she is in labor, her hands
are upon her chest and she has no strength to help herself bring it
forth" (12:5); through Samuel, the "milk" of Hannah's "breasts" will
serve "as a fountain for the twelve tribes" (51:2); Dedila will be "as a
mother chastening her son" (44:9); and Deborah commands the
people to obey her "like your mother" (33:1).

The maternal theme may well have been drawn from the
stories of mothers in Judges and I Samuel; it is also possible that
Pseudo-Philo was influenced by the characterization of women,
particularly that of Rebekah, in *Jubilees*.[63] But Pseudo-Philo goes
far beyond his biblical source. The maternal role — giving birth,
nurturing, or chastening — is a major theme in his depiction of
women. Save for noting women's beauty, he does little with the
erotic; his treatment of the romantic is limited to the beautiful
lament composed for Seila; and nowhere are women treated in
supportive spousal roles. There is at most a passing reference
demonstrating David's trust in Michal (62:7), but neither her
character nor their relationship is developed.

Presenting biblical history as a handmaid to theology, Pseudo-
Philo rewrites narratives so that they consistently demonstrate the

---

[62]Compare the description of Isaac in God's instructions to Abraham (Gen
22:2). Isaac is also called the "fruit of his [father's] body" in Deborah's
description of the Akedah (*Bib. Ant.* 32:4). In general, the description of
Seila's identification with Isaac is built on Deborah's hymnic recollection of
the Akedah.

[63]See *Jub.* 19:17ff.; 25-27; 35; and Endres, *Biblical Interpretation*, chap. 3.

hand of God. Within the context of this theology, women have a specific function: they are either the instruments or the active agents of God. For the various types of instruments and agents Pseudo-Philo develops different patterns of characterizations. But within these patterns all strong female characters are associated in one way or another with motherhood, be it in the role of parent, villainess, or leader of Israel. Conversely, when the biblical story offers no context for a maternal characterization, Pseudo-Philo either underdevelops the portrait or portrays the woman as ineffective and dependent.

Revelatory Experiences Attributed to Biblical Women in Early Jewish Literature

Randall D. Chesnutt

For all their obvious differences, the midrashic works *Jubilees*, *Joseph and Aseneth*, and the *Testament of Job*[1] share a striking common feature: each greatly expands the role of a woman or women known from the Bible. Rebekah, already a bold and resourceful character in Genesis, is elevated even further in *Jubilees*, where she overshadows her rather docile husband and achieves a significant role in salvation history. Aseneth[2] is mentioned only in passing in Gen 41:45, 50, and 46:20 as the wife of the patriarch Joseph, but in the apocryphal romance it is she — not the patriarch — who is the leading character. Women play almost no role in the biblical book of Job: Job's wife appears only long enough to suggest that he curse God and die (2:9); and nothing is mentioned concerning his daughters other than their names, their exceptional beauty, and their roles as coheirs with their brothers (42:13-15). In the *Testament of Job*, however, the women in Job's family appear regularly, and Job's daughters receive especially complimentary treatment. Moreover, each work attributes to the women some sort of revelatory experience which enhances their role in promoting the central ideals of the book.

To the extent that these portrayals represent post-biblical expansions, they provide important data for studying the varying perceptions of and roles assigned to Jewish women in the Hellenistic era. The purpose of this study is to examine how the revelatory experiences attributed to these women function within the respective writings, how they relate to other Jewish traditions of roughly

---

[1]The overworked and imprecise word "midrashic" is used loosely with reference to these three works because they all adapt and retell biblical narratives in such a way as to address contemporary concerns. Other terms (romance, testament) are more appropriate for generic classifications of at least two of these texts, but it is the "midrashic" element in the sense mentioned above which is of primary interest here. Among the many attempts to qualify and refine the term, see G. G. Porton, "Defining Midrash," in J. Neusner (ed.), *The Study of Ancient Judaism*, Vol. I (New York: KTAV, 1981), 55-92; J. Neusner, *Midrash in Context: Exegesis in Formative Judaism* (Philadelphia: Fortress, 1983); and idem, *What is Midrash?* Guides to Biblical Scholarship (Philadelphia: Fortress, 1987).

[2]This spelling, used throughout the present study, transliterates the form found in the Greek text of *Joseph and Aseneth* (Ασενεθ) rather than that of the Masoretic text (אָסְנַת). The Septuagint reads Ασεννεθ.

comparable date, and what they suggest about women's roles in the Judaisms of the Hellenistic age.

Although the three apocryphal works are difficult to date, they are considered here in the probable order of their composition. The generally acknowledged approximate dates are: *Jubilees*, mid-second century B.C.E; *Joseph and Aseneth*, first century B.C.E. or C.E.; and *Testament of Job*, first century C.E.[3]

Rebekah in *Jubilees*

In rewriting Israel's primeval and ancestral traditions, the author of *Jubilees* embellished the portrait of Rebekah more than that of any other character.[4] Although Isaac is treated sympathetically in this text, he is not presented as having any particular quality that makes him heroic or worthy of emulation. Rather, it is his wife who assumes the mantle of leadership in their marriage and provides the bridge from Abraham to Jacob. P. van Boxel is therefore correct in observing that Rebekah "plays such a central part in this salvation history that she can rightly be called a matriarch of Israel."[5]

The elevation of Rebekah in *Jubilees* is evident as early as the initial scene, which depicts her preference for Jacob over Esau. Genesis gives no reason for her partiality and leaves the reader to assume that it is arbitrary. However, in the pseudepigraphon no less a person than Abraham also favors Jacob; indeed, he commands Rebekah to do the same so that Jacob's advancement may be ensured and that God's purposes may be accomplished through him (19:15-31).[6] The author further justifies Rebekah's favoritism by adding an indication that Jacob was morally superior to Esau (19:13-14; cf. Gen 25:27) as well as by making Rebekah's blessing of Jacob divinely inspired (25:14-23). Rebekah's preference for Jacob is thus given patriarchal, ethical, and theological legitimation. Her culpability in deceiving Isaac to acquire the paternal blessing of the firstborn for Jacob is likewise mitigated by the added detail that a dispensation from heaven facilitated the ruse (26:18). These addi-

---

[3]See J. H. Charlesworth, *The Pseudepigrapha and Modern Research with a Supplement*, SBLSCS 7S (Chico, CA: Scholars Press, 1981), 134-40, 143-47, 291-95, and the works cited there.
[4]J. Endres, *Biblical Interpretation in the Book of Jubilees*, CBQMS 18 (Washington, D.C.: Catholic Biblical Association, 1987), 217. I am heavily indebted to Endres throughout this section on Rebekah.
[5]"The God of Rebekah," *Service international de documentation judéo-chrétienne* 9 (1976): 18.
[6]Cf. Gen 25, where Abraham is already dead when Esau and Jacob are born.

tions exonerate Rebekah from any charge of ethical impropriety. Actions which in Genesis not only lack clear motivation but are in fact deceitful become in *Jubilees* commendable acts by which Rebekah furthers divine purposes and provides a crucial link in the drama of salvation history.

After Abraham's death Rebekah assumes an especially prominent leadership role. The strong admonition to Jacob not to marry a Canaanite woman (25:1-3) and the lengthy parental blessing for Jacob (25:11-23) come not from Isaac, but from Rebekah. Isaac is in fact conspicuously absent from this chapter.[7] In the preceding generation it was Abraham who blessed Jacob (22:10-30) and warned him against exogamy (22:20). These parallel functions of Abraham and Rebekah are among the indications that Rebekah, not Isaac, is the bridge between Abraham's generation and Jacob's. In view of the author's conflict with the assimilationists of the day[8] and his vehement opposition to intermarriage with gentiles,[9] it is noteworthy that he allows a woman such a prominent role as a spokesperson for his ideal of endogamy.

Even more striking is Rebekah's blessing of Jacob. Not only is this matriarchal blessing without precedent in the biblical text, Rebekah is said to have been inspired to utter it by the descent of a "spirit of truth" upon her mouth (25:14).[10] Moreover, it is significant that in this blessing a woman — this time gifted with prophetic speech — again articulates one of the author's most cherished ideals, namely, the purification of the Jerusalem sanctuary (25:21).[11] Rebekah's expanded role as the more imperious partner in her marriage is highlighted still further in *Jubilees* 25 by her laying hands upon Jacob (25:14) — a gesture not performed by anyone else in the text — and by Jacob's unqualified submission to her wishes (25:9-10).

The revelatory experiences ascribed to Rebekah do not end

---

[7]Cf. Gen 28:1, where it is Isaac who forbids Jacob to marry a Canaanite. In *Jub.* 27:9-11, Isaac counsels and blesses Jacob not only much later than Rebekah does, but also much more briefly. He merely recapitulates what Rebekah has already done.

[8]See, *inter alia*, J. C. VanderKam, *Textual and Historical Studies in the Book of Jubilees*, HSM 14 (Missoula, MT: Scholars Press, 1977), 241-46.

[9]See especially *Jub.* 30:11.

[10]Ethiopic manuscript C reads "holy spirit." Unless otherwise noted, all quotations of the Pseudepigrapha are from Charlesworth, *OTP*.

[11]From 1:29 and 4:26 it is clear that the author equates this sanctuary with the Temple in Jerusalem. *Jub.* 23:21 describes the pollution of the Temple which renders it unfit to be the authentic holy place. See G. L. Davenport, *The Eschatology of the Book of Jubilees*, SPB 20 (Leiden: Brill, 1971), 15f., 29-31, and 85f.

with her inspired blessing of Jacob. According to 27:1 Esau's murderous intentions toward Jacob "were told to Rebekah in a dream."[12] On the basis of this revelation she orders Jacob to flee to Haran and seek refuge with her brother, Laban. Isaac later instructs Jacob to the same effect, but he does so only upon Rebekah's urging (27:7-11); this is yet another indication of who the leader is in this marriage. Rebekah's announcement to Jacob of her impending death and her testamentary speeches to her family are likewise prompted by a revelatory dream (35:6).

The author continues to highlight Rebekah's stature as familial leader and as a vital link in salvation history up to the account of her death in chapter 35. Even the fatherly actions attributed to Isaac replicate actions already taken by Rebekah. Thus, in *Jubilees* 31 Isaac follows Rebekah's lead in pronouncing a blessing upon Jacob, and in so doing he is influenced by a "spirit of prophecy" (31:12) just as Rebekah was earlier (25:14). Similarly, Isaac's testamentary speech and final joyous meal with his two sons in chapter 36 replicate Rebekah's final actions in chapter 35; this recapitulation suggests that Rebekah held sway over her husband even after her death. Since Rebekah's testamentary admonitions to familial harmony seem to reflect the internecine strife and the Jewish-Idumaean hostilities of the mid-second century B.C.E.,[13] the author has once again employed a woman to address pressing contemporary problems.

Numerous other subtle alterations protecting Rebekah's reputation[14] combine with her advocacy of the author's most cherished ideals to establish her as an important example for the Jewish community of the author's day to emulate. Endres has called attention to the importance *Jubilees* assigns to the ancestors as examples of covenantal fidelity:[15]

> Since human fidelity to the covenant greatly concerned this author, his redaction of the story downplays the role of divine gratuity. In the biblical tradition, God's love and favor shone the more highly because of, and not in spite of, human frailty. For this author, however, the frailty, peccadilloes, and sins of

---

[12]Gen 27:42 does not indicate the means by which she learned of Esau's scheme.

[13]Endres, *Biblical Interpretation*, 173-76; VanderKam, *Studies*, 230-38; G. W. E. Nickelsburg, *Jewish Literature Between the Bible and the Mishnah* (Philadelphia: Fortress, 1981), 76.

[14]For example, all hints of the possible sexual violation of Rebekah by Abimelech of Gerar are carefully eliminated (*Jub.* 24:12f.; cf. Gen 26:6-11).

[15]*Biblical Interpretation*, 49.

the ancestors (especially of Jacob) proved an embarrassment; thus he deleted them whenever possible. As a result, the forebears play a significantly different role in Jubilees: they no longer function primarily as the recipients of divine favor, but as *exempla* for imitation by the Jewish community.

As a moral example, therefore, as well as a familial leader, Rebekah takes her place alongside the patriarchs of Israel. At the conclusion of her blessing of Jacob, her love is even cited as paradigmatic for God's love (25:23) — a striking indication of the esteem in which this author held Rebekah.

All these data combine to suggest that Rebekah is for the author of *Jubilees* "the matriarch *par excellence* of the Jewish people."[16] Taking the leadership role that her unassuming husband did not, she conveys the election from Abraham to Jacob and assures the continuity of salvation history. As a moral exemplar and outspoken opponent of exogamy, the contamination of the Temple, and familial discord, she embodies the ideals which the author considered indispensable for the survival of Judaism through the traumas of the second century B.C.E. Especially significant for our study is Rebekah's role as an agent of divine revelation. Although for *Jubilees* it is Levi and his priestly descendants who are primarily responsible for preserving and interpreting Israel's sacred traditions,[17] Levi is said to have received the bulk of these traditions from Jacob (45:15); and he in turn had received at least some of them from Rebekah as a result of her revelatory experiences.[18] Thus Rebekah functions as one of the mediators of the sacred traditions that, according to *Jubilees*, remain normative for God's people.

Aseneth in *Joseph and Aseneth*

Aseneth so dominates the apocryphon which narrates her conversion and marriage to Joseph that the title now commonly used for the work, *Joseph and Aseneth*, must be judged a misnomer. In the first part of this double novella, chapters 1-21, Joseph appears at the beginning and end but is absent throughout the heart of the story; there, Aseneth's conversion occupies center stage. In

---

[16]The language is that of ibid., 217.
[17]Ibid., 120-54, 233f., *et passim*; and A. Hultgård, *L'eschatologie des Testaments des Douze Patriarchs*, Vol. I, Acta Universitatis Upsaliensis, Historia Religionum 6, 7 (Uppsala: Almqvist and Wiksell, 1977-82), 15-45.
[18]Jacob's other sources include the testamentary speech of Abraham (25:5; 39:6), theophanic dreams and visions (32:20-26; 44:1-6), and especially the seven heavenly tablets which he saw in a night vision (32:20-26).

the the second novella, chapters 22-29, Aseneth again eclipses Joseph, not only by the frequency of her appearance in contrast to Joseph's usual absence, but also by her role alongside Levi as a prime example of and advocate for the ethical ideals which the text promotes.

In no way does this elevation of Aseneth imply that the author either denigrates Joseph or exalts Aseneth at his expense. Joseph is no less a paradigm of virtue here than he is in so many other early Jewish sources.[19] Indeed, the very esteem in which Joseph was held furnished this author a primary means for extolling Aseneth. The terms describing Aseneth so closely parallel those used for Joseph as to betray a concern to elevate Aseneth to a status commensurate with that of the revered patriarch. Thus, just as Joseph is said to have been so handsome that he was the desire of all the women of Egypt (7:3), so Aseneth's beauty occasioned intense rivalry for her hand (1:4-6). Yet, just as Joseph rejected these advances and remained a virgin (παρθένος; 4:7; 8:1; see also 7:4f.), so Aseneth was "a virgin (παρθένος) hating every man" (7:8; see also 1:4-6; 2:1). Exalted attributes are ascribed to Joseph: he is "the Powerful One of God" (3:4; 4:7; 18:1f.; 21:21), "the son of God" (6:3, 5; 18:11; 21:4); but even these lofty epithets find counterparts in the description of Aseneth as one "adorned like a bride of God" (4:1) and as "a daughter of the Most High" (21:4). The portrait of Joseph in 6:2-6 comes close to ascribing angelic status to him, but the same can be said of the descriptions of Aseneth in 18:9-11 and 20:6f.: she is likened to the sun just as Joseph is; heavenly beauty is ascribed to both; each is said to radiate great light. Joseph is clad in an exquisite white tunic, wears a golden crown with precious stones, and carries a royal staff when he first arrives at the house of Pentephres (5:5); later Aseneth also dresses in a radiant white garment, wears a golden crown with costly stones, and bears a scepter (14:12-15; 18:5f.). When the plot against the couple is narrated in chapters 22-29, the Lord is said to guard Aseneth (26:2) as well as Joseph (25:5) "like an apple of the eye," and to fight for Aseneth (28:1) as well as Joseph (25:6) against the antagonists. As R. C. Douglas has observed, "Aseneth and Joseph are almost mirror images of each other."[20]

The most likely explanation for Aseneth's exaltation is that the Jewish community behind the apocryphon had experienced some

---

[19]See G. W. E. Nickelsburg (ed.), *Studies on the Testament of Joseph*, SCS 5 (Missoula, MT: Scholars Press, 1975); H. W. Hollander, *Joseph as an Ethical Model in the Testaments of the Twelve Patriarchs* (Leiden: Brill, 1981); and M. Niehoff, "The Figure of Joseph in the Targums," *JJS* 39 (1988): 234-50.
[20]"Liminality and Conversion in Joseph and Aseneth," *JSP* 3 (1988): 31-42.

disharmony concerning the perception of gentile converts and especially the propriety of marriage between one born Jewish and a proselyte.[21] The exalted portrayal of Aseneth demonstrates that the true convert is deserving of full acceptance into the community of Israel and is indeed worthy to be the wife of one who is born a Jew.[22] Of the various means by which the author labors to establish this point, none is more fully developed or more important for our purposes than the extended narrative of Aseneth's epiphanic experience in chapters 14-17.

In chapter 14, a man from heaven, later identified as God's chief angel (15:12), appears amid great emanations of light to the penitent Aseneth; he commands her to replace her mourning garments with glorious clothing consonant with her new status as one of the people of God (14:12f.). Next, he informs Aseneth that her repentance has been duly acknowledged (15:2f.), that her name has been written irrevocably in the heavenly book of the living (15:4), that God has given her to Joseph as a bride (15:6), that her name will be changed to "City of Refuge" in view of her role as the prototypical proselyte (15:7), and that in converting she has eaten the same food as that eaten by the angels of God in paradise and so has become a participant in life, immortality, and incorruptibility (16:14-16). As D. Sänger has perceived, this angelic visitation is neither the cause nor the occasion of Aseneth's conversion; rather, it functions both to provide heavenly confirmation of a conversion that has already taken place and to articulate the benefits of belonging to the people of God.[23] That Aseneth was worthy to receive the heavenly visitor and the glorious blessings announced by him proves that her conversion and her marriage to Joseph have been divinely sanctioned and that she deserves full recognition as one of the people of God.

In addition to the general revelatory character of this heavenly visitation, the "man from heaven" indicates to Aseneth that "the ineffable mysteries of the Most High" have been revealed to her (16:14). The context suggests that the content of these "ineffable mysteries" is the source of the divine life in which Aseneth participates symbolically by eating from the honeycomb provided miraculously by the

---

[21]This understanding of the social world of Joseph and Aseneth is developed at length in R. D. Chesnutt, "The Social Setting and Purpose of Joseph and Aseneth," *JSP* 2 (1988): 21-48.

[22]Ibid., 30-43.

[23]"Bekehrung und Exodus: Traditionshintergrund von 'Joseph und Aseneth,'" *JSJ* 10 (1979) 29f.; and idem, *Antikes Judentum und die Mysterien: Religionsgeschichtliche Untersuchungen zu Joseph und Aseneth*, WUNT 2.5

angel. Eating the honey, in turn, is equated with eating the bread of life, drinking the cup of immortality, and being anointed with the ointment of incorruptibility (16:16; 19:5; cf. 8:5, 9; 15:5; 21:21). This formulaic language suggests that to live faithfully as a Jew and avoid the contamination of gentile food, drink, and oil — the staples of life most susceptible to gentile defilement — is to share the divine food and hence the immortality of angels in paradise.[24] These μυστήρια are revealed to Aseneth (16:14), and through her story, to all who follow in her steps of renouncing idols and turning to the Lord.

In the second novella, Aseneth receives yet other revelations from Levi, her brother-in-law (22:13). This text holds Levi in high esteem as a prophet gifted with unusual powers to read what is written in people's hearts (23:8; 28:15) and to perceive events happening at a distance (26:6; 28:15-17). As a prophet Levi also had insight into the heavenly mysteries, and he shares these secrets with Aseneth:

> And Aseneth loved Levi exceedingly beyond all of Joseph's brethren, because he was one who attached himself to the Lord, and he was a prudent man and a prophet of the Most High and sharp-sighted with his eyes, and he used to see letters written in heaven by the finger of God and he knew the unspeakable (mysteries) of the Most High God and revealed them to Aseneth in secret, because he himself, Levi, would love Aseneth very much, and see her place of rest in the highest, and her walls like adamantine eternal walls, and her foundations founded upon a rock of the seventh heaven. (22:13)

The author of Joseph and Aseneth thus clearly values higher revelation. Not only Levi, but also Joseph, is said to have received revelations in some form (6:6; 19:9). However, since in this text it is Levi who serves the primary role of recipient and purveyor of re-

---

(Tübingen: Mohr, 1980), 156f., 182.

[24]On the problematic bread-cup-ointment triad, see C. Burchard, *Untersuchungen zu Joseph und Aseneth: Überlieferung-Ortsbestimmung*, WUNT 8 (Tübingen: Mohr, 1965), 121-33; idem, "The Importance of Joseph and Aseneth for the Study of the New Testament: A General Survey and a Fresh Look at the Lord's Supper," *NTS* 33 (1987): 109-17; B. Lindars, "'Joseph and Asenath' and the Eucharist," *Scripture: Meaning and Method. Essays Presented to A. T. Hanson for His Seventieth Birthday*, ed. B. P. Thompson (Hull: Hull University Press, 1987), 181-99; and R. D. Chesnutt, "Bread of Life in Joseph and Aseneth and in John 6," in J. E. Priest (ed.), *Johannine Studies in Honor of Frank Pack* (Malibu, CA: Pepperdine University Press, 1989), 1-16. In a forthcoming study I argue more fully for the interpretation summarized above. Parallels to the triad in other Jewish sources confirm that gentile food, drink, and oil were considered so contaminated by association with idolatry that the Jewish avoidance of them served as a representative expression for the life *more judaico*.

vealed knowledge, it is significant both that Levi conveys supernatural knowledge to Aseneth and that Aseneth is carefully portrayed to resemble Levi closely. She has access to "the ineffable mysteries of the Most High" (16:14) as does Levi (22:13); she urges clemency toward enemies with the same magnanimous language used earlier by Levi for the same purpose (28:7, 10, 14; cf. 23:9-12; 29:3); she ranks among "those who attach themselves (οἱ προσκείμενοι) to the Most High God" (15:7; cf. 16:14) just as Levi is characterized as "one who attached himself (προσκείμενος) to the Lord" (22:13). Thus the convert to Judaism is placed on equal footing with another of the most revered members of the Jewish community, and a woman is assigned revelatory experiences comparable to those attributed to the leading male characters.

Job's Wife and Daughters in the *Testament of Job*

The study of the role of women in this third ancient text is complicated by uncertainty concerning the relationship of chapters 46-53 to the rest of the book. Foremost among the factors which convince many of a separate origin for these concluding chapters is a markedly different image of women from that which emerges in chapters 1-45. Although women figure prominently in 1-45 as well as in 46-53, only in the latter are they depicted in a complimentary fashion. Whether chapters 46-53 represent (1) an interpolation into a work which originally ended after chapter 45 with the resolution of the major conflicts in the narrative,[25] (2) a part of the original designed to bring to a climax and resolve other elements in the book, including the inferior status to which women had been relegated,[26] or (3) a different source from which the author drew without ironing out the discrepancies with the material in chapters 1-45,[27] is beyond the scope of this study. Here it is sufficient to probe the exalted depiction of women in chapters 46-53 in order to inquire first how it differs from that in chapters 1-45, and second, how it

[25]This was argued in detail by M. R. James, *Apocrypha Anecdota*, 2d Ser., Texts and Studies 5.1 (Cambridge: Cambridge University Press, 1897), xciv-xcvi. So also R. Spittler, "The Testament of Job: Introduction, Translation, and Notes" (Unpublished dissertation, Harvard University, 1971), 58-69, summarized in idem, "Testament of Job," *OTP* I, 834; and E. von Nordheim, *Die Lehre der Alten I: Das Testament als Literaturgattung im Judentum der hellenistisch-römischen Zeit*, ALGHJ 13 (Leiden: Brill, 1980), 131-32.

[26]So J. J. Collins, "Structure and Meaning in the Testament of Job," in G. MacRae (ed.), *Society of Biblical Literature 1974 Seminar Papers* (Cambridge, MA: Society of Biblical Literature, 1974), 48; and Nickelsburg, *Jewish Literature*, 246f.

[27]P. van der Horst, "The Role of Women in the Testament of Job," *Neder-*

relates to the elevated portrayals of women and especially the revelatory experiences attributed to them in the other documents here under consideration.

Throughout the *Testament of Job* a contrast is drawn between the transitory material world, which is the arena of Satan's activity, and the permanent realities of the heavenly realm. Job has insight into this distinction, and the plot revolves around his interaction with those who do not.[28] The first major section (chapters 2-27) depicts Job in direct conflict with Satan. By means of an angelophanic revelation, Job is made aware of supramundane reality; he is by this knowledge set apart from those who remain subject to Satan's deceptions. Job is able to penetrate, in four distinct episodes, the disguises with which Satan successfully deceives others. In two cases, those deceived by Satan's wiles are women: a servant girl and Job's wife, Sitidos.[29] Satan appears in chapter 7 in the guise of a beggar asking for bread. Job immediately recognizes him and tells his servant girl to give him a burnt loaf. However, not knowing that the beggar is Satan, she gives him her own good loaf instead. Far more developed is the episode in chapters 23-27 involving Job's wife. This time Satan has bread for sale and Sitidos is the beggar. Although Sitidos unselfishly sells her hair in order to buy bread for Job, she is deceived by Satan and becomes an accomplice in his effort to entice Job to sin. Job, on the other hand, readily unmasks the disguised Satan and reveals to Sitidos that she has been led astray. The function of these women, as Collins has suggested, is to provide "a foil to show off Job's superior handling of the situation."[30]

It is possible to exaggerate the negative light in which these women are cast. In one sense they are portrayed sympathetically: they are utterly loyal to Job, and even when they act improperly

---

lands *Theologisch Tijdschrift* 40 (1986): 283.

[28]Collins, "Structure and Meaning," 40: "Throughout the book Job stands in opposition to some other party. In the first half of the book we have a conflict between Job and Satan, in the second half a confrontation between Job and his friends. These two oppositions may be said to form the core of the book." My understanding of the literary structure and purpose of the Testament of Job is heavily indebted to Collins's important article and to Nickelsburg, *Jewish Literature*, 241-48.

[29]This spelling of the name will be used throughout, although there is considerable variation in the manuscript tradition. Some scholars, assuming that "Sitidos" is the genitival form which came to be mistaken for the nominative, prefer the spelling "Sitis"; but cf. van der Horst, "Role of Women," 275f.

[30]"Structure and Meaning," 40. See also van der Horst, "Role of Women," 278: "She [Sitidos] is used in order to create a symmetry in the plot, so that two mirror images complement each other. Job and God are on the one side. ... The Satan and the wife are on the other side." Van der Horst cites private correspondence from A. Brenner as the source for this statement.

they are victims rather than willing agents of satanic illusions. For example, even though the servant girl fails to recognize Satan, she acts out of kind-hearted generosity in giving bread to a beggar (7:11).[31] And Sitidos is consistently depicted as a devoted wife: she even suffers the humiliation of cutting and selling her hair in order to buy food for her husband (23:6-11). Indeed, by her actions on behalf of Job she carries the plot along for a significant portion of the book.[32] Nevertheless, in terms of spiritual awareness she is conspicuously deficient; her lack of perception is contrasted with the superior insight of Job.

In the second major section of the book, chapters 28-45, Job's superior insight is again contrasted with others' lack of perception. The primary foils here are four visiting kings,[33] but Sitidos also demonstrates a failure to perceive parallel to that of the kings. In chapter 39, as she laments the death of her children, Sitidos requests that the kings' soldiers dig through the ruins of the fallen house and recover the bones of the children in order to give them a decent burial. The kings agree, but Job forbids them; he insists that the children have been taken up to heaven and therefore that the search for their bones would be futile. Although Sitidos and the kings think Job has gone mad, the superiority of his insight is proved when all see a vision of the children in heaven, "crowned with the splendor of the heavenly one" (40:3). The vision leads Sitidos and three of the four kings to acknowledge the heavenly reality to which Job is already attuned. Even though Sitidos finally receives this awareness of spiritual reality, it is clear that she does so only through Job's mediation: it was he who revealed to her that she was being led astray by Satan, and it is he who now discloses to her the glorious heavenly status of their deceased children. On her own she has no such insight; rather, she misperceives reality and errs repeatedly. In fact, for the short time that she lives following her vision, she resumes an earthbound existence by taking rest and refreshment and then continuing the duties of her servitude (40:4-6).

The portrayal of Job's wife is all the more uncomplimentary because she never intentionally takes Satan's side; she, like the servant girl earlier, is simply so spiritually imperceptive that she becomes Satan's unwitting accomplice. Although men as well as

---

[31]Her action parallels Job's acts of generosity (9-12; 53:2f.) and contrasts with the concern of Job's daughters for their own living (46:2; 47:1).
[32]I am indebted to A.-J. Levine for this insight.
[33]The identification of these friends as kings is found in the LXX (Job 42:17e).

women serve as foils for Job, the text leaves the strong impression
that women — precisely because they are women — are spiritually
unintelligent and therefore easy prey for Satan. That we are justified
in deducing such a general estimate of women from the particular
characters in the narrative is confirmed by 26:6, where Sitidos is
ranked as "one of the senseless women who misguide their husbands' sincerity."[34]

The picture is radically different in chapters 46-53. A premium
remains on insight into heavenly reality, but it is Job's three
daughters, not his sons, who are heirs to this insight.[35] Job divides
his earthly possessions among his seven sons, but to his daughters
he bequeaths something better: three golden boxes containing the
three strands of the therapeutic girdle by which his own health had
been restored and by which the Lord had revealed to him "things
present and things to come" (47:9). Each of the girls dons her cord
as a sash and, to cite the first daughter's experience as typical, "she
took on another heart — no longer minded toward earthly things —
but she spoke ecstatically in the angelic dialect, sending up a hymn
to God in accord with the hymnic style of the angels" (48:2-3). When
Job dies three days later, only his daughters — not the sons — see
his soul conveyed into heaven in gleaming chariots (52:1-11). As
Job's body is taken to the tomb, the daughters, girded with their
charismatic sashes and singing hymns to God, lead the way; in
contrast, Job's seven sons and his brother can only weep and
lament (52:12-53:4).

J. Collins maintains that the rather low view of women's
spiritual abilities continues even into chapters 46-53, since here
Job's daughters, like his first wife, gain insight into heavenly reality
only through Job's mediation.[36] However, as P. van der Horst
observes, the fact that Job plays some role in both cases does not
justify such a conclusion.[37] The enlightenment of Job's doormaid

---

[34]See also the vivid translation in R. Thornhill, "The Testament of Job,"
Apocryphal Old Testament, ed. H. F. D. Sparks (Oxford: Clarendon, 1984),
633: "one of those brainless women who subvert their own husbands'
integrity."
[35]These are Job's daughters by his second wife, Dinah, the daughter of the
patriarch Jacob. Given the way Sitidos is portrayed, it is not surprising that
she, unlike Job's wife in the biblical story, dies before Job's fortunes are
restored. The tradition that Job married Dinah is also attested, *inter alia*, in
LAB 8:7f.; *Gen. Rab.* 57:4; and *Tg. Job* 2:9.
[36]"Testaments," in M. E. Stone (ed.), *Jewish Writings of the Second Temple
Period*, CRINT 2.2 (Assen: Van Gorcum, 1984), 352f.; and idem, *Between
Athens and Jerusalem: Jewish Identity in the Hellenistic Diaspora* (New York:
Crossroad, 1983), 223.
[37]"Role of Women," 280f.

and his wife were *ad hoc* and temporary; they undergo no permanent transition from satanic deception to spiritual perception. Following her vision Sitidos requires rest and refreshment before returning to the duties of her earthly servitude (40:4-6).[38] This earthbound status contrasts sharply with that of Job's daughters; the language employed to describe them after their transforming revelatory experience comes close to an ascription of heavenly or angelic status. Each daughter is so radically transformed that she disregards earthly things and praises God in angelic languages. These women become the leading characters in chapters 46-53; the role of their father is minor, and that of their brothers and uncle unflattering. In a reversal of the stereotypes prominent in the earlier chapters, the "feminine" lack of perception attributed to Job's maidservant and his wife is here ascribed to the helpless male characters. The men are not only unaware of the glorious fate of Job's soul, they even assume the typically "female" role of expressing the lament.[39] The women, on the other hand, are now the knowledgeable ones who, like Job, do not become distraught over earthly afflictions but take comfort in heavenly reality.

Women thus play a remarkably positive role in chapters 46-53. The revelatory experiences of Job's daughters provide the climactic testimony for an order of reality which enables those aware of it to endure in a troubled and transient world of satanic illusions. Collins's statement that "womankind in *T. Job* symbolizes ... the human state of ignorance" is therefore valid for chapters 1-45, but hardly so for chapters 46-53. The revelations and ecstatic behavior attributed to the daughters in these chapters, *vis-à-vis* the rather dull male characters, project an image of women which contrasts sharply not only with that in chapters 1-45 but also with stereotypes of women in early Judaism.

Patterns and Implications

What patterns emerge from the foregoing discussion of the revelatory experiences and otherwise exalted roles assigned to biblical women in the three works considered? What, if anything, can be

---

[38]In the immediately following narrative of her death, some witnesses indicate that she "died disheartened" while others read "died in good spirits" (40:6).

[39]Van der Horst, "Role of Women," 282; and see further M. Alexiou, *The Ritual Lament in Greek Tradition* (Cambridge: Cambridge University Press, 1974), 10-23 and 212 n. 107: "The prominence of women in funeral lamentation is attested from earliest times in archaeology, epigraphy, and literature."

inferred about the status of Jewish women in the Greco-Roman era? Two kinds of conclusions, both tentative, are appropriate. The first concerns the affinities between these apocryphal works and other early Jewish sources in which women are said to have received revelations, and the second concerns the implications of our study for the social position of women in early Judaism.

The variety of functions served by the revelations to women in the three works makes generalizations hazardous. Rebekah's revelations support her vital role in the salvation history of *Jubilees*: she represents the bridge from Abraham to Jacob and an early link in the all-important chain of levitical tradition. Her ethical admonitions and her role as a model of covenant faithfulness are also strengthened by references to her revealed knowledge. The revelations to Aseneth in *Joseph and Aseneth* amplify her role as the prototypical proselyte: through her experiences divine approval is assured, and social acceptance is sought, both for gentiles who sincerely convert to Judaism and for marriage between born Jews and such proselytes. The weight of Aseneth's exemplary conduct in the face of hostility, as well as her appeal for clemency and nonretaliation in such situations, is also augmented by her revelations. By means of the heavenly realities revealed to Job's daughters, the *Testament of Job* 46-53 emphasizes a heavenly order of reality which enables those sensitive to it to endure the satanic afflictions of the material world. As functionally and substantively different as these revelations are, it is nonetheless significant that in three discrete and diverse early Jewish texts, portraits of women known from the Bible are embellished with revelatory experiences which play a central part in the message of the book.

Moreover, the works considered here are not alone among Jewish texts in ascribing revelations to biblical women. Rebekah is a favorite subject of such traditions; the targums and rabbinic midrashim often refer to her as a prophetess. *Genesis Rabbah* 67:9 (cf. 67:2) and *Targum Onqelos* on Gen 27:13 attribute Rebekah's knowledge of Esau's plot to prophetic revelation, and *Targum Pseudo-Jonathan* on Gen 27:5 and 27:42 cites revelations by the Holy Spirit as the means by which Rebekah came to know both of Isaac's intention to bless Esau and later of Esau's plot against Jacob.[40] Even Josephus, who typically downplays assertiveness or

---

[40]See further P. Schäfer, *Die Vorstellung vom heiligen Geist in der rabbinischen Literatur*, SANT 28 (Munich: Kösel-Verlag, 1972), 55f.; and Ginzburg, *Legends* I, 341; V, 271 n. 15, 272 n. 18, 281 n. 72, and 287 n. 113.

initiative on the part of biblical women,[41] credits Rebekah with wisdom and foreknowledge and allows her a significant role as a divine agent.[42] The tenacity of such traditions is attested by late midrashim which report that Rebekah foresaw the destruction of the temple by Titus and the martyrdom of great Jewish scholars by the Romans.[43]

Jewish sources attribute revelations to other biblical women as well. Based on Gen 18:15, several rabbinic texts represent Sarah as having received direct communication from God.[44] B. Megillah 14a recognizes seven prophetesses in Scripture: Sarah, Miriam, Deborah, Hannah, Abigail, Huldah, and Esther.[45] Some texts simply assume that all the matriarchs were prophetesses.[46] In Pseudo-Philo's Liber Antiquitatum Biblicarum 9:9f., Miriam receives the Spirit of God and has a revelatory dream in which an angelic being foretells the illustrious career of her yet unborn brother, Moses. The same work presents Deborah as one who "enlightens" Israel (30:2; 33:1), a visionary who sees the stars and lightning defeat the enemies of God's people (31:1).

Non-biblical women are also cast as recipients and purveyors of divine revelation in early Jewish and Jewish-Christian literature. In the very Jewish context of the Lucan infancy narratives, Anna is

---

[41]On the reduction of Rebekah's role, see T. W. Franxman, Genesis and the 'Jewish Antiquities' of Flavius Josephus, BibOr 35 (Rome: Biblical Institute Press, 1979), 176, 182, 184. See also B. H. Amaru, "Portraits of Biblical Women in Josephus' Antiquities," JJS 39 (1988): 143-70. Concerning Josephus's portrayal of Sarah, for example, Amaru writes (p. 145): "Sarah is most notable for her submissiveness and her chastity. Josephus effects the first quality by giving her no direct speech in his narrative, and by deleting the few acts of initiative attributed to her in the biblical text. Whatever her significance to the biblical story line, in every scene shared with her spouse her role is diminished and her presence made unobtrusive, consistently permitting Abraham to hold 'centre stage.'" Amaru (p. 146 n. 12) correctly relates this tendency of Josephus to the hellenistic notion that assertiveness and independence are undesirable qualities for women. With reference to hellenization in Josephus's portrayals of women generally, see L. H. Feldman, "Josephus' Portrait of Deborah," in A. Caquot, M. Hadas-Lebel, and J. Riaud (eds.), Hellenica et Judaica (Leuven and Paris, 1986), 115-28; and idem, "Hellenizations in Josephus' Version of Esther," TAPA 101 (1970): 143-70.

[42]Ant. 1.19.1-5. See further Amaru, "Portraits,"150f.; and J. L. Bailey, "Josephus' Portrayal of the Matriarchs," in L. Feldman and G. Hata (eds.), Josephus, Judaism, and Christianity (Detroit: Wayne State, 1987), 161-65.

[43]Midrash ha-Gadol to Gen 27; Leket Midrashim 22a. See Ginzburg, Legends, V, 271 n. 15, and 287 n. 113.

[44]Gen. Rab. 20:6; 45:10; 48:20; 63:7; and J. Sotah 21b; but cf. n. 48 below on the Sages' attempts to qualify this admission.

[45]Cf. the longer list of biblical characters designated "prophetesses" in Ginzburg, Legends VII (Index), 387f.

[46]Gen. Rab. 67:9; S. 'Olam Rab. 21.

called a prophetess (Lk 2:36), and the reference in Rev 2:20 to Jezebel's appropriation of the same title implies that prophetesses were accepted and respected in at least some early Christian circles. Other women who prophesied in the early church include the four virgin daughters of Philip (Acts 21:9) and the worshipers envisioned in I Cor 11:5. One of the very signs of the messianic age according to Acts 2:17-21, with its quotation of Joel 2:28-32, is that women as well as men would receive outpourings of God's spirit and would prophesy. Lk 24:22f. reports that the women who visited Jesus' tomb saw a vision of angels. The genre of sibylline oracles in early Judaism and Christianity depends for its long-standing popularity upon the premise that women could receive and utter ecstatic prophecies. In the Egyptian Therapeutic community described by Philo, both men and women had ecstatic experiences.[47]

From these diverse revelatory experiences attributed to women in early Jewish tradition, sweeping generalizations are impossible. Certainly no linear development is discernible. Further, some strands of Jewish thought carefully suppress even the hint that women received divine revelations.[48] Nevertheless, the three portrayals of women which form the subject of this study are significant tributaries to those streams of tradition from which emerge other currents with prominent roles for women. These diverse currents include the phenomenon of prophetesses in early Christianity, the rabbinic characterization of the matriarchs as prophetesses,

---

[47]*On the Contemplative Life* 1-11. See R. S. Kraemer, "Monastic Jewish Women in Greco-Roman Egypt: Philo Judaeus on the Therapeutrides," *Signs* 14 (1989): 342-70.

[48]For example, Josephus eliminates Rebekah's direct communication from God (Gen 25:23); instead he has Isaac receive the divine oracle regarding Jacob and Esau (*Ant*1.18.1). Other examples of this tendency in Josephus are discussed in Amaru, "Portraits," 143-53. In a similar vein, rabbinic midrash on Gen 18:15 acknowledges that God spoke to Sarah but qualifies this admission carefully: some Sages insisted that Sarah was the only woman with whom God ever condescended to speak directly and that he did so only because of the peculiar circumstances of the case; others argue that God spoke to her through some intermediary such as an angel or Shem, the son of Noah (*Gen. Rab.* 20:6; 45:10; 48:20; 63:7; and *J. Sotah* 21b). Philo's pejorative use of feminine terminology to describe the irrational soul reflects a similar perception of women as lacking spiritual insight (e.g., *Questions and Answers on Exodus* 1:8). See R. A. Baer, *Philo's Use of the Categories Male and Female* (Leiden: Brill, 1970), 40-44, and the article by J. Romney Wegner in this volume. For a convenient if somewhat tendentious collection of Jewish texts evidencing the perception of women as ignorant and easily misled, as well as texts projecting a more positive image of women, see L. Swidler, *Women in Judaism: The Status of Women in Formative Judaism* (Metuchen, NJ: Scarecrow, 1976).

Merkabah mysticism,[49] Gnosticism,[50] and Montanism.[51]

To extrapolate information about the actual social status of women from literary embellishments of biblical characters is extremely difficult. What is feasible for women in literary fiction is not necessarily feasible in social reality; nor do women's roles in literary fiction necessarily represent an author's social ideal. In the case of *Joseph and Aseneth*, for example, it is extremely doubtful that one can infer from the singular case of Aseneth the initiatory patterns regularly followed in the author's community. Aseneth's conversion is by all estimates a special case; she is a larger-than-life figure whose unique characteristics and actions befit her prototypical status but may not reflect social reality or actual ritual practice.[52] Even so, if an exalted and influential position for a woman had simply been out of the question in the social environment from which the apocryphon came, Aseneth's story could not have been expected to serve the purposes the author intended. One might argue that misogyny typified the apocryphon's community and that one of the author's very purposes was to correct it, but there is little in *Joseph and Aseneth* itself to suggest that this was the axe the author wished to grind. An exemplary and influential role for a woman is assumed rather than argued; it is a premise from which the author proceeds to deal with other concerns.[53] The Jewish world of this

---

[49]The connection between *Asen.* and the Merkabah mystical tradition, however, is not as close as H. C. Kee suggests in "The Socio-Religious Setting and Aims of 'Joseph and Asenath,'" in G. MacRae (ed.), *Society of Biblical Literature 1976 Seminar Papers* (Missoula, MT: Scholars Press, 1976), 183-92; and idem, "The Socio-Cultural Setting of Joseph and Aseneth," *NTS* 29 (1983): 394-413. The alleged affinities are superficial and exaggerated, and fundamental differences are overlooked. Much closer, but still requiring extreme caution, are the affinities between *T. Job* and Merkabah mysticism. See H. C. Kee, "Satan, Magic, and Salvation in the Testament of Job," in G. MacRae (ed.), *Society of Biblical Literature 1974 Seminar Papers*, Vol. I (Cambridge, MA: Society of Biblical Literature, 1974), 53-76.

[50]See K. L. King, ed., *Images of the Feminine in Gnosticism*, Studies in Antiquity and Christianity (Philadelphia: Fortress, 1988).

[51]Jewish elements in Montanism are unmistakable even if J. M. Ford, "Was Montanism a Jewish-Christian Heresy?" *JEH* 17 (1966): 145-58, overstates the Jewish-Christian character of the sect. See W. H. C. Frend, "Montanism: Research and Problems," *Rivista di storia e letteratura religiosa* 20 (1984): 521-37, esp. 533.

[52]See Nickelsburg, *Jewish Literature*, 261-263; and C. Burchard, "Der jüdische Asenethroman und seine Nachwirkung. Von Egeria zu Anna Katharina Emmerick oder von Moses aus Aggel zu Karl Kerényi," *ANRW* 2.20.1 (Berlin: De Gruyter, 1987), 656.

[53]Significant in this connection is the very positive feminine imagery used in the description of Μετάνοια, the "exceedingly beautiful and good daughter of the Most High" (15:7). Other Jewish texts using feminine imagery for divine entities, such as personified Σοφία, are notoriously misogynistic; see especially the Wisdom of Jesus ben Sirach; see also n. 48 above on Philo's use

text was therefore likely one in which women served (or could serve) as leaders who exemplified and spoke out for the principles central to the life of community.

The same may be said concerning the portrayal of Rebekah in *Jubilees*. On the one hand, it would be naive to suppose that in the social world behind the narrative women typically enjoyed a status commensurate with that accorded Rebekah; on the other hand, had some semblance of proper familial and societal structures not been maintained in the *Jubilees*, the rewriting of Rebekah's story as a means of addressing problems in the Jewish community would have been self-defeating. *Jubilees* clearly does not throw social convention to the wind but shows great concern for proper relationships within family and society. For example, along with explicit appeals for familial love and unity, the text pictures Jacob dutifully caring for his aging parents (29:14-20); Esau becomes the archenemy of social order for failing to support his parents and respect their wishes.[54] Jacob's loving relationship with Leah is also emphasized (36:21-24), even though the biblical narrative implies that he was less than kind to her.[55] Thus, it is within a context of respect for proper familial and social patterns that the author of *Jubilees* assigns Rebekah the dominant role of leadership in the home and a prominent position among the leaders of God's people, while Isaac is depicted as manifesting tenderness in the touching scene in which he consoles his grieving wife (27:13-18). Since these vignettes of the ideal family life of the forebears function as examples for the Jewish community to emulate,[56] we may conclude that in the author's social world it was both possible and desirable for a capable woman to assume an aggressive role of leadership as the situation demanded.

The person who composed *Testament of Job* 46-53 may have been more self-consciously attempting to counter the denigration of women than were the authors of the other two works considered here. Certainly the author of chapters 1-45 was aware of, and in some measure contributed to, such denigration. However, in chapters 46-53 this situation is reversed, whether by the same author or a redactor. Therefore, the book as it now stands offers an exceptionally positive portrayal of women: they embody the author's most

---

of feminine imagery for the irrational soul.

[54]For example, see 29:18, where Esau apparently steals from his father's flocks and marries a third time in defiance of his parents' wishes. See further Endres, *Biblical Interpretation*, 118.

[55]On the upgrading of Leah in *Jubilees*, see further Endres, *Biblical Interpretation*, 179.

[56]Ibid., 49, 203, *et passim.*

cherished values. Moreover, to the extent that readers are expected to have revelatory experiences akin to those attributed to characters in the story, men and women are on equal footing. Since the spiritual knowledge so highly prized in the *Testament of Job* cannot come from natural human insight but only from divine revelation, men and women are dependent on the same means for attaining it.

This brief attempt to extrapolate social reality from three narrative sources highlights the need to take fully into account the indirect and problematic nature of the literary evidence concerning the status of women in antiquity. Justice is done to the literature neither by those who, obsessed with offsetting the sexism therein, focus on one issue and seek at all costs to discover evidence of dignified roles for women, nor by those who perpetuate such sexism by their insensitivity to the complimentary images of women which do appear. Careful treatment of narrative sources, with due regard for the context and function of stories about women, is likely to yield conclusions which are neither as sweeping and revolutionary as the former group would like nor as meager as the latter group might suppose. The revelatory experiences attributed to women in the three documents considered here not only reinforce the important functions those women serve on the literary level, but they also provide significant if indirect evidence for at least some elevation of women's position in the real world of early Judaism. This study therefore contributes to a growing body of evidence indicating that not all Jewish women in the Hellenistic age were as oppressed and repressed as some stereotypes, both ancient and modern, would suggest.

Patriarchy with a Twist: Men and Women in Tobit

Beverly Bow
and
George W. E. Nickelsburg

Religious belief and practice combined with a dominant concern for family life lie at the heart of the fictional composition known
as the Book of Tobit. Although we cannot be certain to what extent
Tobit's story world reflects the real world of the second century
B.C.E. author,[1] the text does seem to treat certain events as commonplace. The Book of Tobit thus provides a glimpse of the everyday
life and belief of families in the period of formative Judaism. Moreover, the story is compelling; through narrative and dialogue, the
members of the two families, joined by marriage, emerge as full
personalities rather than as static figures. The consequent humanity of these characters crosses the boundaries of time; the modern
reader can identify with the wife's irritation at her husband's false
accusation, the mother's worry over her son on his journey, the
father's joy at his daughter's wedding.

In this essay, we shall focus on the manner in which the Book
of Tobit depicts religious and family life in relation to men and wom-
en. We shall argue that there is a definite dichotomy in the portrayal
of the two sexes: while women are normally confined to the family
and its practical concerns, men operate in a sphere that encom-
passes religious activity and the world outside the family and household. Nonetheless, although the text presents a patriarchal worldview in describing the social and religious functions of its characters,
certain elements in the story strain against this ideological norm. In
other words, there are twists that express the tension between the
patriarchal social structure and elements of characterization depicted within it.

Narrator and Characters

In the following literary analysis of the Book of Tobit we limit
ourselves to a discussion of the narrator and the characters. Ini-

---

[1]On the dating, see Frank Zimmerman, *The Book of Tobit* (New York: Harper
and Brothers, 1958), 23-24; George W. E. Nickelsburg, *Jewish Literature
Between the Bible and the Mishnah* (Philadelphia: Fortress, 1981), 35; the
introduction to Tobit in Bruce M. Metzger (ed.), *Oxford Annotated Apocrypha*
(New York: Oxford University, 1965, 1977), 63.

tially, the narrator speaks in the first person through the title character (1:1-3:6). The reader, reading the "I" of the narrator, identifies with Tobit. In 3:7, the narrator introduces the story of Sarah, and the voice switches to the third person thereafter, even when the story returns to Tobit.[2] This shift may be seen as logically necessary, for the character Tobit is not in the position of the omniscient narrator. However, the shift is more than a conventional nicety; it serves to distance the reader. Now reading "he" instead of "I," the reader no longer identifies as closely with the character Tobit. Moreover, the third-person narrative implies throughout the narrator's presence as omniscient observer.

Directly or indirectly the narrator reveals the characters by having them speak or act, and by having other characters react to them.[3] In a well-told story like Tobit, where characters are "living" or developed (as opposed to "cardboard" or underdeveloped), the reader can evaluate them as one would evaluate a real person. The characters appear to "come to life," so that the reader learns who they "are," or what personal qualities or traits they have.[4] In the Book of Tobit, the narrator provides a substantial amount of information about the title character: his faith that God rewards righteousness; his generosity; his despair at being blinded. On the other hand, the primary actor is Tobias, who takes a journey with an angel and marries into a wealthy family, but the reader learns little about his personal traits. The most fully developed female character is Anna, whose words and actions suggest a fully formed personality. Sarah's prayer (3:10-15) reveals her grief, her concern for her father, and her trust in God, but after this initial characterization she does little and speaks less (one other word, 8:8). The text offers, in comparison with the depictions of Tobit and Anna, less about Sarah's parents both as individuals and in terms of their spousal relationship. We are told simply that Raguel and Edna treat guests well, are sympathetic to Tobit's blindness, and are concerned for their daughter's welfare.

Religious Life

Under the rubric of religious life, we include such motifs as

---

[2] Cf. 1QapGen, where the narrator also shifts from first person (Abraham) to third. For a detailed discussion, see Irene Nowell, "The Narrator in the Book of Tobit," in David J. Lull (ed.), SBLSP (Atlanta, Scholars, 1988), 27-38.
[3] David Rhoads and Donald Michie, Mark as Story: An Introduction to the Narrative World of a Gospel (Philadelphia: Fortress, 1982), 101.
[4] Ibid., 101-103.

prayer, ritual duties or duties prescribed by the Israelite Law, and interaction with supernatural beings. Although women within the text also participate in some aspects of the religious sphere, in the story world of the Book of Tobit it is principally males who inhabit this realm.

Prayer. All of the main characters address God directly in prayer or evoke the deity's name in some fashion. Tobias prays with his new wife after the demon has been banished (8:4-8); Edna invokes God in blessings (8:18 [Gk. 17]; 10:12), as do Raguel (8:15-17) and Tobit (11:14, 17); in Chapter 13 Tobit utters a lengthy poetic blessing. And even Anna appeals to the Lord indirectly in her rebuke of Tobit (5:19). It is the prayers of Tobit and Sarah, however, that are the most carefully constructed. Set in parallel to one another, they function as literary pivots for the plot.

The characters address a double problem in their prayers which the angel Raphael ultimately will resolve. In turn, this resolution will unite the two families through marriage.[5] Both prayers are preceded by a description of the situation which prompts the characters to seek divine aid: Tobit's piety, his blindness, and his reproach by another; Sarah's (presumed) innocence, the demon, and her reproach by others.[6] The prayers are, further, similar in structure and vocabulary. Deep grief (περίλυπος, ἐλυπήθε, λύπη) prompts both Tobit and Sarah to pray. Both begin their prayers with the formulaic "Righteous [so Tobit]/Blessed [so Sarah] are you, O Lord." Both mention having heard reproach (ὀνειδισμός), and they ask to "be released" (ἀπολυθῆναι), since dying seems to be the only solution to their problems. Both speak of sin (ἁμαρτία, ἀκαθαρσία) and captivity (αἰχμαλωσία).

Thematically, however, the differences between the prayers point to a distinction in the religious roles of Tobit and Sarah. A patriarchal worldview is upheld in that the male character, Tobit, is paradigmatic of Israel. He mentions divine judgment and speaks of "my sins and those of my fathers," which are responsible for the people's present state of exile. Sarah, the woman, is paradigmatic neither for Israel nor even for other women in her situation;[7] her prayer concerns only her own personal dilemma. In contrast to

---

[5]Or, as Nickelsburg puts it (*Jewish Literature*, 30), the situations of Tobit and Sarah are two plots resolved by a third: Raphael's mission.
[6]Nickelsburg, ibid., notes the "close literary symmetry" and places these elements in parallel columns.
[7]Cf. Jdt 8:32-34; 9:2-14; 16:2-17.

Tobit's "my fathers," Sarah speaks only of "my father."

Yet there is a twist to this patriarchal presentation. The tones of the prayers reveal Sarah as the more admirable character of the two. Although Tobit uses all the "right" (i.e., conventional) phrases, the tone of his prayer is self-centered and whining. Tobit presumptuously assumes that his desire to die is also divine will: "Deal with me according to your pleasure (κατὰ τὸ ἀρεστόν); command my spirit to be taken up." Sarah, who herself also sees death as the only solution, acknowledges that God may not see the situation in the same way; she prays, "If it is not pleasing (δοκεῖ) to you to take my life," ease my pain another way. Tobit flatly states that "it is better for me to die than to live";[8] in other words, he sees only this one option. In contrast, Sarah's prayer is wiser, less self-centered. She has considered suicide but rejects it because she is concerned about her father's feelings and reputation. She asks, "Why should I live?" This question, combined with what immediately follows, implies the request: "Give me a reason to live" (which she soon receives). Furthermore, while Tobit admirably gives a "proper" confession of his sins, Sarah more admirably is "innocent of any sin with man."

Another point of difference serves to emphasize the distinction between the ways in which Tobit and Sarah view divine-human interaction. At the end of his prayer, Tobit says, "Do not turn (μὴ ἀποστρέψῃς) your face away from me." At the beginning of her prayer, Sarah says, "I have turned (ἀνέβλεψα) my eyes and face toward you." In Tobit's religious purview, the normal orientation of God's "face" is toward humanity; humans can turn away from God not only by sinning (which is implied in his previous words), but they can also cause the deity to turn away from them. Tobit repeats this understanding in 13:6: "If you turn (ἐπιστρέψητε) to him... then he will turn (ἐπιστρέψει) to you and will not hide is face from you." But the wording in Sarah's prayer assumes God's constant orientation towards humanity. She seems to see the role of the human as that of supplicant: I am in need, so I have turned to you. Sarah's words do not reflect an understanding that her actions can in any way cause a change in the divine relationship to humanity.

Although a personal tragedy occasions each prayer, only Tobit's recitation goes beyond his particular problem to encompass all Israel. Conversely, Sarah is praying because she has been

---

[8]The words are very similar to what Jonah says in Jon 4:3, 8. This wish is one of a number of connections between Tobit and Jonah; others include the setting in Nineveh, the fish "who would have swallowed the young man" (Tob 6:2), and the mention of the "prophecies of Jonah" in Tob 14.

married seven times and has not managed to produce an heir; in her despair she wants to die. Tobit briefly comments that he has heard false reproaches, but he never mentions his blindness or his impoverishment; in contrast, he goes on and on about Israel's sins and exile.

It is difficult to prove that the differences between these two specific prayers reflect general views about men's and women's piety. We cannot conclude that women stereotypically pray only in response to specific situations of individual concern while men's prayers would usually include larger issues and other people. Sarah's is the only prayer by a woman in the story. However, on the two occasions in which Edna evokes the deity in blessings, her concerns are particular: to comfort Sarah when she weeps (7:17-18), and to express a wish to see her grandchildren (10:12). In the prayers and blessings of the male characters, even when they concern particular situations, the focus is on others. Raguel expresses joy over the marriage of Sarah and Tobias (8:15-17) and wishes for their prosperity (10:11). When Tobit regains his sight, he blesses God and all the holy angels (11:14-15); when he meets Sarah, he blesses her and her parents (11:17). Tobit's long blessing in Chapter 13 does not concern himself at all but concentrates on the nation. While Tobias's prayer (8:4-7), in which Sarah presumably joins although as a silent partner, is specifically oriented toward marriage, he also mentions the entire human race who sprang from Adam and Eve.

Despite the differences, Tobit and Sarah's prayers of supplication are equally effective. Although neither is answered in the way each expects, God hears both and sends Raphael to heal them (3:16-17). The personal tragedies that prompted them to pray are rectified: Tobit's blindness is cured, and Sarah gets a husband who lives through the night.

Ritual/Prescribed Duties

Charity. The performance of charitable deeds is the responsibility only of the male characters. Twice Tobit indicates his diligence in helping those less fortunate (1:16-17; 2:2). In his first testamentary address to Tobias, he emphasizes the importance of charity and its rewards (4:7-11, 16); in his final testament he again mentions almsgiving (14:11). Raphael similarly reveals to Tobit and Tobias the good that giving alms accomplishes (12:8-9).

The injunction to be charitable applies to both rich and poor, as Tobit announces in his initial testament: those who have few possessions should give "according to the little you have" (4:8). But such giving is a special responsibility of propertied men. Despite the fact that Tobit himself has had his property confiscated by the king (1:20), the book as a whole is addressed to the wealthy. Nor is Tobit left fully destitute: he has a considerable sum in trust in Rages (1:4).[9] Raguel is also wealthy, as his bestowing upon his new son-in-law half his property "in slaves, cattle, and money" (8:21; 10:10) indicates. Tobias inherits the rest when his in-laws die (14:13).

None of the women has any responsibility for performing charitable deeds. In fact, they appear to have no control over family property as long as a male family member is present. Sarah's inheritance clearly belongs to Tobias (6:11-12; 8:21; 14:13). The sole indication that women can retain control over property is Raguel's stipulation that Tobias will receive the remainder of his property only after both he and Edna have died (8:21). The implication is that if a husband dies first, the wife inherits (cf. Jdt 8:7). Anna outlives Tobit (14:11-12), but Tobias is then living in his parents' home and apparently controls the family possessions; the text says that he inherits the property "of his father Tobit" (14:13). The women in this story thus have no possessions from which they can give alms.

Burial of the Dead and Mourning. This theme occurs repeatedly throughout the Book of Tobit. Interring is an extremely important ritual act[10] that supersedes other concerns such as the king's displeasure (1:18) and the celebration of Pentecost (2:1-5). In the text, the act crosses the boundaries between the private and the public spheres. It is a familial duty for Tobias; twice his father tells him to see to the proper burial of himself and Anna (4:3; 14:10).[11] Raphael himself digs a grave for Tobias, in case his latest son-in-law fails to survive the wedding night (8:9). It is also a service that Tobit provides for others, and which does not go unnoticed in heaven. Raphael specifically mentions Tobit's burial of the dead as a reason for his being sent to heal him (12:12-13). Like charity, interring is strictly a male responsibility, perhaps because of its connection to the public world. Or perhaps burial, like giving charity, is a male duty

---

[9]At least $10,000, according to the note in the *Oxford Apocrypha.*
[10]See the comments by Nickelsburg in "Tobit," in James L. Mays (gen. ed.), *Harper's Bible Commentary* (San Francisco: Harper and Row, 1988), 793; Zimmerman, *Book of Tobit,* 51.
[11]Anna must be buried in the same grave (4:3; 14:10, 12); cf. *Apoc. Mos.* 31:3; 42:4-7.

because in this story world there is always a male head of household; we cannot know whether a woman householder would have had a similar responsibility.

For a text so interested in burial of the dead, the Book of Tobit provides little indication of mourning rituals. Tobit performs some kind of ritual washing after handling a corpse (2:5), and he is then reminded of Amos 8:10: "Your feasts shall be turned into mourning." He does sleep outdoors after an interring (2:9),[12] but he engages in no specific ritual of mourning. Neither Tobias nor Sarah is said to mourn when their parents die; the narrator merely reports the deaths and that funerals were given.

Religious/Ethical Instruction. To educate children in the Law and the correct way to live is primarily a male duty in the Book of Tobit. Thinking he will soon die, Tobit calls his son and instructs him about keeping the commandments, the importance of charity, proper marriages, and correct behavior (4:5-12); he repeats some of this in his second testament (Chapter 14).[13] But here we find another twist in the patriarchal structure. According to 1:8, because his father was dead Tobit's grandmother taught him the Law.[14] In this casual reference, the narrator informs the reader that women apparently knew the Law, and that in the absence of a male relative performed the duty of providing religious instruction. How and to what extent women might have learned the Law is unclear; there is no indication that Anna, Sarah, or Edna knew the Law.

Endogamy is an injunction that applies to both sexes in the story world of the apocryphon. Tobit marries a member of his family (1:9), and he strongly enjoins Tobias to do the same (4:12-13). Sarah bemoans in her prayer that there is no relative left for her to marry (3:15), and Raphael informs Tobias that as Sarah's only relative he is entitled to her hand (6:11). This is a view Raguel echoes (7:10, 12). The emphasis placed on endogamy fits the diaspora setting of the story, since it would have been more difficult to find an eligible, nongentile spouse outside of Israel than it was in Israel before the

---

[12]See Nickelsburg's comments in *Harper's*, 794; Zimmerman, *Book of Tobit*, 56-57.

[13]Typically, testamentary literature concerns male family members: fathers and sons. For a discussion of the genre and some examples, see Nickelsburg, *Jewish Literature*, 231-53.

[14]Cf. IV Macc 15-16, where the mother of the seven martyred brothers encourages them to uphold the Law even if it meant death; she is called "vindicator of the Law" (15:29).

exile.[15]

Interaction with Supernatural Beings. Contact with the otherworldly lies at the center of the religious content of the text. There are two supernatural beings in the Book of Tobit: a demon and an angel. One is responsible for the problem that prompts Sarah's prayer; the other rectifies the situations that occasioned the prayer of Tobit as well as that of Sarah. But, not surprisingly, the manner in which Asmodeus and Raphael interact with the characters demonstrates the dichotomy in the text's portrayal of men and women.

Only the male characters have "good" contact with supernatural beings. The angel Raphael freely talks with all the male characters (5:4-16; 7:8-9), instructs Tobit and Tobias (12:6-11), and travels with Tobias (Chapter 6). Tobias, instructed by Raphael, performs the ritual that banishes the demon (8:2-3). On the other hand, none of the women interacts in a positive way with these beings. The demon plagues Sarah, but the text does not even indicate that she is aware of Asmodeus's existence. The angel is responsible for Sarah's healing, but he accomplishes this indirectly through Tobias and apparently for Tobias's benefit. Raphael never speaks to the women, and he even appears to go out of his way to avoid prolonged association with Sarah (11:3). In fact, in Tobit's world the realm of the supernatural is off-limits to women. The one instance of any such interaction involves an evil demon who victimizes a female character. Perhaps the author wanted to avoid the kind of disastrous results of such an association between women and heavenly beings as found in Genesis 6 or *I Enoch* 6-11, where the union between heavenly male creatures and beautiful earthly women is followed by increasing wickedness and violence.[16]

To summarize: in the religious world of the Book of Tobit, the male characters have more freedom and responsibility than their female counterparts. Although women may pray or otherwise call upon the deity, their prayers are particularized to their own situations. The male characters, by contrast, pray on behalf of others. Except for the duty of marrying within one's tribe, which applies equally to both sexes, female characters are only ascribed ritual duties in the absence of a male family member who would normally

---

[15]On the problems of the geographical provenance of Tobit, see G. W. E. Nickelsburg, "Tobit and Enoch: Distant Cousins with a Recognizable Resemblance," *SBLSP* (1988): 68.
[16]Cf. ibid., 57-58.

have had the responsibility. Only the male characters have any direct positive contact with supernatural beings.

Family Life

The Book of Tobit portrays family life by presenting interactions among various family members: spouses, parents, children, in-laws. Family members have gender-defined roles in terms of responsibilities and familial obligations, but occasionally exceptions to these role appear. In general, the female characters have more autonomy in the domestic sphere than they do in the religious realm; the male characters conversely play a role in both spheres.

Spouses. Of the couple who gets married during the course of the story, the male partner makes the arrangements for the marriage himself while his fiancée has no say regarding wedding preparations. Although Tobit is concerned that his son have a proper marriage, he has nothing do to with the wedding itself and indeed learns of it only after the fact. Tobias, at the urging of Azarias, a person he has only just met, conducts the deal with Sarah's father. Like a piece of property, Sarah is given to Tobias (7:13), just as Raguel gave her to her seven previous husbands (7:11).[17]

The story also contains an element of heavenly matchmaking which is described as a benefit only for the male partner. It is an angel who suggests to Tobias that he marry Sarah (6:10). When the youth expresses his fear that Sarah's demon will kill him too, the angel informs him that "she was destined for you from eternity" (6:16 [Gk. 18]). This wording demonstrates that the story is being told from an androcentric viewpoint: the angel does not say to Tobias: "You are destined for her." The recipient of divine favor is the groom, not the bride. Once again, she is object; he is subject. Even heaven here regards Sarah as a commodity.

Such heavenly matchmaking suggests a belief in a provident God who arranges matters in human affairs, and indeed this theme underlies the entire book.[18] Biblical marriages often contain the same element: in Gen 24:14, Abraham's servant prays to find "the one whom [God] has appointed for thy servant Isaac"; in the Book of

---

[17]Arrangement by the bride's father is biblical, according to Louis M. Epstein, *The Jewish Marriage Contract: A Study in the Status of the Woman in Jewish Law* (New York: Jewish Theological Seminary of America, 1927), 231. But cf. Gen 24:58, where Rebekah is given the option of saying no; compare as well Jdt 16:22 and *Asen.* 4:5-12.

[18]Nickelsburg, *Jewish Literature*, 30-35.

Ruth, where the direction of events according to divine purpose is implicit throughout, a marriage occurs which works for the good of all concerned.[19] In the Book of Tobit, where female characters have no direct contact with angels, it is only the male character, Tobias, who learns that his spouse has been pre-selected by heaven.

These divisions between men and women most often break down once the marriage has taken place: in the interaction between husbands and wives. The conversations and arguments of the pairs, especially those of Tobit and Anna, indicate a potential equalizing of gender-determined roles. Anna is the least passive of the female characters; she is not the kind of wife who is controlled by her husband. Tobit and Anna have four conversations in the story, and in three of these the wife rebukes the husband. After Tobit is blinded, Anna becomes the wage-earner and engages in "women's work" outside the home (2:11-14).[20] Her job provides the setting for their first interaction as well as her first rebuke. Anna has received a kid as a bonus from her employers, and Tobit unjustly accuses her of stealing it. Anna's reply is eloquently direct: "Now we can see what you are."[21]

Such a negative presentation of Tobit and positive depiction of Anna tend to equalize their positions and offset the prevailing patriarchal social structure. The narrator is silent about Tobit's motivation for the accusation.[22] To this point, the character has been described only in terms of his exemplary righteousness. It is curious, then, that in his first reaction Tobit immediately assumes that the kid is stolen, and in his second he refuses to believe Anna's explanation. Perhaps the narrator is reformulating the initial description of Tobit's personal piety to indicate a hint of self-righteousness. An alternative but not mutually exclusive interpretation would see this relationship as paralleling the earlier interaction between Sennacherib and Tobit; in both cases, the stronger unjustly oppresses the

---

[19]Including all Israel, since the son born to Ruth and Boaz became David's grandfather (Ruth 4:22).

[20]The texts vary considerably in this section. Zimmerman assumes Anna did some type of weaving (*Book of Tobit*, 59).

[21]In recension S; B has "You seem to know everything!" See Nickelsburg, *Harper's*, 794-95.

[22]Cf. Robert Alter on ambiguity in characterization, *The Art of Biblical Narrative* (New York: Basic Books, 1981), 22, 33, 117-18, 126. Alter notes that "the initial words spoken by a personage ... [constitute] an important moment in the exposition of character" (74), and that the biblical writers stipulate or suppress "motive in order to elicit moral inferences and suggest certain ambiguities" (44).

weaker.[23]

Anna's other rebukes to Tobit also serve to equalize her position in relation to her husband. In their second conversation (5:17-19), Anna in effect tells her husband to straighten his priorities: their son is more important than money. Tobit temporarily quiets his wife's fears; at least, she stops weeping. But when the narrative next returns to the couple (10:1-7), her fears resurface. Her third rebuke to Tobit — "Be still and stop deceiving me!" (10:17) — suggests either that Anna thinks her husband is lying to her or that she does not want him to dismiss her fears so lightly. The narrator has already noted that Tobit is also worried; the implication of Anna's words is thus at the very least the desire that she not be shut out from her husband's concern over their son.

Despite the rebukes, the narrator gives the impression that the couple care for each other. As soon as Anna sees Tobias returning, she shares the good news with her blind husband (11:6). Tobit seems to be genuinely trying to comfort his wife about their son's safety in 5:20-21. However, he may simply want her to shut up, as his considerably shorter response to her weeping in 10:6 suggests: "Be still and stop worrying; he is well." In his first testamentary address, Tobit urges his son to take care of Anna after she is widowed (4:3-4). However, in all the instruction that follows, including admonitions to treat the poor and employees well, Tobit says nothing about how a man should treat his wife. In other words, Tobit tells Tobias "be good to your mother, also to employees and unfortunate strangers," but he omits "be good to your wife."

In comparison to Anna and Tobit, who act individually, Edna and Raguel act together as a couple: both greet guests and make them welcome (7:8); they (and also Sarah) weep at hearing of Tobit's misfortune (7:7-8). Both deliver separate farewell addresses to the newlyweds when the latter leave for Nineveh (10:11-12). These examples present less a demonstration of teamwork, however, than an indication of Edna's lack of autonomy.

Contrasted with Anna-as-wife, Edna's role in the domestic sphere is more subservient. On two occasions (7:16; 8:12), Raguel tells Edna to do something, and she complies. Unlike Anna and Tobit, Edna and Raguel are never in conflict with each other. In their first interaction, Raguel remarks to his wife about Tobias's resemblance to his relative Tobit (7:2). The mildness of this initial exchange stands in sharp contrast to the first interaction between Anna and

---

[23]Suggested by A.-J. Levine in correspondence.

Tobit.

Edna does have some limited functions as the "woman of the house," but on the whole her role is subordinated to that of her husband. Indeed, her character is hardly definable outside her relationship with Raguel. Although the narrator in Chapter 3 and the angel in Chapter 6 have already mentioned Raguel, the reader encounters Edna only when Tobias and Raphael arrive at their house, subsequently only in conjunction with Raguel. Edna may function as a witness to the marriage contract (or she may merely fetch the scroll[24]), but she takes no part in the negotiations with Tobias; Raguel calls her only after he has given Sarah to her new fiancé (7:12-14). Edna apparently does have authority over the household servants. The maids belong to Raguel (3:7), but it is Edna — albeit at her husband's request — who sends a maid to check on Tobias (8:12). This authority over servants seems not to extend to the other woman in the family, as one might judge from the maids' behavior toward Sarah (3:7-9).

Sarah's primary function in the story is to provide a wife for Tobias. Once she is wed, her role is diminished. She speaks only one more word (8:8), and she is mentioned by name on only three other occasions (10:10-12; 11:17; 12:12-14). It is therefore difficult to describe the couple's relationship. In terms of the plot, it is not their interaction that is important, but their marriage; the wedding resolves the two conflicts: Tobias finds a suitable wife, and Sarah finds a suitable husband. What we do sense is that Tobias dictates the contours of their relationship.[25] Having fallen in love with her sight unseen (6:17), he determines to marry her. (Perhaps he is partially motivated by the inheritance to which Raphael has twice told him he is entitled.) Tobias arranges the marriage with Raguel; Sarah is not asked her opinion about the union (7:8-13). He tells her to pray with him after he vanquishes the demon (8:4). And in his prayer he indicates what their relationship is to be: she will be a helper like Eve was to Adam (8:5-7). Tobias has added "and support" to Eve's role as helper, which may mean that he would expect her to earn money if he were to become disabled, like his mother did for his father. Overall, Sarah-as-wife is a completely passive character, as she was the passive victim of the male demon.

Nevertheless, Tobias does seem to care about this woman he

---

[24]S: "He called his wife and said, 'Fetch a scroll,' and he wrote a marriage agreement on the scroll"; B: "He called Edna his wife, and taking a scroll he wrote an agreement, and they set their seals to it."
[25]A.-J. Levine, in correspondence.

has just met and married, and he does express the touching wish that they grow old together (8:7). He also remarks in his prayer, in a bit of a *non sequitur*, that he is not taking Sarah "out of lust" (8:7). This reference, which may stand as a contrast to Asmodeus's sexual desires, assures that Tobias's motives are pure. Further, twice he calls his new wife "sister" (8:4, 7; cf. 5:20 and 7:16, where Tobit and Raguel address their wives similarly).

There may be in this address an implied comparison to Abraham's wife Sarah, whom he also called his sister (Gen 12:11-19). The name Sarah in the Book of Tobit recalls the biblical matriarch; there are other parallels as well between the two women. Childlessness creates a personal problem for each, although only with Abraham's wife is the problem attributed to barrenness (Gen 16:1-2). Both Sarahs have confrontations with maids: Hagar "looked with contempt on her mistress" (Gen 16:4), and "Sarai dealt harshly with her" (Gen 16:6). Raguel's maids insult and taunt Sarah, and they accuse her of beating them (Tob 3:7-9). In this section of the Book of Tobit, the word "reproach" is used, and the expression is often employed as a technical term to indicate barrenness (e.g., Gen 30:23; Luke 1:25). Raguel's maids do not call Sarah barren, but their reproach is apparently connected to her childless state.

Parents and Children. It would be helpful if we could compare how parents in the narrative would treat children of both sexes in the same family, but Tobias and Sarah lack siblings. Nevertheless, we can determine that certain functions of parents and children appear to be gender-related. In general, the male roles are characterized by duty, while the female roles are relational in orientation.

Fathers, but not mothers, have obligations toward their sons but not their daughters in the areas of religious instruction and inheritance. If a father is present, it is his duty to teach his son the correct way to live; this duty is manifested in Tobit's testamentary addresses (4:5-21; 14:3-11; cf. 1:8). Sarah receives no similar instruction, except for 10:12.[26] Neither Anna nor Edna instructs her child. Thinking he is going to die soon, Tobit sends his Tobias to Rages because he wants to leave him an inheritance (4:1-2). The matter of an inheritance is also present in Sarah's story (8:20-21), but here the property goes to her husband. This property appears to be a dowry (which replaces the biblical custom of the bride price).

A father's (not a mother's) duty toward his daughter but not

---

[26]See below, under *In-Laws.*

his son involves arranging her marriage. Both Tobit and Raguel show substantial interest in their children's prospective spouses. Tobit's concern is evident when he admonishes Tobias to marry the right kind of woman. Anna says nothing about her son's wife either before or after he marries. While Tobit is concerned, only Raguel arranges his child's marriage. Edna does not participate in these arrangements, but at the couple's departure she tells Tobias, "I am entrusting my daughter to you" (10:12).

The mothers do not show an interest in such practical matters as instruction and property, perhaps because the fathers of Tobias and Sarah are still alive (contrast 1:8). Rather, Sarah and Edna's relationship to their children is depicted only in emotional terms. Anna weeps when her son leaves (5:17), worries while he is gone (10:4-5), and weeps again when he returns (11:9). Edna comforts her daughter when she is distressed (7:17), expresses a wish to see her grandchildren, and warns Tobias not to grieve her daughter (10:12). This emotional role is shared, along with their interest in practical concerns, by the fathers. Tobit worries over his son's delay (10:1-2), and cries and embraces Tobias when he returns (11:14). Raguel kisses his daughter goodbye when she leaves with her husband (10:12).

As son, Tobias has more responsibilities and more freedom than Sarah the daughter. A respectful and obedient attitude is one such responsibility. Tobit tells his son to respect his mother because of the danger she faced while pregnant: "Honor her all the days of your life; do what is pleasing to her, and do not grieve her" (4:3-4).[27] Tobias respectfully obeys his father and does whatever Tobit asks of him (2:2-3; 5:1, 3-4). Tobit admonishes his son to "do what is pleasing" to his mother, but there is no instance of Anna telling him to do anything. Whether Tobias would be as obedient to his mother is therefore unknown. Nevertheless, he is concerned for both his parents' feelings (6:14), even more than with his own wedding festivities: he wants to return home so that his parents will no longer be worried (10:7-9).[28]

Tobias is frequently reminded by Tobit of his responsibility for seeing to the proper burial of his parents (4:3-4; 14:10). The question

---

[27]Edna uses almost the same words to Tobias: "Do nothing to grieve [Sarah]" (11:12). Does this mean that wives were owed the same respect as mothers, or is there an implied reference here to the dangers of pregnancy? The text in general is implicitly concerned with producing children (3:9, 15; 4:12; 10:12; 14:3), and perhaps therefore with the biological role of women.
[28]Cf. Gen 24:56, where Abraham's "good servant," in a similar situation, says, "Do not delay me. ... let me go that I may go to my master."

of who would bury Tobit and Anna were Sarah's demon to kill him —
not who would care for them while they still lived — is the objection
Tobias raises when Raphael proposes that the couple marry (6:14).
Sarah apparently has no such responsibility; Tobias gives the funerals for his parents and for hers (14:11-13).

In addition, Tobias has much more freedom of movement than
does Sarah. He travels (5:5, 16), interacts with strangers outside the
home (2:2; 5:4-8), learns magic healing arts (6:6-8, 16-17), and has
what might be termed adventures (6:1-13). Although Sarah does
greet strangers at her home (7:1), she does not leave the house until,
with her husband, she departs for Nineveh (10:11). Not only thus
constrained and dependent, Sarah is primarily characterized in·
emotional rather than practical terms. Such emotionalism is particularly manifested in her concern for Raguel's feelings. Although
she considers hanging herself, she hesitates for fear of disgracing
her father or bringing him sorrow in his old age (3:10). Precisely
what the disgrace would be is not clear: that he had a child who
committed suicide, or that he died without an heir to inherit his
property and continue his line (3:15).

Sarah is certainly an obedient daughter: she marries without
comment the man her father chooses. Her prayer indicates that she
will do what is good for her father (i.e., marry and produce an heir)
even if it is not what she wants (she wants to die). And she does
marry the man her father chooses, even though the marriage
results in a loss for her. That is, she "loses" her home by going with
her husband to his. Tobias, as we have seen, is similarly obedient,
but in his case obedience to his father (i.e., going to Rages) results in
a gain. Not only does he obtain his inheritance from Tobit, he also
finds a wife and acquires half her father's property.

In-Laws. The notion of blessing is a constant theme in the
relationship between in-laws. Raguel blesses his daughter and son-
in-law immediately after the wedding (7:13) and again when they
leave (10:11). Edna also pronounces a blessing to Tobias upon the
departure (10:12), and Tobias blesses Sarah's parents as he begins
his journey home (11:1 [Gk. 10:13]). In turn, Tobit blesses Sarah and
her parents when he meets his new daughter-in-law (11:17). Only
Anna and the passive Sarah, who do not interact at all, fail to bless
their new relatives.

As a daughter-in-law, Sarah is brought to live in her husband's
home, and her familial affiliation transfers to her husband's parents. In the only instruction she receives from her father, he tells

her, "Honor your father-in-law and your mother-in-law; they are now your parents" (10:12). Tobit calls Sarah "daughter" when he meets her (11:17); by so doing, he effectively keeps her in a dependent position. In contrast, Edna addresses Tobias as "dear brother" (10:12), and thus she elevates his position in relation to his in-laws from that of son to that of brother. Tobias is respectful toward his wife's parents, and even though Raguel tells him (only in recension S), "I am your father and Edna is your mother," his primary allegiance remains with his own parents, to whose home he adamantly insists upon returning (10:7-9).[29] Only after his parents die and he leaves Nineveh, as his father urged, does Tobias return to live with his in-laws (14:11-13).

Conclusions

The story world of the Book of Tobit portrays a patriarchal system in which gender determines roles played by the characters. Women operate primarily within the domestic sphere. Their concerns are the family (husbands, children, parents) and the home (servants, guests). Occasionally, however, the text evidences a tension between the patriarchal structure and characterization; this tension is most pronounced in the depiction of Anna. She is the only female character who ventures into the public sphere (she works), even if that situation is necessitated by her husband's incapacitation. Within the family, women show varying degrees of autonomy. Again, Anna is the strongest of the three: she speaks her mind and is often in conflict with her husband. Edna is never in conflict with Raguel and seems quite subservient to him, but she does have authority over the servants. Sarah is the most passive of the three. She is victimized by a demon and reproached by the servants; she passes from being controlled by her father to being controlled by her husband.

The male characters operate within a public sphere as well as within the private world of the family. Of the three men, only Raguel is never seen outside the sphere of his home. Aside from familial concerns, the male characters deal with economic matters (inheritances), ritual duties (burial, charity), and law (instruction of children); they also form relationships with non-family members (Azarias). Within the family, all three male characters direct their

---

[29] In his earlier references to Adam and Eve and the role of a wife (8:6), Tobias did not include what Gen 2:24 adds: "Therefore a man leaves his father and his mother...."

wives; Tobit, however, is less successful in eliciting the desired response than the other two.

Matters of religion are largely the prerogative of the male characters. Both men and women pray and have their prayers answered, but the differences in the prayers suggest another twist in the patriarchal system. Tobit, speaker for the exiled nation, prays in a theologically normative way. In this sense, his prayer is not self-centered. Ironically, however, the tone of his prayer is quite selfish. Sarah's prayer focusses only on herself and her personal problem, but its tone is not self-centered: she is concerned for her father, not for herself. Thus, in light of the two prayers, Sarah emerges as the more admirable of the two characters. The men, however, dominate in the other religious areas. Only the male characters have ritual duties and, unless there is no male householder, only the men provide religious instruction. The men alone interact positively with supernatural beings. Female characters have only a limited function in the religious world of the Book of Tobit; the religious realm belongs to the men.

To what extent the world described in the Book of Tobit, set centuries before the author's own time, reflects the real world of the author is difficult to determine. We cannot easily extract which elements belong to the author's world, and which ones the author contrived to reflect his (or her) conception of the time period in which the text is set. It would seem that society in the author's time had a patriarchal structure. But what does one make of the twists in the narrative? Are they pure, wishful fictions, or do they reflect those points at which everyday human relationships can break with societal order? If the latter is the case, it is striking that the author has chosen to cherish these human moments and to weave them into the texture of this narrative.

Aseneth and Her Sisters
Women in Jewish Narrative and in the Greek Novels

Richard I. Pervo

Introduction

A number of biblical[1] and similar writings — including Ruth, Esther, Judith, *Joseph and Aseneth*, the Susanna-episode of the Greek book of Daniel, and various novellas[2] — feature a woman as principal character. When these works are compared with the major Greek romantic novels of the Imperial era, they reveal qualities that may properly be described as feminist, a characteristic shared in part with some of the early Christian writings, for which they probably served as models.[3]

The history of the surviving Greek romantic novels begins with tantalizing fragments and ends with a showpiece of baroque complexity.[4] When the genre emerges into the full light of day (Chariton's Callirhoe, first century C.E.), the view of women is rather positive and independent. However, the form was adopted by representatives of the Atticizing tradition of the Second Sophistic,[5] who were able to domesticate, in several senses of that word, the genre.

The roles and characterizations of women in the major Greek romantic novels have recently been examined by Briggite Egger,[6]

---

[1]Embracing the "Apocrypha" of Christian Bibles.

[2]For example, the tales about Rahab, Tamar, Bathsheba, Deborah, and the matriarchs, especially as retold in post-biblical settings. For an apparent transposition of such a tale into the key of *Cupid and Psyche* in The Exegesis on the Soul (NH II,6), see M. Scopello, *L'exégèse de l'âme*, NHS 25 (Leiden, Brill, 1985), 45-55.

[3]I refer in particular to (parts of) the various Apocryphal Acts of Apostles and to subsequent hagiography. See, for discussion and references, V. Burrus, *Chastity as Autonomy. Women in the Stories of the Apocryphal Acts* (Lewiston, NY: Edwin Mellen, 1987); E. Clark, *The Life of Melania the Younger* (Lewiston, NY: Edwin Mellen, 1984); and S. Davies, *The Revolt of the Widows. The Social World of the Apocryphal Acts* (Carbondale: Southern Illinois University, 1980), as well as my reviews of Burrus in *CBQ* 51 (1989): 264-65, and of Davies in *SecCent* 2 (1982): 47-49.

[4]A modern English translation of each of the complete Greek novels and the larger fragmentary pieces is now available in B. P. Reardon (ed.), *Collected Ancient Greek Novels* (Berkeley: University of CA, 1989). The "Big Five" identified by the author are: Chariton, Xenophon of Ephesus, Longus, Achilles Tatius, and Heliodorus, from approximately the first to the third century C.E.

[5]In particular, Longus, Achilles Tatius, and Heliodorus.

[6]B. M. Egger, "Women in the Greek Novel: Constructing the Feminine" (Diss., University of CA-Irvine, 1990).

who has demonstrated that the power of romance heroines is quite restricted and largely apparent. These young women[7] are so stunningly beautiful that their *parousias* usually have the characteristics of an epiphany.[8] Men are drawn to them as if by magnets. Their attractiveness seems to place them in positions of power, but they chiefly use it to extricate themselves from the difficulties it has created.

These heroines rarely travel of their own volition. If their adventures take them around the Mediterranean world (and they often do), the women are usually captives, or worse. Even while in foreign lands they normally remain within the home. In public they are basically silent (although tears are permitted).[9] Male attention, more often than not unwelcome, is their principal experience.[10] Egger concludes that, although these women exude power, their capacity to exert it is subverted by all-too-familiar hidden messages stressing the impropriety of transgressing established limitations. She finds the typical romantic novel both a force for conservatism in that the established order is affirmed and a picture of reaction in that the circumstances of women depicted resemble those of a by-gone age rather than the realities of the Imperial Era.[11]

One aspect of the comfort and consolation both men and women could draw from reading such works derived from the security portrayed in the affirmation of traditional sex roles.[12] Egger characterizes this viewpoint as "emotional gynocentrism but

[7]Or, often, girls; Anthia (Xenophon of Ephesus), for example, is fourteen when the novel begins.
[8]For example: "As he approached the country house, Theron thought up the following move: he uncovered Callirhoe's head, shook her hair loose, and then opened the door and told her to go in first. Leonas and all the people in the room were awestruck at the sudden apparition — some of them thought they had seen a goddess, for people did say that Aphrodite manifested herself in the fields" (Chariton 1, 14, trans. Reardon in *Collected Ancient Greek Novels*, 36); "Often as they saw her in the sacred enclosure the Ephesians would worship her as Artemis ... some were amazed and said it was the goddess in person ... but all prayed and prostrated themselves and congratulated her parents" (Xenophon of Ephesus 1, 2, trans. G. Anderson in Reardon, 129).
[9]Egger, "Women in the Greek Novel," 63.
[10]Ibid., 272ff., 292. These statements are typical, not universal. There is a wide range of variation among even these five novels.
[11]Using here evidence from such works as S. Pomeroy, *Women in Hellenistic Egypt. From Alexander to Cleopatra* (New York: Schocken, 1984).
[12]Egger, "Women in the Greek Novel," 392. Egger does not suggest that the romantic novels were tracts. A factor she does not deeply explore is the simultaneous development of romantic love as the basis for marriage (on which see P. Veyne, "La famille et l'amour sous le haut-empire romaine," *Annales ESC* 33 [1978]: 35-63) and the contemporaneous emergence of the typical Greek romance.

practical androcentrism."[13] The author of the Pastoral Epistles would find a great deal to approve in the conduct of these heroines.

Little more than fragments remains of the (probably not large) output of serious realistic ancient Greek novels.[14] Thanks to the careful note-taking of the late Patriarch of Constantinople, there is a summary of Iamblichus's *Babylonica*,[15] which reveals in Sinonis a resolute and aggressive heroine. Fictional women could be strong and assertive so long as they were not ideals.

Their counterparts in the romantic novels are "bad" women: the rivals and antagonists of the heroines. These dreadful creatures are sexually and otherwise aggressive, independent, ruthless, willful, and domineering.[16] Most of them are devious and evil creatures who abuse their slaves and disrupt households.[17] Fortunately, the providence that guides romance will bring them in due course to the esthetic bench of poetic justice, from which will descend exquisitely apposite and edifying sentences.

Squeaky Clean: Susanna

Susanna is the Jewish heroine who most closely conforms to model of the romantic novels.[18] She is as beautiful, wealthy, and virtuous as any.[19] She is, however, a matron, with children, with a husband whom we should expect to protect her, but who does not.[20]

---

[13]Ibid., 365.
[14]Realism was generally restricted to comedy. Some fragments of apparently comic realistic Greek novels survive, as well as the Ὄνος of Pseudo-Lucian, and the Latin tradition includes the serio-comic novel of Apuleius and the (incomplete) *Satyricon* of Petronius.
[15]A translation of Photius's summary, together with the longer fragments by G. N. Sanday, appears in Reardon, *Collected Ancient Greek Novels*, 783-97.
[16]They are rather more interesting, often more appealing than the actual heroines, to modern readers.
[17]The subjects are those of the "Household Codes" (Col 3:18-4:1; Eph 5:22-6:9; 1 Pet 2:18-3:7), and the "bad women" of the romantic novels are everything the codes warn against.
[18]Unless otherwise noted, citations refer to the version of Theodotion (Θ).
[19]Egger notes that the female leads of romantic novels can be introduced with brief, coded references emphasizing their status, wealth, and extraordinary beauty. She goes on to state: "With surprisingly few strokes of standard praise narrators expect to arouse interest in her and the fate of her love story, and establish her as the positive female type and main female focus of attention of the story" ("Women in the Greek Novel," 55). The exception is Chariclea, in Heliodorus.
[20]He is not named among those at the trial (parents, children, other relatives in Θ, v. 30; parents, five hundred servants, and four children in the LXX). For her transformation into actual widow see H. Engel, *Die Susanna-Erzaehlung*, Orbis Biblicus et Orientalis 61 (Göttingen: Vandenhoeck & Ruprecht,

Susanna does not run about town but remains properly se-
cluded. The wicked elders had to spy her out in her παράδεισος.[21]
She is adamant in preservation of her virtue, and she prefers death
to being blackmailed into adultery. Susanna speaks only to her
maids. Rather than reply to the elders' proposal, she offers a brief
soliloquy. At her trial she is silent.[22] Only after condemnation does
she pray (vv. 42-43), but this ejaculation has no effect upon the
human actors. She is largely an object, vigorously virtuous, but quite
passive. This allegedly feminine quality makes her an ideal model for
the sapiential expression of the principle that vengeance belongs to
the Most High.[23]

Susanna's experience of accusation and trial is shared with
many romance heroines,[24] but this story is just a bit more indeli-
cate than ideal novels permit. For example, the LXX v. 32 has her
stripped for the voyeuristic pleasure of the judges.[25] No protagonist
of an ideal romance had to undergo such an indignity.[26] Such
details were more likely to occur in realistic novels. Jewish narrative,
like subsequent Christian acts and hagiography, frequently
exhibits a realism that learned critics would have found quite vulgar.

A Not Very Nice Pagan Girl: Aseneth

Aseneth also opposes human vengeance, and she does so in

1985).
[21]Θ establishes a rationale by making Joakim's home a Jewish community
center and giving opportunity for the elders' lust to mature. The LXX prefers a
lightning bolt of lust. The garden was a traditional site for seduction, as in
Achilles Tatius 1,15,1.
[22]There is, however, no suggestion that her testimony was sought.
[23]Susanna's providential delivery would not be out of place in a romantic novel
(see R. Pervo, Profit with Delight. The Literary Genre of the Acts of the
Apostles [Philadelphia: Fortress, 1987], 74). The use of retardation to
increase suspense is quite obvious, as the spirit of Daniel could have been
stirred up during the trial.
[24]See ibid., 42-50.
[25]Θ softens this by having her unveiled only. For voyeuristic interest this
edition introduces the bath motif, although the elders do not actually see her
in the bath. The Acts of Peter (BG 8502,4 132, 8-15) offers a parallel, in
addition to the famous Shepherd of Hermas, Vis. 1,1,2, on which see the
commentaries of M. Dibelius, Der Hirt des Hermas, HNT Ergaenzungs-Band
(Tübingen: Mohr, 1923), and P. Brown, The Body and Society (New York:
Columbia, 1988), 70. On Susanna v. 32, see Engel, Die Susanna-Erzaehlung,
101-2, and C. A. Moore, Daniel, Esther and Jeremiah. The Additions, AB 44
(Garden City, NY: Doubleday, 1977), 103. The Mishnaic Tractate Sota 1.5 is
usually introduced (anachronistically?) into discussions of this verse.
[26]See Egger, "Women in the Greek Novel," 62. Those interested in sex will be
better served by the Apocryphal Acts than by the "Scriptores Erotici."

word and deed.[27] As her story opens, however, she resembles the normal heroine of a romantic novel. Her beauty is a threat to the social order: Men literally fight over this marvel who, strikingly, does not in the least resemble the typical Egyptian beauty, but rather the women of Israel, especially Sarah.[28] Lest one imagine some suitor, besotted with admiration, murmuring, "That's funny; you don't look Egyptian," we should recall that Aseneth in her virginity is all but hermetically sealed within the ancestral palace, which came equipped with the proverbial tower. Seven maidens who have not so much as spoken with a male child attend her. Young men enter the picture only at the gates of the wall surrounding the courtyard of the house: seventy-two of them guard it (Chapter 2). Aseneth is thus the archetypical protected maiden. No male has so much as gazed upon her. That her ardent suitors must have based their claims on hearsay evidence is yet another tribute to her desirability.

Aseneth was probably not the last adolescent girl to be seen as difficult. She is first depicted as boastful, arrogant, and openly contemptuous of men (2:1). Indeed, when her father proposes to marry her to Joseph, she has a temper tantrum and proclaims the candidate wanting in both social background and ethical standards. She will have no other spouse than the crown prince (4:7-11).[29] Since, however, marriage and admiration for the other sex are not to be equated, her requirements for a husband do not necessarily

[27]*Asen.* is often discussed in conjunction with Greek novels. For references see C. Burchard in *OTP* 2, 183 n. 23 and *JSHRZ* 2.4 (Gütersloh: Gütersloher Verlagshaus Gerd Mohn, 1983), 51-52. Both M. Philonenko, *Joseph et Aseneth* (Leiden: Brill, 1968) and Burchard (especially in *JSHRZ*) give many instances of parallel motifs. Comparison with romantic novels is made easier by the surface love-story plot as well as its lack of canonical status. Egypt is one of the favorite "foreign" locales for Greek novels, and it may have been the place where the genre took shape. In this point see G. Anderson, *Ancient Fiction. The Novel in the Greco-Roman World* (London: Croom Helm, 1984). C. Grottanelli, who is an historian of religion, relates biblical narratives to the ancient novel more directly than do most classicists. See "The Ancient Novel and Biblical Narrative," *Quaderni urbinati di cultura classica* n.s. 27 (1987): 7-34.

[28]*Asen.* 1:3-6. I follow Burchard's edition, which forms the basis for his presentation and translation of the text in *OTP*. For competition among suitors (a motif already found in Homer), see, e.g., Chariton 1, 1-2. On the beauty of Sarah see *Legends* 5:261 n. 90; 6:273 n. 132. See also the *Genesis Apocryphon* (1QapGen 20:2-8); J. A. Fitzmyer's *The Genesis Apocryphon of Qumran Cave I. BibOr* 18a, 2d ed. (Rome: Biblical Institute, 1971); and S. J. D. Cohen, "The Beauty of Flora and the Beauty of Sarai," *Helios* 8 (1981): 41-53. Aseneth was very tall (1:4), an attribute shared with the goddesses of romantic novels. When the story opens she is eighteen, rather old for the role. As Burchard observes (*OTP* 203 n. J), she had already been besieged by suitors for several years.

[29]Burchard states that she simply wants the best man; see *OTP* 201 n. A.

mitigate the force of the statement that she despised men. The best parallel from a romantic novel to this variation on the Hippolytus-motif comes in the person of (H)abrocomes (Xen. Eph. 1,1). Habro-comes despised Eros and paid the price. Like him, Aseneth will be struck by a lightning-bolt.[30] Her stance is quite unusual for the heroine of a first century C.E. novel,[31] whence the need to turn to Habrocomes.

Aseneth is never a helpless, simpering virgin. Fully conscious of her high status and of the rights and privileges thereunto apper-taining, she has the demeanor of a hellenistic queen.[32] In the absence of her parents the young woman takes charge of the ances-tral estate that she will inherit. Her regal behavior and insistence upon the husband of her choice nicely contrast with her subsequent dejection and thus help the plot, but had Aseneth been a good girl — filial, deferent, and obedient — the story would have ended much sooner, with her acquiescence to the parental choice and, no doubt, her dutiful adhesion to the religious practices of her new lord and master.[33]

But nothing so exemplary takes place. By resolutely and in-temperately rejecting her father's plans and by stomping out of the hall in anger, she sets up the plot. Girls who blow up at their fathers *should* get into trouble in ancient novels, and Aseneth's trouble turns out to be neither better nor worse than the usual fate of heroines: love at first sight.[34] Joseph, who is constantly harassed by utterly brazen women, catches her staring at him and presumes the worst (7:2-7). Aseneth thus finds herself assigned to the role of the bad woman who threatens the virtue of chaste males.[35]

This was a dreadful mistake, of course, and, after the suspect has been identified, Aseneth's parents send for her and command a decorous kiss. However, each potential lover hates the other sex.

---

[30]"And Aseneth saw Joseph on his chariot and was strongly cut (to the heart), and her soul was crushed, and her knees were paralyzed, and her entire body trembled, and she was filled with great fear" (6:1; cf. 8:8). The parallel scene is Xen. Eph. 1, 2-3. Both characters deliver a soliloquy in their torment: *Asen.* 6:2-8; Xen. Eph. 1, 4.

[31]Chariclea, the heroine of Heliodorus, is rather independent and strong — as well as a virgin — but she has become involved with her intended long before the story opens.

[32]If Joseph is a kind of Alexander Helios, Aseneth is a Cleopatra Selene.

[33]Popular philosophers of the Imperial period took considerable pains to state that wives should follow the religion of their husbands.

[34]She is astute enough to observe not only Joseph's physical virtues but also his insight (6:2-7).

[35]For more information about such women see Egger, "Women in the Greek Novel," 67-94.

Readers will have to wait a long time for that kiss: a good third of the book.[36] For now there will be no kissing at all. Aseneth is a stranger and an idolater (7:7-8:5). The author is here clearly playing with the conventions of romance to construct the story, but Aseneth is by no means the contemporary (male) ideal of the "good wife," nor will her conversion be for the sake of getting the boy of her dreams.

That boy, Joseph, offers a sympathetic benediction and then heads off for eight days on the grain circuit. Aseneth is left to fend for herself, without catechesis or admonition. This plot device helps create suspense, but the outcome is that Aseneth is neither instructed nor converted by any male. Even her heavenly visitor does not play the role of mystagogue. For the lengthiest and most crucial section of the novel Aseneth holds center stage, usually alone. Her repentance and conversion derive from her own choice, insight, capacity to accept revelation, and courage. She does not rule Joseph's emotional world, nor could she, for emotions do not control him. The universe of which she is the center is that of her parents, and it is a universe she presently rejects.

Unless the narrator is to be charged with utter incompetence, the language of Aseneth's repentance must be considered metaphorical. Love-sickness quickly gives way to spiritual remorse. Aseneth describes herself as a victim of persecution and as an orphan (11:3-4). This all seems a bit unreal, as her parents have not rejected her, nor will they. In due course Aseneth will get Joseph and all that she ever wanted. In part this dissonance stems from her role as typical and representative proselyte, one who experiences as the model and patron of other converts the sufferings and alienation a change of religion may bring. Her story thus constantly threatens to slip into allegory. Nonetheless, it is worthy of note that such an important symbolic role is assigned to the figure of a woman.

Her prayer of repentant self-description, a prayer based upon feeling rather than experience, is scarcely a woman's lament at being treated as an object for enhancing family status through an advantageous marriage. Devotees of ancient romantic stories were (and are) quite familiar with heroes who lose their true status and must both stave off, in captivity or servitude, lustful admirers and undergo any number of physical trials. There is relatively little of this surface adventure in *Asen.* Her trials and tribulations — Joseph has none — are emotional and spiritual in nature. The external element of this novel comes at its end (chaps. 23-29), a kind of required

---

[36]The wait is worthwhile; the benefits of the kiss include life, wisdom, and truth (19:10-11).

adventure with interesting ramifications. The core of the novel, its structural and thematic center, is internal. *Asen.* comes closer to being a novel of emotion and of personal development than do most of its longer and more sophisticated Greek counterparts. The emotional and spiritual do not stand apart from the practical.[37]

Alienated from family, wealth, and servants, from all of the sources of status and security, Aseneth prays for courage (11:11, 18), and God answers her prayer. She is a different kind of protagonist from the young women who preserve their sexual purity through hell and high water for their true male loves. *Asen.* reads like a cross between a Greek romance and a piece of early Christian hagiography. The narrator does not disparage the love she feels for Joseph, as her conversion is not to celibacy. Nevertheless, the love of God is what makes realization of her romantic passion possible.

Asen. thus has one answer to the question of how women might convert to Judaism.[38] Presumably marriage constituted one route. Aseneth converts prior to marriage, not after, and of her own volition, not at the instigation of her family or future spouse. Repentance, a creedal confession, renunciation of paganism with all its pomps and all its ways, and adoption of Jewish practice, especially in the matter of diet, are the marks of her conversion.[39] The result is a transformation that makes her more beautiful than ever,[40] an outward and visible sign of inward and spiritual grace.[41] And, Aseneth converts without the mediation of a human coadjutor, οὐκ ἀπ' ἀνθρώπων οὐδε δι' ἀνθρώπου.

---

[37]That change comes through miraculous revelation is ordinary in ancient literature, which does not deal with character development. This is in accordance with ancient anthropology, just as θειοὶ ἄνθρωποι πρῶτοι εὕρεται stand in the place moderns attribute to evolution.

[38]See S. J. D. Cohen, "Crossing the Boundary and Becoming a Jew," *HTR* 82 (1989): 13-33.

[39]Ibid., 21, states that Aseneth did not observe Jewish laws, other than abstaining from food offered to idols. The parallel construction of 8:5 and 16:16, however, suggests that she did at least meet the demands for community membership stipulated by Joseph.

[40]*Asen.* 18:7-9, with a shift to biblical similes (8:4).

[41]The obvious parallel here is Apuleius, *Metamorphoses* 11. C. Burchard prints a synoptic comparison in *Untersuchungen zu Joseph und Aseneth*, WUNT 8 (Tübingen: Mohr, 1965); cf. his *Der Dreizehnte Zeuge*, FRLANT 103 (Göttingen: Vandenhoeck & Ruprecht, 1970), 59-105. The imagery of putting on new garments is common in initiation rites and is probably one of the reasons earlier researchers (e.g., Batiffol) thought that the work was written by a Christian. Without denying the use of initiatory symbolism, I would point to Isa 61 as a specific source. The language and themes of Deutero- and Trito-Isaiah permeate *Asen.* The principal example of metamorphosis in the Hebrew Scriptures is, of course, that of Moses. Once again a male model provides the context.

It is no less significant that the wedding of Joseph and Aseneth is not the happy ending of this short novel. The heroine does
not pass from the jurisdiction of her father to the jurisdiction of
Joseph and then live quietly in peace at home. For her, conversion
means the abandonment of her earthly protector for a heavenly patron, human father for divine parent. As a child of the Most High she
becomes a new person endowed with powerful gifts. Once a spiritual
refugee, she becomes a refuge for others. Once enclosed within a
fortress, she becomes a fortress for others. She is identified with
Wisdom and heavenly Zion, symbols of female power, sagacity, and
nurture. She is citadel and rock rather than mother.[42] The importance of the final portion of the novel for the character of Aseneth is
to exhibit her acting out these roles, without the benevolent protection of her husband. Here, again, the contrast with ancient romantic
novels is noteworthy.

Neither villains nor shipwreck[43] separate Joseph and Aseneth. She can ride in a chariot and hold hands with a brother-in-law
(22:12). While Joseph goes about his business, she sets out to
inspect her ancestral estate, with a detachment of six hundred
armed men (26:1-5). This is not the normal setting for the perils of
an ancient romantic heroine. Joseph is less anxious about leaving
her alone than she is about being left alone. That he can dispatch her
to look after her estate while he is on the road not only displays her
regal status but also seems to present what is probably a woman's
view of the ideal husband: one willing to trust his wife with important
responsibilities rather than locking her up at home. The religious
warrant for his liberated behavior is trust in the protection of the
Almighty.

That Levi, rather than Joseph or even Pentephres, should
offer Aseneth instruction in esoteric wisdom is quite acceptable
(22:13). This is an actualization of her endowment with wisdom and
of the suitability of her character for the reception of such material.
Aseneth becomes something of a charismatic figure, able to exercise
her will through means different from her earlier arrogant temper
tantrums.

---

[42]The identification with Wisdom is quite apparent in 17:6. For rock and
heavenly citadel see 19:8 and 21:13. In various Christian writings (the later
level of Q; Matthew; John; Paul), Jesus is identified with Wisdom. The image
of the rock is, of course, applied to Peter. For Sarah as rock, see Isa 51:1-2.
[43]N. Frye, with an eye on Xenophon of Ephesus, says that the shipwreck is
"the normal means of transportation" in Greek novels; see his *The Secular
Scripture. A Study of the Structure of Romance* (Cambridge, MA: Harvard,
1976), 4.

But life after conversion is not ease in Zion. When the unrequited rage of Pharaoh's son explodes into a murderous plot into which some of Joseph's brothers are drawn, Aseneth trusts in God, who in turn brings miraculous deliverance (27:10-11). Wisdom embodied, she eschews revenge and stays the righteous rage that would slay the rebellious brothers. Aseneth is also asylum personified, the city of refuge for Jews no less than gentiles. She is quite prepared to argue with Simeon and the others (28:9). As dispenser of clemency she fulfills a regal role.[44]

Marriage for Aseneth is thus rather the symbol of her new status than its realization. To be sure, she can have her cake and eat it too, for her parents are perfectly pleased with the marriage and appear to embrace the faith, while the officiating minister is none other than the Pharaoh, who makes the event a compulsory national holiday.[45] In the end Aseneth becomes the veritable queen of Egypt, achieving the objective announced at 4:11. She married the heir after all. This is as much gratification as anyone could require, but it is tempered by and imbued with irony. Aseneth does not get to marry the object of her longings because the last bandit and the final tyrant had had their chance. She achieves her goals through a personal change that also altered her longings. Becoming Queen of Egypt is less important than becoming a child of God. Worldly success belongs to the realm of appearances.[46]

Both as symbol (the modern expression is 'role model') and actor, then, Aseneth, an imperious, independent, resourceful, and powerful woman, who is refuge and haven for converts, Wisdom, rock, and Zion, reflects traits that distinguish her from the run-of-the-mill romantic heroine. Since it is quite unlikely that the author of *Asen.* was not familiar with Greek romantic novels, known to us or unknown, comparison is warranted. There are doubtless numerous explanations for the contrasts, not the least of which are the work's religious themes and allegorical proclivities. Yet one could easily construct a novel with the same themes that nonetheless reflects the main lines of female characterization commonly found in ancient novels.

In comparison with these novels *Asen.* displays characteristics that could be called, *mutatis mutandis*, feminist. The book pre-

[44]Callirhoe is also an agent of clemency, so Chariton 8, 3-5. This is quite remarkable, as Egger, "Women in the Greek Novel," 101, notes.
[45]*Asen.* 21:2-8, with the death penalty for working during the holiday (cf. Matt 22:1-14). On the banquet see Esth 1:1-8.
[46]A view alluded to in Sirach and vigorously embraced in Wisdom.

sents conversion to Judaism as a positive advantage to women seeking to break out of the (ivory or prison) towers within which their lives have been circumscribed. Aseneth is no less a striking model and vivid image for women of Jewish origin who might find in her story some encouragement and inspiration of their own.[47]

Widows Might: Judith and Melite

The author of the Pastoral Epistles recognizes two types of widows: genuine (ὄντως) and indulgent (σπαταλῶσα).[48] The outstanding example of a widow in the romantic novels is Melite, of Ephesus,[49] who has found her way into the prestigious TDNT with the epithet "notorious."[50] She is nonetheless interesting for all of that, since she is, in the words of a servant, "a very beautiful woman, a living work of art ... rich and still young. Her husband just recently died at sea."[51] Modern readers are liable to prefer her refreshing candor, independence, and energy to the ultimately tiring protestations of the beleaguered heroines.[52]

Melite operates with a great deal of freedom. Bound to neither spouse nor parent, she is the arbiter of her own life and can travel freely (5,11) and manage her own household. Melite (like Aseneth) visits her estate and deals with its manager (5,17). She acts as her own agent, disposing of her goods to help friends and retaining lawyers when hauled into court (7,8; 6,14). She is also sexually forthright and aggressive and not above a bit of deceit and dissembling. Melite is not evil; she does not play the role of wicked tyrant,

---

[47]And, if it is not too much to hope for, men. Characters and situations in novels are, to be sure, fictional constructs and ought not to be treated as tout court reflections of reality. The world of Asen. is an ideal world. The ideal differs from that of most of the ancient romantic novels.

[48]1 Tim 3:5-6. For the meaning of σπαταλῶσα see Sir 21:15; Jas 5:5. The theme of the "flighty" (we should say "merry") widow appears in the Talmud: b. Sota 22a; j. Sota 3, 4, and is common in folklore and popular story. G. Staehlin, Χηρα, TDNT 9: 454 n. 131, gives numerous references to primary texts about ancient widows. B. Thurston's recent study, The Widows. A Women's Ministry in the Early Church (Minneapolis: Fortress, 1989), surveys some material in a rather incomplete and critically questionable form.

[49]Achilles Tatius 5-8. Ephesus was the "homeland" of "Milesian Tales" (and of the Pastorals) and the home of probably the best known of such widows, the "Matron" of Satyricon 111-12, who did not observe a particularly solemn or lengthy period of mourning.

[50]Staehlin, Χήρα, 454 n. 131, with many references.

[51]Ach. Tat. 8,11, 4-5, trans. J. J. Winkler in Reardon, Collected Ancient Greek Novels, 238. All but widowhood are the normal attributes of the protagonists.

[52]The author may have wished it so. Achilles Tatius often seems to be a parody (like Joseph Andrews) of the more ideal novels. For a catalogue of modern admirers see Egger, "Women in the Greek Novel," 76 n. 2.

but she is not "good." She wants to have sex with the hero Cleitophon, who is the intended of Leucippe, and she does, but she will not get to keep him. Melite settles for what she *can* get, and she does so with grace.[53]

Moralists were unlikely to let such widows off lightly. Jerome may serve as mouthpiece for the breed:[54]

> Gentile widows are wont to paint their faces with rouge and white lead, to flaunt in silk dresses, to deck themselves in gleaming jewels, to wear gold necklaces, to hang from their pierced ears the costliest Red Sea pearls, and to reek of musk. Rejoicing that they have at length escaped from a husband's dominion, they look about for a new mate, intending not to yield him obedience, as God ordained, but to be his lord and master. With this object they choose poor men, husbands only in name, who must patiently put up with rivals, and if they murmur can be kicked out on the spot. (*Epistle* 127, 3)

Like most of the romantic novels,[55] the Book of Judith is set in the historical past and includes military adventures. Judith, like most romantic heroines, has to confront the lust of a foreign potentate,[56] and she is not the only heroine to kill an adversary. The most notable difference is, of course, that she embarks upon this course of her own volition. She has to be a widow (or a prostitute) in order to possess a credible amount of the requisite sexual experience and freedom of action.

Judith has much in common with Melite: she is rich, beautiful, and independent, a wealthy widow who has, so to speak, kept her

---

[53]For a discussion of Melite's character and role see ibid., 75-79, 245-56.

[54]*Selected Letters of St. Jerome*, trans. F. A. Wright (Cambridge: Loeb, 1933), 445. Clearly Jerome was even more upset by the independence of these women and the reversal of sex roles than by their clothing and makeup. He proceeds to contrast this type with his subject, Marcella: "Our widow, on the other hand, wore clothes that were meant to keep out the cold, not to reveal her bare limbs. Even a gold signet ring she rejected, preferring to store her money in the stomachs of the needy rather than to hide it in a purse. Nowhere would she go without her mother, never would she interview without witnesses one of the monks, or clergy. ... Always her retinue consisted of virgins and widows, and they were all staid women; for she knew that a saucy maid is a reflection on her mistress' character, and that women usually prefer the company of people like themselves."

[55]Students of the ancient novel have generally neglected Judith, despite Wilamowitz's observation that it is "a typical Hellenistic novel," as noted in C. Moore, *Judith*, AB 40 (Garden City, NY: Doubleday, 1985), 72.

[56]Greek novels show that the racist stereotype of lusty, sexually unprincipled, and uncontrolled "barbarians" has a long history. Properly reared Hellenic males of good standing often seek to marry the heroines. Bandits, slaves, and foreigners are commonly prepared to rape them.

looks and her figure (8:7). Like Melite she is also quite intelligent.[57] This is not the poor exploited widow to be pitied in the same breath with orphans. Judith runs her own estate and appears to be the uncrowned queen of Bethuliah. When she learns that the male leadership has pledged to surrender the town within five days she dispatches her slave/confidante[58] to summon those insipid elders to her house. They arrive and are given a tongue-lashing (8:9-27). A.-J. Levine says, "Only the text's females act in a fully efficacious manner; only Judith displays well-directed initiative; only her maid competently follows instructions. The men are weak, stupid, or impaired."[59]

Her observation has been stated, in the form of a complaint, by male critics of the Greek novels for over a century. The relative weakness and ineptness of the male protagonists, not to mention most of the antagonists, in comparison with their female counterparts has caused many tongues to cluck.[60] Next to the women the men tend to look colorless.[61] Worse yet, they seem less resolute and resourceful. Would-be virile Victorians had grave reservations about the desirability of allowing their (young male) students to ponder such role models.[62]

Against this background of craven and incompetent males ruled by their emotions Judith shines like a beacon. Many men wished to marry her (16:22), but without avail. No wonder, for she requires no male to protect her, and she wants for nothing in the material, social, and spiritual realms. Nor does her widowhood require the consolation of a son to become his father's heir.[63] Judith

---

[57]Piety plays a rather larger role in Judith's life than in Melite's, of course.

[58]On such confidantes (who are usually slaves) see Egger, "Women in the Greek Novel," 94-119. She observes that the romantic novels have little to say about female friendships. Judith's eventual emancipation of her servant (16:22) is typical. Such rewards for faithful service tend to come in the closing paragraphs of the novels, as part of the final summary to indicate that all get their due. The opposing character to Judith's maid is Holofernes's eunuch, Bagoas, whose name, estate, and behavior are entirely typical for such novels.

[59]"Character Construction and Community Formation in the Book of Judith," in D. Lull (ed.), SBLSP (Atlanta: Scholars Press, 1989), 564.

[60]Egger, "Women in the Greek Novel," 175-79, provides numerous references. The Joseph of Asen. may be delectable in appearance, but his manner is priggish and his role relatively minor.

[61]This is no mean feat, given the frequently monochromatic characterization of the heroines.

[62]Even Josephus is excluded from the traditional English school and university curriculum because he was a turncoat.

[63]Despite lip-service to the joys of motherhood, the Greek romantic novels leave realization of this ideal on the periphery of their plots. See Egger, "Women in the Greek Novel," 329-39.

is no Jephthah. The heritage she leaves is neither children nor
wealth, but secure peace for her nation (16:25). All in all, she is a good
candidate for allegorization.[64]

Alone of her people, this wealthy and resourceful widow is
prepared to resist. The weapons she uses are feminine wiles. After
suitable prayer and devotion, she gets herself tarted up and sets out
to subdue her enemy.[65] Like the heroines of romantic novels she is
so gorgeous that her very presence draws a crowd (10:18-19).
Through artful seduction and deceitful deception of would-be deceiv-
ers she entices Holofernes to his artfully arranged doom and her
skillfully contrived escape.[66] Judith delivers the fatal blows herself,
tosses the torso under its bed, stuffs the trophy into her grocery-
bag, and heads smiling off on the pretext of devotion — and its
reality. Rather than private prayer there will be a corporate celebration, with women leading men in a bacchanal of triumph.[67] The
world has been turned upside down.

That it will not long remain so is the observation of A.-J. Levine,
whose careful study reveals both the overt, surface meaning of the
text and its latent content. She may overstate the extent to which
Judith is safely domesticated by the resumption of her former life
and ultimate burial in her husband's sepulcher,[68] but she is certainly correct in observing that the circumstances do not produce
permanent social change. The model, however, remains.[69] One
cannot imagine such a character as Judith in an ancient ideal
romance, which had little use for the ὄντως χήρα and no central role
for the σπαταλῶσα. To find a woman so independent one must turn

---

[64]Especially by Christians, and usually christologically. This is not to deny that
she is a symbol, "The Jew(ess)," a personification of national courage and
resourcefulness based upon piety and faith. Jews, Greeks, and Romans, as is
well known, commonly personified cities and nations as female.
[65]See 9:1-10:9. Her preparation, and the resultant metamorphosis, can be
compared with that of Aseneth (18:5-11) and Esther (15:1-5).
[66]T. Craven's study, *Artistry and Faith in the Book of Judith*, SBLDS 70 (Chico,
CA: Scholars Press, 1983), has brought to light the many levels of irony
employed by the author. Moore, *Judith*, 219 on 12:7, reports a conjecture of
Dancy that, in an earlier version of the tale, menstruation was used as the
excuse for her declining Holofernes's advances. Leucippe makes use of this
same stratagem, Achilles Tatius 4,7,6. Judith's "dishonesty" has been the
object of moralistic criticism. Craven contributed an (unpublished) paper in
defence of Judith to the 1989 SBL Pseudepigrapha Seminar (Anaheim, CA, 20
Nov.). Members of the Seminar agreed that Judith's dissembling was justified.
[67]Well characterized by Levine, "Character Construction," 569.
[68]A correction made in her revision of the seminar paper for the forthcoming collection on Judith, ed. J. VanderKam, for Scholars Press.
[69]See the remarks of E. Schüssler Fiorenza, *Memory*, 115-18, who compares
Judith to personified Wisdom.

to Melite.

To find a woman so ruthless and powerful one must turn to Heliodorus's Arsace, a tyrant acting as satrap of Memphis in her husband's absence and a model of female sexual aggression in its unrestrained "barbarian" manifestation.[70] She, too, is a widow *pro tem* and willing to use any tactic to satisfy her lusts. When this vicious specimen comes to a suitable end, mourners and honors are in short supply. Ancient novels had room for man-killing widows, but not in the featured position.[71] How ὄντως would the author of the Pastorals have found her? She is both a heroine and the sort of widow of whom Jerome could not fully approve.

All's Well That Ends Well

Only in the heroine of the latest of the ancient Greek romances, Heliodorus's Chariclea,[72] does there emerge a character who resembles Aseneth or Judith. Like them she is both καλη and σοφη (Hel. 3,4.1). Chariclea is well educated and out-spoken, gifted with rhetorical skills and informed by theological training. She is aggressive and competent, able to dispatch a batch of pirates with a quiver of arrows and to outwit formidable rivals. She cares for the fiancé she has selected against (foster-) parental advice and successfully negotiates the full repertory of adventures in store for her breed. For Chariclea virginity is a bit more than waiting until marriage.[73] She operates with both the freedom and the restrictions of

---

[70]Heliodorus, Books 7-8; see Egger, "Women in the Greek Novel," 86-90.

[71]Levine, "Character Construction," 563-64, has an insightful interpretation of the death of Judith's husband, aphoristically summarized as "Were all women to be like Judith, not only Holofernes would lose his head" (563). Since men tend to fear precisely this, the threat Judith raises is not fully mitigated. It would be more comforting had Manasseh perished in battle. The biblical prototypes of Jael and Deborah, explored by S. A. White, "In the Steps of Jael and Deborah: Judith as Heroine," in D. Lull (ed.), *SBLSP* 1989 (Atlanta: Scholars Press), 570-78, cannot be dismissed, but Greek myth and legend had their equivalents also. The surviving romantic novelists ignored or transformed them. Semiramis, for example, a legendary Oriental queen, appears in the fragments of Ninus as a tongue-tied, blushing maiden (trans. G. Sanday in Reardon, *Collected Ancient Greek Novels*, 803-8). Pseudo-Philo's edition of the Deborah-legend (chaps. 30-32) has numerous resemblances to Judith and so provides another witness to the transformation of biblical traditions.

[72]The date of Heliodorus is disputed; it might be as late as the fourth century C.E.

[73]Joseph asserts: "It does not befit a man who worships God to sleep with his wife before the wedding" (*Asen.* 21:2). In a rigorously moral context this sounds redundant, if not anticlimactic.

the women featured in early Christian literature.[74] With renunciation of sexuality comes emancipation.

Judith may have renounced sex, but her sexuality remains undenied. Aseneth marries for love and has children.[75] These two female fictional characters[76] contrast rather sharply with the ideal young heroine of the Greek romantic novels. Numerous explanations may be put forth for these differences, including their nationalistic (Judith)[77] and symbolic (*Asen.*) character, and their clear variation in type,[78] but the effect of such qualifications is limited. Historical novels are, after all, novels.[79]

The survival of these relatively early popular Jewish texts suggests that there may once have existed a less sophisticated and literary body of writings much less interested in reinforcing traditional social roles than were the "Scriptores Erotici." Further, their survival suggests that "pagan" counterparts to *Joseph and Aseneth,* Judith, and the Apocryphal Acts may well have been composed and read: novels showing independent and resourceful women achieving love and freedom, or at least freedom, with heroines more like Judith or Sinonis than like Leucippe or Anthia.

To read works like Judith and *Joseph and Aseneth* against the romantic novels helps give profile to each and to suggest the various options open to the authors of ancient novels. Both options taken and options not taken are revelatory. The options taken by the authors of *Joseph and Aseneth* and Judith present challenges to the established order, challenges that some readers, at least, would scarcely have been content to brush off as exceptions. The romantic novels, according to Egger's persuasive analysis, showed women (and men) what women were supposed to want. These Jewish novels, on the other hand, more accurately describe what I strongly suspect many women actually wanted.

---

[74]Egger, "Women in the Greek Novel," 281-91, treats her as a special case. Photius, who has little good to say about the novels he read, gives Heliodorus high marks on the topic of chastity. See Pervo, *Profit,* 182 n. 82.

[75]As does Susanna. Aseneth is evidently a mother (21:9) when she undergoes her adventure with Pharaoh's son.

[76]An only slightly less strong case could be made for the character of Esther. The parallels between Judith and Esther are significant, regardless of their interdependence.

[77]See Pervo, *Profit,* 115-21.

[78]Especially in the case of Judith.

[79]The Greek novels developed from, and began as, historical novels. For a recent view see T. Hagg, "Callirhoe and Parthenope: The Beginnings of the Historical Novel," *Classical Antiquity* 6 (1987): 184-204.

From Narrative to History:
The Resurrection of Mary and Martha

Adele Reinhartz

The women disciples of Jesus make only rare and brief appearances in the canonical gospels. Of these shadowy figures, only two —
the sisters Mary and Martha — emerge with any clarity. The three
passages in which they appear (Lk 10:38-42; Jn 11:1-44; 12:1-7)
depict Martha in the acts of serving (Lk 10:40; Jn 11:1-44), com-
plaining (Lk 10:41) and confessing (Jn 11:27), and Mary as engaged
in studying (Lk 10:39), mourning (Jn 11:20, 31), and anointing (Jn
12:3). We surmise that they, along with their brother Lazarus,
constituted an independent Jewish household from which parents
and spouses were absent. But the most important detail about
them, from the evangelists' perspective, was their contact with
Jesus, whom they apparently believed to be the messiah (Jn 11:27).
This composite picture leaves many questions unanswered: What
was the nature of their relationship to each other and to the man
who was the focus of their activities? What were their places in, and
feelings about, the various social and religious groups and institutions of their community? Were they even historical figures, and/or
role models for the early Christian churches? To answer these
questions requires nothing less than an act of resurrection which
would release Mary and Martha from the narratives and commentaries in which they are entombed, and make them breathe, act, and
most important, speak to us.[1]

Such resurrections, far from being restricted to the prophets
of old, are attempted regularly by scholars who draw on the narrative materials in the New Testament in order to compose the history
of the early church. While we usually assume that the people named
in the Pauline epistles were historical figures,[2] the same cannot be
said for many of the others mentioned in early Christian literature.
It is possible that all or some of the latter correspond to the "real"
women and men of the early movement, but the fact remains that
they are known to us only through texts which, while claiming to tell
a "true" story, nevertheless exhibit many of the characteristics of

---

[1]For a detailed discussion of the methodology in this task, see Bernadette
Brooten, "Early Christian Women and their Cultural Context: Issues of Method
in Historical Reconstruction," in Collins, 65-91.
[2]The historicity of Phoebe (Rom 16:1), Prisca (16:3), and Junia (16:7), for
example, is assumed by Florenza, *Memory*, 171-72.

fictional narrative.[3] The anonymous writers of these texts,[4] although often basing their accounts on early tradition, exercised great liberty in their choice of stories and had no misgivings about writing their own interests — as well as those of their communities — into their narratives. As a result, the gospels actually present two simultaneous stories: the accounts of Jesus and his followers, situated in the early decades of the first century C.E., at the same time reflect the experiences, concerns, and theologies of the evangelists' implied audiences at the end of that century.[5] In so doing, the narratives express not only the creativity but also the biases of their authors.[6]

What then do we make of Mary and Martha? The paucity of detail in the gospels clearly indicates that the evangelists were not interested in describing the sisters for their own sakes. Rather, their inclusion serves other purposes, such as the presentation of a particular view of the life of Jesus and his significance for the implied audience. Nevertheless, the fact that they are mentioned by both Luke and John, and in different contexts, suggests that they were not evangelistic creations but were already present in, or known to, a pre-redactional, shared stratum of tradition.[7] While this observation in itself does not demonstrate their historicity, it supports the assumption that Mary and Martha, or figures like them, did exist at

---

[3]The gospels contain elements such as plot, characters, narrators, and implicit commentary, which are also characteristic of fictional narrative. R. Alan Culpepper's *Anatomy of the Fourth Gospel* (Philadelphia: Fortress, 1983), is only one of the many examples of attempts to analyze the gospels by using the methodologies of literary criticism.

[4]Although it is customary, and convenient, to refer to the gospels by the names of the individuals to whom they were traditionally attributed, it is the most recent scholarly consensus that the evangelists cannot be identified in any absolute way. It is likely that the evangelists were male; hence my use of the masculine pronoun.

[5]This point is made by J. Louis Martyn, *History and Theology in the Fourth Gospel*, 2d ed. (Nashville: Abingdon, 1979), 37 and *passim*; the same approach can be used with the other gospels. For a discussion of "implied audience" as well as related terms (e.g., narrator, author, implied reader), see Culpepper, *Anatomy*, 15-17, 205-27.

[6]With the advent of redaction criticism in the post-World War II period, this observation has become a cornerstone of gospel criticism. See Norman Perrin, *What is Redaction Criticism?* (Philadelphia: Fortress, 1969).

[7]Some scholars have argued for a direct literary knowledge of Luke on the part of John, especially in the anointing scenes (Jn 12:3-7; Lk 7:36ff). See, for example, Werner Georg Kümmel, *Introduction to the New Testament*, rev. ed., trans. H. C. Kee (Nashville: Abingdon, 1975), 203. However, R. E. Brown seems to represent the majority view in stating that there is no direct literary contact between the third and fourth gospels, but that there is the possibility of access to similar traditions as well as of cross-influences at an oral stage in the history of gospel composition. See Brown, *The Gospel According to John*, AB 29 (New York: Doubleday, 1966), xlv, xlvii.

the time of Jesus and/or in the early years of the Christian movement.

In our efforts to give these women life, we cannot simply exhume them intact from their narrative contexts and dust them off. If the evangelists, or the tradition from which they drew, turned real people into literary characters in the service of their narrative, so do we need to reverse that process. As we consider how others have mapped the path from narrative to history and then take some tentative steps along the trail ourselves, it will soon become apparent that the path is not clearly marked. Indeed, it seems to lead in several different directions. Nevertheless, by placing Mary and Martha at the center of our investigation, and by paying attention to their roles as literary figures, we might glimpse something of their identities as Jewish, Christian women. In the process, we may also catch sight of other women, those unnamed, silent and faceless individuals in the early church who knew and reacted to these narratives.

Luke 10:38-42

The references to Mary and Martha in the third gospel come at the end of Chapter 10. This chapter records the mission of the seventy (or seventy-two) disciples (10:1-24) and Jesus' subsequent conversation with a lawyer (10:25-37), which concludes with the parable of the Good Samaritan (10:30-37).[8] Immediately after the parable, Luke notes that Jesus, presumably accompanied by his disciples (10:38), entered a village where he was received by Martha. While her sister Mary sat at Jesus' feet and listened to his teaching (10:39), Martha "was distracted with much serving" (10:40). Annoyed with Mary's behavior as well as with the apparent indifference of her guest, Martha asked Jesus, "Lord, do you not care that my sister has left me to serve alone? Tell her then to help me" (10:40). Instead of the sympathy she expected, however, Martha received a gently worded rebuke: "Martha, Martha, you are anxious and troubled about many things; one thing is needful. Mary has chosen the good portion, which shall not be taken away from her" (10:41-42).[9]

Attempts to recover the historical sisters from Luke's account require a judgment as to the meaning of Jesus' response in 10:41-42. Were these words spoken by Jesus himself, or were they placed

---

[8]All biblical citations are from the RSV, 1952.
[9]For a discussion of the textual problems in these verses, see Joseph A. Fitzmyer, *The Gospel According to Luke (X-XXIV)*, AB 28a (New York: Doubleday, 1985), 894, and Bruce M. Metzger, *A Textual Commentary on the Greek New Testament*, corr. ed. (London: UBS, 1975), 153-54.

in his mouth by the evangelist? Do they simply express approval of female discipleship ("sitting at his feet"), or are they a critique of an activity traditionally seen as female (serving at table)? These questions in turn require further investigation into the *Sitz-im-Leben* of the passage as well as the social mores of the Greco-Roman world. Does the pericope pertain to life in the time of Jesus, i.e., early first-century Palestine, or to the later situation of Luke's Diaspora community? Would the original readers have perceived serving at table to be women's work? Both the foreground and the background of the scholarly discussions of the historical sisters depend in large part on answers to these questions.

Ben Witherington III examines Lk 10:38-42 in his *Women in the Ministry of Jesus: A Study of Jesus' Attitudes to Women and their Roles as Reflected in his Earthly Life.*[10] The main purpose of his book is to show that "Jesus ... not only countered the negative evaluations of women [that were prevalent in the Jewish environment], but also endorsed and extended women's rights beyond the positive evaluation" which Witherington admits also existed within first-century Judaism.[11] This aim sets the agenda for his book and also determines the contours of his exegesis. According to Witherington, the pericope is an accurate account of an event in the life of the historical Jesus, although written by Luke in his own language and style.[12] Jesus' words "are neither an attempt to devalue Martha's efforts at hospitality, nor an attempt to attack a woman's traditional role; rather, Jesus defends Mary's right to learn from Him and says this is the crucial thing for those who wish to serve Him."[13]

Witherington does not dwell on the connotations of his statement, however. Instead, his principal interest is in contrasting the roles of Martha and Mary as portrayed in this passage with those of their non-Christian, Jewish contemporaries. First, he claims that it would have been questionable for a Jewish male to be alone with two women who were not related to him.[14] Second, he argues that Jesus, in condoning Mary's role as disciple, was breaking new ground. Although Jewish women could study, Witherington asserts that it was highly unusual for a rabbi to come into a woman's house and teach her.[15] Finally, he suggests that Martha's act of serving,

---

[10](Cambridge, Cambridge University Press, 1984).
[11]Ibid., 10.
[12]Ibid., 101.
[13]Ibid.
[14]Ibid.
[15]Ibid.

though apparently seen by some to have been a traditionally female role, may have been atypical: "In a Jewish context ... women were not allowed to serve at meals if men were in attendance, unless there were no servants to perform the task."[16] On these grounds, Witherington asserts the superiority of the early Christian movement to its Jewish matrix: Jesus frees humankind from the restraints imposed by Jewish law and custom. Though he does not explicitly say so, Witherington thus implies that Mary and Martha, in their allegiance to Jesus, have moved outside the Jewish community, and that their experience of liberation was typical of, or paradigmatic for, women in the early church.

While this analysis has its merits,[17] it is marred by a disturbing bias. It is also open to criticism on exegetical grounds. For example, it is not clear from the context that Jesus was alone with the two women.[18] Lk 10:38 refers to a group of people travelling together; while only Jesus is specifically mentioned as having entered the house, is the reader to understand that the rest stayed outside? If Jesus were her only guest, why was Martha so preoccupied? Her words convey a feeling of harassment with which those who have provided hospitality for an unexpected, large crowd can identify. Furthermore, the text offers no indication that the contact between Jesus and the sisters was perceived to be unusual, by Jesus, the women, any onlookers, or the narrator. John 4 here offers a useful contrast: the Samaritan woman (4:9), the narrator (4:9), and the disciples (4:27) note the irregularity of Jesus' behavior in stopping to converse with and request hospitality from a woman, and a Samaritan at that.

Next, Witherington's assertions concerning the place of wom-

---

[16]Ibid. Witherington contradicts himself here. On the one hand, he assumes that serving at table was a traditional female role (100, 103, 118), but on the other hand part of his argument is built on the notion that serving in mixed company was a radical act (101, 112).

[17]For example, Witherington in ibid., 100, is probably correct in saying that Luke was not interested in the story for the sake of the sisters but only insofar as it provided a vehicle for Jesus' words in 10:41-42.

[18]For Witherington's argument, such as it is, see ibid., 101, and 190 n. 135. Witherington cites Metzger, *Textual Commentary*, 153, in support of his claim, though in fact Metzger's comment refers only to the phrase "in her house." That the disciples are not specifically mentioned as having entered the house with him does not mean that we are necessarily to understand Jesus as having entered the house alone. Rather, it could simply mean that Jesus, as the central character, is the only one who needs to be mentioned. For parallels, see Gen 12:14, in which only Abram is mentioned, though both he and Sarai have entered Egypt; Gen 22:19, in which only Abraham is mentioned as having returned to his men, though Isaac apparently did too; for Lukan examples, see 2:4 and 7:6.

en in Judaism are inadequately documented, if at all. He cites no primary evidence, rabbinic or otherwise, for his claims that two women and an unrelated man could not be alone together, that women did not serve in mixed gatherings, or that women did not study. Although the role of women in first-century Judaism is a complex issue, Witherington's categorical statements appear to be the product of his apologetic interests rather than of an independent, critical examination of the relevant sources. In other words, his claim that "a low view of women [in Judaism] was common, perhaps even predominant before, during and after Jesus' era"[19] is necessitated by his view that Jesus ushered in a new era of liberation from Judaism.[20]

A very different picture of Martha and Mary emerges in Elisabeth Schüssler Fiorenza's "A Feminist Interpretation for Liberation: Martha and Mary: Lk. 10:38-42."[21] As a Christian feminist historian and theologian, her perspective differs greatly from that of Witherington. Schüssler Fiorenza's goal is to take the "*ekklesia* of women ... as the hermeneutical center and canon of a critical feminist interpretation and re-reading of the Bible."[22] In doing so, she seeks to "develop a new model of biblical interpretation that can explore and assess the oppressive or liberating dynamics of biblical texts and their function in the contemporary struggle of women for liberation."[23] Her attempt at a critical re-reading and re-appropriation of the text for contemporary women shapes her reconstruction of the figures of Mary and Martha, just as Witherington's agenda

---

[19]Witherington, *Women*, 10. His sources for this assertion are several passages from the English translation of *Genesis Rabbah*, the Babylonian Talmud, Philo and Josephus, as well as some secondary sources. He does qualify his statement somewhat by saying that the views of Jeremias and Bonsirven are overly negative, and by citing Judith Hauptman's "Images of Women in the Talmud," in R. R. Ruether (ed.), *Religion and Sexism, Images of Women in the Jewish and Christian Traditions* (New York: Simon and Schuster, 1974) as presenting a more balanced view.
[20]The tendency to cast Christianity and its portrayal of women over against Judaism is not unique to Witherington. As Brooten, "Women," 72, comments, "on the question of women, Judaism is regularly used as a negative backdrop against which to view early Christianity." Brooten supports her observation by citing some of the most influential studies of women in the early church, including those of Joachim Jeremias, George Tavard, G. W. Trompf, Evelyn and Frank Stagg, Leonard Swidler, and Johannes Leipoldt.
[21]*Religion and Intellectual Life* 3 (1986): 21-36. See the similar treatment in her *Theological Criteria and Historical Reconstruction*, Protocol of the 53d Colloquy: April 10, 1986 (Berkeley: Center for Hermeneutical Studies in Hellenistic and Modern Culture, 1986).
[22]Schüssler Fiorenza, "Lk. 10:38-42," 23; cf. *Criteria*, 1-2.
[23]Schüssler Fiorenza, "Lk. 10.38-42," 23.

has shaped his.[24] Yet although she operates explicitly from a feminist perspective, she avoids any comparison of Mary and Martha with Jewish or indeed other women outside the Christian movement, and hence she also avoids the anti-Judaism that characterizes so many other studies of Christian women.[25] Schüssler Fiorenza rejects both the theory that Luke's pericope is an accurate portrayal of an event in the life of Jesus and the claim that the words placed on Jesus' lips were spoken by him. Instead, she situates Luke's story in the context of the community to which he writes,[26] and sets Martha and Mary squarely within the early Christian housechurch.[27]

In order to determine the import of the passage, Schüssler Fiorenza first engages in a limited literary-critical analysis. Her discussion, which underlines the androcentric dynamic of the text,[28] focuses on the nature of the contacts between Jesus and each of the sisters. She considers the relationship between Martha as host and Jesus as guest to be one of independent equals. This egalitarian relationship is rejected, however, by the Lukan Jesus in favor of one of dependency such as he has with Mary "who chooses the position of a subordinate student" dependent on her master.[29] This, she argues, is not descriptive of the actual place of women in the time of Jesus. Rather, it represents the evangelist's own (androcentric) notions of what the role of women should be.[30] For Luke, Schüssler Fiorenza suggests, Martha and Mary represent women engaged in

---

[24]This is discussed in William Anderson's response to Schüssler Fiorenza's analysis in *Criteria*, 17, 19, in which he bluntly comments that Schüssler Fiorenza "has shaped the material to fit her prejudices." For Schüssler Fiorenza's own discussion of value-laden and value-free scholarship, cf. *Memory*, xviff.

[25]Cf. *Memory*, 105, in which she comments that "historical reconstructions of Christianity over and against Judaism can be continuing resources for Christian anti-Judaism because they perceive Christian origins in light of the historical fact of Christianity's separation from and partial rejection of its Jewish roots and heritage." See also *Criteria*, 6.

[26]*Criteria*, 29-30. According to Schüssler Fiorenza, this is linguistically signalled by the title κύριος, which appeals to the authority of the resurrected Lord. Herman Waetjen, *Criteria*, 36, suggests that on textual-critical grounds the reading should be "Jesus" and not κύριος. See Fitzmyer, *Gospel*, 893, who also seems to favor this reading. Such a shift in terminology does not, however, invalidate Schüssler Fiorenza's position, which can be supported with reference to other evidence of the evangelist's redactional activity (e.g., the Lukan Sermon on the Plain, which betrays the author's specific interests). See Hans Conzelmann, *The Theology of St. Luke*, trans. G. Buswell (Philadelphia: Fortress, 1961), 45-46.

[27]*Criteria*, 30.

[28]Ibid., 29.

[29]Ibid.

[30]Ibid.

two different activities: Martha is actively engaged in preaching the word in the housechurch; Mary listens passively to the teaching of Jesus.[31] Luke criticizes the former model while urging the latter upon his readers, some of whom were likely women engaged like Martha in preaching activity. In Schüssler Fiorenza's words:[32]

> Lk. 10:38-42 pits the apostolic women of the Jesus movement against each other and appeals to a revelatory word of the resurrected Lord in order to restrict women's ministry and authority. Its rhetorical interests are to silence women leaders of housechurches who like Martha might have protested, and at the same time to extol the silent and subordinate behavior of Mary.

This reconstruction therefore presents the sisters as examples of women who were not only members of the church, but also leaders and preachers in their own right. As such, they were thorns in the sides of some of the male members of the church hierarchy. Luke, a member of this hierarchy, sought to alter the situation by presenting the silent, sitting Mary as a behavioral model preferable to that of the active and assertive Martha.

As our discussion has demonstrated, Ben Witherington and Elisabeth Schüssler Fiorenza take different routes on their way from the gospel narrative to early Christian history, and they arrive at different destinations. The fact that their pictures of Martha and Mary bear the stamp of their respective agendas leads one to suspect that this will be true of all such journeys; there may in fact be no "objective" destination at all. We will not allow this suspicion to scuttle our own travel plans, but we should plan our own itinerary carefully and, perhaps, buy some cancellation insurance as well. In contrast to the primarily historical approaches of Witherington and Schüssler Fiorenza, our own journey will linger much longer at its point of departure, that is, on a literary analysis of the Lukan narrative. Only after so doing will we decide how far down the road to history and in which direction our vehicle will carry us. The following literary analysis of the pericope will focus on two main points: its larger context in chapter 10 and in the Lukan gospel as a whole; and its characterization of Mary and Martha.

Although many scholars see little or no connection between Lk

---

[31]Ibid. According to the Mishnah and Gemara, rabbinic disciples did not simply listen to their teachers, but they engaged in discussion with them. Cf. also the dialogues between the Lukan Jesus and his disciples and would-be disciples (e.g., 11:1-4; 8:39-50), and the comments by Waetjen in *Criteria*, 36.
[32]Schüssler Fiorenza, "Lk. 10:38-42," 32.

10:38-42 and its immediate narrative context,[33] it is possible to demonstrate otherwise. Chapter 10 begins with the sending out of a large number of disciples who are given specific missionary instructions (10:4-11). Among these is the directive: "Whenever you enter a town and they receive you, eat what is set before you" (10:8). This suggests that those who receive the disciples will also serve them by taking care of their physical well-being. For their part, the disciples heal the sick and preach the word (10:9). Receiving the disciples by serving them and hearing their word is tantamount to receiving and hearing Jesus and indeed God as well (10:16). If this is the case, then the women in 10:38-42, who serve Jesus and sit at his feet, epitomize true belief. This reading suggests that we have come upon Martha and Mary in the very act of conversion, of turning to Jesus as savior.

What then is the significance of Jesus' rebuke? It may indicate that while serving, that is, taking care of physical needs,[34] and hearing the word are both elements of discipleship, concern for the former should not overshadow the importance of the latter. True service consists not only of attention to physical needs (and its accompanying distraction) but also, and primarily, of listening to the gospel. While serving others food and drink is an altruistic act, it should be placed in the same category as anxiety about one's physical needs, against which the Lukan Jesus cautions: "Do not be anxious about your life, what you shall eat, nor about your body, what you shall put on. For life is more than food, and the body more than clothing. ... For all the nations of the world seek these things; and your Father knows that you need them. Instead, seek his kingdom, and these things shall be yours as well" (12:22-23, 30-31).[35]

Even more significant for our analysis are passages such as 22:26-27 in which the Lukan Jesus inverts the conventional relationship between master and servant: "Let the greatest among you

---

[33]For a brief discussion, see Fitzmyer, *Gospel*, 892. Waetjen in *Criteria*, 35, referring to the Parable of the Good Samaritan also argues that the larger context needs to be considered.

[34]Schüssler Fiorenza's decision to limit the meaning of διακονέω in this pericope to "preaching" may be challenged. While preaching is clearly one meaning of the verb, other Lukan passages imply the broader translation of "to serve." Such service is ascribed not only to women (4:39; 8:3; 10:40) but also to male servants (17:8) and to Jesus himself (12:37; 22:26-27). Furthermore, Acts 6:2 uses the verb specifically to mean service at table, in contrast to preaching the word. For more detailed discussion, see Schüssler Fiorenza, "Lk. 10:38-42," and Hermann W. Beyer, "διακονέω, διακονία, διάκονος" in *TDNT* II, 81-93.

[35]In his response to Schüssler Fiorenza, William Anderson in *Criteria*, 19, also draws a connection between the two pericopes.

become as the youngest, and the leader as one who serves. For which is the greater, one who sits at table, or one who serves? Is it not the one who sits at table? But I am among you as one who serves." But what kind of meal is it that Jesus serves? The answer is: a spiritual one. Whereas Jesus' disciples serve him in various ways, he serves them by offering the word and eternal life. Lk 10:38-42 may thus provide a graphic illustration of the inverted master-servant dichotomy. Though Martha is called upon to serve the Lord, it is Mary who provides him with an opportunity to serve her.

These parallels suggest that Jesus' remarks were not intended to limit women's activity to passive listening to the word preached by men, as Schüssler Fiorenza suggests. Nor do they depict women's new freedom to be disciples of a great teacher, as Witherington argues. Rather, they emphasize that while service to others is important, hearing the word for oneself is the essential ingredient of discipleship. Because Luke provides male and female examples of both serving and hearing the word, it would seem that a differentiation of roles is not his primary message. The place of Lk 10:38-42 in the larger narrative and theological context of the third gospel suggests that Jesus' words to Martha convey the evangelist's attitude toward discipleship in general, not his views on women disciples specifically.

A similar conclusion emerges from an analysis of the Lukan characterization of the sisters. As Schüssler Fiorenza notes, Martha and Mary are portrayed only in their relationship to Jesus.[36] While she interprets this as evincing Luke's androcentrism, the pericope is not manifestly concerned with issues of equality between men and women, or the subordination of women to men, or even the right of women to assume functions that an androcentric church would prefer to limit to men. A glance beyond the passage reveals that in the third gospel all activities and relationships — whether associated with male or with female characters — are christocentric. This literary feature of the gospel is inherent in the narrative itself, as the implied author points out in his address to Theophilus (Acts 1:1). Therefore the characterization of Mary and Martha should be understood less as androcentric than as christocentric. That the sisters are depicted only in their relationship to Jesus reflects not a male bias but the inevitable focus of the gospel narrative.[37] In other

---

[36]"Lk. 10:38-42," 29.

[37]This is not to deny Luke's overall androcentrism, which is evident in other passages (e.g., Acts 18:26ff.). Cf. ibid., 31. But Waetjen in *Criteria*, 18, argues that most of Schüssler Fiorenza's arguments regarding Luke's androcentric bias are from silence and so are not particularly strong.

words, had the same story been told about male siblings such as the brothers Zebedee (Lk 5:10), the christocentric focus of their characterization would have been similar (cf. 5:1-11).

A second element of the characterization of Mary and Martha concerns its effect on the gospel's implied audience. Clearly the evangelist, as implied author, would like his audience to understand and accept the point conveyed in the passage, whatever we understand that point to be. But I suggest that he does so by using the specific literary technique of frustrating and thereby modifying the expectations he imputes to his readership.[38] Such expectations are articulated by Martha in 10:38-42. The passage derives its impact from the fact that Martha initially appears to have justice on her side. It seems unfair that she should do all the work while her sister sits. The expectation that Mary should help serve is also implicit in and therefore reinforced by 10:8, in which service is a sign that one has received the disciples and accepted their message.

Jesus' unexpected reply therefore functions in the first instance to frustrate Martha's expectations as well as those of the implied readers: if Martha's complaint is justified and if Jesus is on the side of justice (cf. Lk 6:32-49), why does he rebuke her? In the second instance, however, Jesus' words serve to modify and deepen the implied reader's understanding. Mary's act, while seemingly inconsiderate, is in fact the preferable one since it demonstrates the element of discipleship that Luke considers central. In this way, the characterization of Martha and Mary becomes a vehicle for the Lukan theme that true disciples, like the sisters, will center their actions on the Christ, and that true service consists not of caring for physical needs but of ingesting, and digesting, the message of the gospel.[39]

In summary, our discussion of Luke's narrative has pointed us in a different direction than those taken by Witherington and Schüssler Fiorenza. It has suggested that the evangelist's narrative purpose is not to describe the ideal female disciple in particular, but to illustrate his views on discipleship in general. This observation does not acquit Luke of androcentrism or ignore the use that later

---

[38]On this literary device as it pertains to John, cf. my "Great Expectations: A Reader-Oriented Approach to Johannine Christology and Eschatology," *JLT* 3 (1989): 61-76.
[39]The technique of frustrating and then modifying readers' expectations also appears in Lk 8:19-21 (Jesus seems to reject the idea that honor is due to one's parents) and 9:60 (he appears to question the honor due to the dead). In both cases, Jesus shocks his narrative audience, and Luke shocks his readers, by subordinating well-established moral values to the radical message

ecclesiastics have made of this and other Lukan passages to bar
women from positions of leadership.[40] Nevertheless, Luke's use of
female figures to express his views on discipleship, while probably
grounded in pre-Lukan tradition, at least implicitly attests to a role
for women in his view of the church. Further, it suggests the willingness of the male members of his implied audience to derive a lesson
from a story in which women are important characters.

These observations lead our attempts at historical reconstruction in two directions. If we assume that the evangelist is drawing
upon a tradition ultimately rooted in historical fact, the story provides a glimpse of two sisters in the process of becoming believers in
the Christ, through the missionary activity of the disciples or
perhaps even Jesus himself.[41] If we see the passage as addressed to
a particular community, we may catch sight, however briefly, of the
women members of that community who would have seen the sisters as role models affirming the legitimacy of their discipleship.[42]

John 11:1-44

Mary and Martha appear as two of the central characters in
the Johannine story of the raising of Lazarus. This final and most
detailed sign[43] of Jesus' ministry serves as a catalyst for the
sequence of events which culminate in Jesus' betrayal, trial, and
execution (cf. 11:47ff.).[44] In comparison with Luke's passage, the
portrait of the two sisters here is lavishly detailed. We are told they
live in a village named Bethany (11:1), and have a brother named
Lazarus (11:2). We also learn that Jesus loved all three siblings (11:3,
5).

---

of salvation through the Christ.

[40]Indeed, this seems to be a part of Witherington's agenda: he exalts the
traditional roles that women found meaningful in the early church, and by
implication, should continue to find satisfactory today. See Witherington,
Women, 117-18, and the brief discussion in Schüssler Fiorenza, Criteria, 5.

[41]In 10:2, Jesus seems to be implying that the seventy are sent out ahead of
him; they therefore prepare the way for his own travels to specific
communities. But 10:16 suggests that the entire chapter is intended also to
support the idea that the apostles and later missionaries can be effective in
bringing the word of God to the people, and that believing through the word
of such a missionary is tantamount to receiving, and being accepted by, Jesus
and God. Consequently, it is difficult to say whether we are to see Mary and
Martha as hearing the word initially from the disciples or from Jesus himself.

[42]This point is also made by Schüssler Fiorenza, "Lk. 10:38-42," 32.

[43]Other signs are recounted in chapters 2, 4, 5, 6, and 9.

[44]Brown, Gospel, 427, sees chapters 11 and 12 as added later to the plan of
the gospel, at which time the cleansing of the Temple was moved from its
place at the end of the ministry to the first Passover (118).

Mary and Martha initiate the action by sending word to Jesus that their brother is ill (11:3). Behind this act lie the expectations that Jesus cares about Lazarus and, more important, that he has the ability to heal him. This latter expectation is implied by the narrator, who reports Jesus' puzzling response to the message: instead of rushing to Lazarus's bedside, Jesus stays two days longer where he is.[45] It is also expressed explicitly by Martha (11:21) and Mary (11:32) as well as by the Jewish crowd in Bethany (11:37). When Jesus does finally arrive, Lazarus is already dead and buried. Martha greets Jesus, and the two engage in a theologically charged discussion. First, she expresses her views that had Jesus been in Bethany, Lazarus would not have died, and that even now God would give Jesus what he asks (11:21-22). Jesus does promise that her brother will rise again (11:23), but Martha understands his comment to be a reference to the "resurrection at the last day" (11:24). As a correction, Jesus makes a self-revelatory statement: "I am the resurrection and the life; he who believes in me, though he die, yet shall he live, and whoever lives and believes in me shall never die. Do you believe this?" (11:25-26). The climax occurs with Martha's ensuing confession: "Yes, Lord; I believe that you are the Christ, the son of God, he who is coming into the world" (11:27).

The narrative now turns to the meeting between Jesus and Mary. Upon hearing from Martha that Jesus had called for her (11:28), Mary rose, presumably from her mourning, and went to meet him outside the village; she was followed by the Jewish friends who had been consoling her (11:29-31). The gospel recounts her mournful reproach: "Lord, if you had been here, my brother would not have died" (11:32). Unlike Martha, Mary makes no further statement regarding Jesus or his powers. Neither does Jesus respond to her directly; rather, followed by Mary (11:45), Martha (11:39), and the crowd (11:45) he immediately heads toward the tomb. Over Martha's practical objection (11:39), he has the stone removed from the entrance to the tomb (11:41) and, after a brief, audible prayer (11:42), he calls Lazarus forth (11:43-44). The remainder of the chapter recounts the responses of the Jewish witnesses to the sign (11:45) as well as that of the Jewish authorities (11:47-53) in a manner which emphasizes the impending passion.

Before offering our own literary analysis and historical reconstruction of the Johannine Martha and Mary, it will be instructive to look briefly at three other studies. Each finds particular details to be

---

[45]This pattern is similar to that in 2:1-11 and 4:48-54. See my "Great Expectations" for discussion and bibliography.

of interpretive significance, and each provides a different perspective on both the *Sitz-im-Leben* of the passage and the nature of Martha's confession.

The first study is that of Raymond E. Brown, who appended an article entitled "Roles of Women in the Fourth Gospel" to his *The Community of the Beloved Disciple*.[46] Brown's purpose was to examine the Johannine evidence pertinent to the contemporary debate about the role of women in the church.[47] Although he does not exclude the strong possibility that the fourth gospel represents an early, possibly historical tradition,[48] he regards the Johannine women characters primarily as representative of the situation in the evangelist's community.

Brown focuses on two narrative details: the note in 11:3 that Jesus loved Mary and Martha; and the conversation between Martha and Jesus in 11:25-27. He claims that the description of the sisters as beloved of Jesus associates them with the Johannine disciple par excellence, the Beloved Disciple.[49] Though they are not equal to this male figure, the women are nevertheless considered to be true disciples.[50] This point is reinforced by Jesus' revelation of his mystery to Martha (11:25-26).[51] Her confessional response indicates that she has both understood his words properly and reached a level of true faith.[52] The parallel between Martha's confession here and that of Peter in Mt 16:16, in Brown's view, exemplifies the fourth evangelist's deliberate tendency to give women a role traditionally associated with Peter.[53] This portrayal of Martha as a near equal to the Beloved Disciple and the synoptic Peter is for Brown a clue to the status of women in the Johannine community. He suggests that women were seen as recipients of revelation and therefore were esteemed members of the church. He does not, however, draw any conclusions with respect to women's position in the community's authority structure.

---

[46](New York, Paulist, 1979), 183-98; the essay was first published in *TS* 36 (1975): 688-99.
[47]Ibid., 183, 185.
[48]Ibid., 185 n. 328.
[49]Ibid., 191.
[50]Ibid.
[51]Ibid.
[52]Ibid., 190. Here he has apparently revised the opinion expressed in *Gospel*, 434, that Martha's confession expresses a similar outlook to that of the Samaritan woman, i.e., a developing but still partial faith.
[53]*Community*, 190. Brown notes that the evangelist takes special care to do so. We may ask, however, how we can tell this to be the case. Do we see John's construction as deliberate because we expect he would most naturally give these roles to men?

Brown's perspective is shared in some respects by Schüssler Fiorenza, who discusses the Johannine account in her article on Luke 10.[54] Like Brown, she uses the reference to Jesus' love for the sisters in 11:3 to suggest that they should be grouped along with the Beloved Disciple as disciples of Jesus.[55] Further, she too considers Martha's words in 11:27 to be a full christological confession comparable to that of Peter in Mt 16:16.[56] But Schüssler Fiorenza goes beyond Brown in considering many more details of the pericope and in suggesting that the narrative reflects the role of women as leaders in the Johannine community. In her description of the sisters as full disciples, for example, Schüssler Fiorenza compares Martha's call of Mary (11:28) with Andrew and Philip's call of Peter and Nathanael (1:35-51). In my view, however, this comparison is inappropriate, since the two situations differ in one important manner. Whereas Peter and Nathanael made their first contacts with Jesus through Andrew and Philip and then became disciples as a consequence of that contact, Mary is clearly already a disciple prior to being called by Martha (cf. 11:3). Hence Martha's words to her sister are not a call to discipleship but a literary device designed to introduce the next narrative segment.[57]

In similar fashion, Schüssler Fiorenza takes the narrator's comment in 11:31, 45 that the Jews who had been consoling Mary followed her out of the house as indicating that she had followers among her people who then came to believe in Jesus.[58] This reading implies that their following had something to do with Mary's leadership. But this theory is not borne out by the text, which states that those who believed did so because they witnessed the raising of Lazarus (11:45).

Finally, for Schüssler Fiorenza, Martha's confession is evidence that she had become the spokesperson for John's christological emphases: "Martha represents the full apostolic faith of the Johannine community just as Peter does for the Matthean community."[59] The implication is that Martha would have been seen by the community as a leader among the disciples, although Schüssler Fiorenza does not state whether this is in rivalry to or partnership

---

[54]"Lk. 10:38-42."
[55]Ibid., 32.
[56]Ibid., 31.
[57]Brown, *Gospel*, 435, comments that the entire scene in 11:28-33 does not really advance the story and, indeed, seems rather artificial.
[58]Schüssler Fiorenza, "Lk. 10:38-42," 32.
[59]Ibid., 31.

with the Beloved Disciple.[60] In conclusion, Schüssler Fiorenza contrasts the Johannine passage favorably with Luke's account. She
argues that John's portrait of Mary and Martha as disciples and
community leaders "indicates how women might have appealed to
the leadership of women in order to legitimate their own ministry
and authority."[61]

Unlike Schüssler Fiorenza and Brown, Witherington situates
some elements of the story (e.g., Martha's rudimentary confession,
Jesus' self-proclamation, the general outline of the sisters' encounter with Jesus) in the *Sitz-im-Leben* of Jesus, although he acknowledges that other details, including the resurrection of Lazarus, may
be redactional.[62] Witherington too sees 11:3 as evidence that Mary
and Martha were disciples of Jesus,[63] but his analysis differs from
that of Brown and Schüssler Fiorenza in its evaluation of Martha's
confession. According to Witherington, the Johannine Martha sincerely believes in Jesus and has faith in his power, but she does not
come to a full confession of faith. Although 11:27 is the most complete confession encountered thus far in the narrative,[64] it falls
short in that it does not go beyond the "orthodox Pharisaic view of
resurrection on the last day."[65] For Witherington, the portrayal of
Martha therefore conveys the message that women have a right to
be taught even the mysteries of the faith and that they are capable of
responding in faith with an accurate, if incomplete, confession.
Hence they are also capable of being disciples of Jesus.[66] In contrast
to Martha, he argues, Mary is not portrayed here in a sympathetic
or favorable manner. She is simply presented as a grieving woman

---

[60]Despite the high regard shown here for Martha, the fourth evangelist still
sees the Beloved Disciple as primary. Though the Disciple makes no full confession — indeed, he says little in the narrative — he is closely aligned with
Jesus throughout the second half of the gospel whereas Mary and Martha
appear only in two chapters.
[61]Ibid., 32
[62]Witherington, *Women*, 106.
[63]Ibid., 108.
[64]Witherington in Ibid., 108-9, concedes that Martha's confession exceeds
that of Peter in chapter 6, though it is unclear to me why he sees this as
ironic.
[65]Witherington in ibid., makes this judgment on literary-critical grounds: "It
is possible that the Evangelist has constructed his Gospel so that alongside
the crescendo of the miraculous, we have a crescendo of confessions. This
would mean that Martha's confession takes on new importance because of its
place in the climactic episode of the series of signs." Hence Thomas's
confession would be the best of all, though it is accompanied by a critique
voiced by the Johannine Jesus himself (cf. 20:29).
[66]Ibid., 109. But Witherington is silent as to whether they might also have
held positions of leadership. Perhaps his apologetic concerns simply prevent
him from considering this as a possibility. Cf. ibid., 117-18.

who points an accusatory finger at Jesus and thereby betrays an attitude of hopelessness and lack of trust.[67]

Behind the varied claims of these three studies lies a common picture of Mary and Martha as disciples, a picture which implies that women were fully accepted as members — and, if Schüssler Fiorenza is correct, even as leaders — in the Johannine community. There are two elements of the passage, however, which this picture omits: the literary technique used by the evangelist to create an impact on the reader and to deepen christological understanding; and the narrative clues which pertain to the place of these women within the Jewish community of Bethany. To these points we now turn.

Our discussion of Lk 10:38-42 noted that the exchange between Martha and Jesus serves to frustrate and then modify certain expectations of the evangelist's implied readers with regard to their understanding of discipleship. The same technique is at work in the conversation between Jesus and Martha conveyed in Jn 11:25-27. Here Martha's first words articulate her expectations concerning Jesus' love of Lazarus and his ability to heal him. That these expressions are echoed by Mary and by the Jewish crowds suggests that they were seen by the evangelist as characteristic also of his implied audience. Jewish in origin, these views were apparently held by those who were already Christians, since Mary and Martha are themselves Christians when they articulate them.

However, these expectations are frustrated not only by Jesus' words concerning resurrection but also by his tarrying instead of responding immediately to the sisters' invocation. The inappropriateness of his response in itself challenges the expectations of the reader, and Jesus' comment to Martha in 11:25-26 serve to modify and correct them. Martha, and probably the implied audience as well, impute to Jesus the power to raise the dead at the last day and so imply a straightforward future eschatology. But Jesus' response asserts that she has misunderstood: resurrection is not future but present. This assertion is then demonstrated dramatically and forcefully by the resurrection of Lazarus. Martha's desire to see her brother alive has been realized magnificently, although not in the way she had imagined. Where she asked for healing, Jesus provided resurrection.

---

[67]Ibid., 109. While it is true that Mary is not as important in the narrative as Martha is, Witherington's comment goes beyond what is warranted by the text. In fact, the seemingly imbalanced treatment of the sisters is corrected in the first pericope of the next chapter: there Mary, not Martha, is central to narrative interests (12:1-7).

There is yet another important element to their conversation.
Jesus' correction of Martha's christological understanding is immediately followed by her confession. She believes what Jesus has just
told her, though she as yet lacks empirical evidence that his assertions are true. Like the nobleman whose son is healed (cf. 4:44ff.),
her belief is prior to the accomplishment of the sign. The sequence
gains significance in light of Jesus' later remark to Thomas: "Have
you believed because you have seen me? Blessed are those who have
not seen and yet believe" (20:29). This analogy settles the question of
whether Martha's confession is rudimentary or profound. While her
balking at the tomb might suggest otherwise,[68] her willingness to
base her faith on Jesus' words implies that she is indeed one of the
blessed. As in the Lukan passage, so here the attribution of a high
confession to Martha would have served both to modify the expectations of the readers — women and men — and to legitimate the right
of women to be active in the church.

To this point in our historical-critical study we have placed
Martha and Mary primarily in the context of the early Christian
community; very little has been said about their own historical context. This silence is appropriate with respect to the Lukan passage
which, pace Witherington, says nothing about them as Jewish
women.[69] The situation is different, however, for Jn 11:1-44. In this
passage the sisters are apparently engaged in the traditional
mourning rites of first-century Palestine.[70] Further, they are con-
soled by the members of their community, and these fellow Jews
show no inclination to distance themselves from the mourners
when Jesus arrives. The observation that Jewish believers in the
Christ were part of the general Jewish community counters the
impression created by 9:22, which has tended to overshadow the
discussion of the relationship between the church and the synagogue in the evangelist's own *Sitz-im-Leben*.[71] In 9:22 the narrator
states that "the Jews had already agreed that if anyone should

---

[68]Witherington in ibid., 108, takes 11:35 to be a sign that her faith is not
complete. Nevertheless, the narrative sequence in John 11 follows closely
that of Mt 16, in which Peter also follows his confession with a comment
(16:22) which casts doubt on the fullness of his understanding. He is then
clearly rebuked by the Matthean Jesus (16:23).
[69]The very placement of this story within the ministry of Jesus would seem to
imply there was a Jewish context.
[70]For discussion of Jewish mourning practices in the Second Temple period,
see Emanuel Feldman, *Biblical and Post-Biblical Defilement and Mourning:
Law as Theology* (New York: KTAV, 1977), and S. Safrai and S. Stern, *The
Jewish People in the First Century*, CRINT II (Philadelphia: Fortress, 1976),
774-75, 781-85.
[71]See Martyn, *History and Theology*, 37-62; Brown, *Gospel*, 380.

confess [Jesus] to be the Christ, he was to be put out of the synagogue." Although it is possible that Jews may have come simply out
of kindness to console even those mourners who had been excluded
from the synagogue, this seems a far-fetched way of avoiding the
contradiction. Whether we seek an explanation for the contradiction
or add it to the list of Johannine narrative difficulties, we may at
least conclude that in the time of Jesus, if not of the evangelist, there
were women disciples who were integrated into their Jewish communities.

As in our analysis of Lk 10:38-42, the picture which emerges
from the portrayal of Mary and Martha in Jn 11:1-44 corresponds
to the two levels on which the narrative may be read. The passage
depicts Mary and Martha as Jewish women who live independently
with their brother in Bethany. Fully integrated into the Jewish
community, they nevertheless have a close enough relationship
with Jesus to call on him in time of trouble. Furthermore, at least
one of them, Martha, has a rather sophisticated understanding of
his identity and his significance for those who believe in him. But the
evangelist apparently writes not only to record an important event
in the life of Jesus but also to speak directly to his audience. In using
Martha to represent a true disciple who attains the profound
understanding of resurrection that he wishes his community to
share, the evangelist also is creating a strong role model for the
women members of the church. Such a model authenticates both
their membership as women and their right — like Martha's — to
"ask whatever you will, and it shall be done for you" (Jn 15:7).

John 12:1-7

We conclude our study with a brief look at Jn 12:1-7, which
immediately follows the raising of Lazarus. In this scene Mary
anoints Jesus at her home in Bethany, six days before his final
Passover (12:1).[72] The occasion was a dinner in Jesus' honor at
which Martha served (12:2). Mary silently "took a pint of costly ointment of pure nard and anointed the feet of Jesus and wiped his feet
with her hair" (12:3). For this act she is criticized by Judas, who
complains sanctimoniously, "Why was this ointment not sold for
three hundred denarii and given to the poor?" (12:5). But Jesus,
defending Mary, responds "Let her alone, let her keep it for the day
of my burial. The poor you always have with you, but you do not

---

[72]For a comparison of the various anointing scenes, see Witherington,
Women, 110; Schüssler Fiorenza, *Criteria*, 3; and esp. Brown, *Gospel*, 449-54.

always have me" (12:6-7).

Elisabeth Schüssler Fiorenza discusses this passage briefly because it provides a counterpoint to her study of Lk 10:38-42. She notes that for John, in contrast to Luke, Mary is not the opposite of Martha but the counterpart to Judas; the true female disciple is an alternative to the unfaithful male disciple.[73] Her act both prepares Jesus for his burial and anticipates his command that the disciples wash each other's feet as a sign of the "agape praxis of true discipleship."[74] Hence Mary, like her sister in the preceding pericope, is a model for female leadership in the Johannine community.[75]

Ben Witherington III, like Schüssler Fiorenza, sees Mary's anointing of Jesus as a prophetic act. From this evidence, he concludes that the gospel writers may be implying that early Christian women legitimately assumed the role or tasks of a prophet.[76] His analysis differs from that of Schüssler Fiorenza in that he sees continuity, not contrast, between the Lukan and Johannine accounts: the Johannine sisters too are seen as having been liberated from the shackles of their Jewish past. Mary demonstrates this liberation by letting down her hair in the presence of men to whom she was not related, an act that, according to Witherington, was considered scandalous.[77] Martha's serving at table in mixed company, an act that violates the rules of Jewish practice, constitutes evidence of her liberation. She performs the function of a free servant to honor the one in whom she believes. "Liberty in Christ is not only freedom from customs which restrict love, but also freedom to take a lower place, to humble oneself to serve."[78]

Witherington has read into his treatment of the Johannine pericope the theme of liberation from Jewish mores as he did in his discussing of Lk 10:38-42. But neither the content nor the context of Jn 12:1-7 provides any hint of this theme. Witherington's comparison of this passage with the Lukan story is on firmer ground. In both cases, Martha — functioning as the head of the household — serves at table while Mary engages in acts of devotion and discipleship. In Jn 12:1-7, however, there is no rivalry between the two sisters; furthermore, Mary's acts in the Johannine passage go beyond

---

[73]"Lk. 10:38-42," 32.
[74]Ibid.
[75]Ibid.
[76]Witherington, *Women*, 115. Witherington agrees with Brown that this possibly gave precedent for women to become deaconesses.
[77]Witherington's main source for this appears to be Jeremias, although he cites two rabbinic sources in English translation. Ibid., 113, 194 n. 209.
[78]Ibid., 112. This exaltation of traditional female roles comports well with

the listening and learning of Lk 10:38-42 both to encompass prophetic elements and to provide a foil for Judas.[79]

Finally, with respect to context, the juxtaposed Johannine passages are among the last, climactic scenes of Jesus' ministry as well as key elements that advance the plot toward the all-important passion narrative. It is consequently not only the particular roles ascribed to Martha and Mary in the fourth gospel but also the crucial juncture at which they appear that compels us to take them seriously both as characters and as vehicles for Johannine theology. In portraying Mary and Martha in acts of serving and anointing, Jn 12:1-7, like the other pericopes we have explored, presents the sisters as disciples. That they hosted a dinner for Jesus, at which others of his inner circle were present, implies that the sisters or women like them were also part of, or close to, this inner circle. Regardless of its historicity, the account would have served to affirm the full membership of women in all aspects of the Johannine community.

Conclusions

Our attempts to resurrect Martha and Mary from their narrative resting places have resulted not in a single picture of each sister, but in a multiplicity of images. The differences among these images are primarily due to the varying perspectives of the scholars who re-created them. Witherington, despite his concession that the Johannine anointing story may impute leadership positions to women, concludes that the account upholds the status quo. In his view, the unique feature of Jesus' women followers is that:[80]

> the traditional roles of hospitality and service are seen by them as a way to serve not only the physical family but the family of faith. Being Jesus' disciples did not lead these women to abandon their traditional roles in regard to preparing food, serving, etc. Rather, it gave these roles new significance and importance, for now they could be used to serve the Master and the family of faith. The transformation of these women involved not only assuming new discipleship roles, but also resuming their traditional roles for a new purpose.

The tone of this and many other sections of his book implies that modern Christian women should be satisfied with these roles as

---

Witherington's apologetic motives. See ibid., 117-18.
[79]Brown, *Gospel*, 435, points out that Mary is always at Jesus' feet.
[80]Witherington, *Women*, 118.

well.

This is a view which Schüssler Fiorenza emphatically rejects.[81] Instead, she declares:[82]

> A hermeneutics of remembrance can show that both Luke and the Fourth Gospel reflect the struggle of early Christian women against patriarchal restrictions of women's leadership and ministry at the turn of the first century. ... The critical exploration of the literary dynamics of Lk. 10:38-42 has shown that the androcentric tendencies of traditional and contemporary interpretations are not completely read into the text, but that they are generated by the text. Even a feminist interpretation that is interested in defending the story as positive for women perpetuates the androcentric dualism and patriarchal prejudice inherent in the original story. This text is patriarchal because it reinforces the societal and ecclesiastical polarization of women. Its proclamation denigrates women's work while at the same time insisting that housework and hospitality are women's proper roles. ... We ought to be not only good disciples but also good hostesses, not only good minsters but also good housewives, not only well-paid professionals but also glamorous lovers.

This does not mean that patriarchal texts cannot be used in preaching and teaching. Rather, since "women and men have internalized the androcentric and patriarchal tendencies of this text as the word of God, Bible studies and sermons must critically explore its oppressive functions and implications."[83]

More difficult than identifying the views, assumptions and contemporary concerns which shape such reconstructions of Mary and Martha is labelling one's own. No doubt mine have already been discerned by many readers. First, as a woman scholar, I am fascinated by the opportunity to imagine women back into a period of history in which their presence has often been ignored, forgotten, or overshadowed. I here stress the element of imagination, not only because of the paucity of the evidence, but also because of the difficulties which are inherent in any attempt to do historical reconstruction on the basis of narrative alone.[84] I am more confident in our

---

[81]In *Criteria*, 5, she expresses this directly by questioning the "scholarly" nature of Witherington's book and deploring its publication in a distinguished New Testament series.

[82]Schüssler Fiorenza, "Lk. 10:38-42," 32-33.

[83]Ibid., 33.

[84]For a discussion of the "historical imagination" and its central role in the

ability to say something about Martha and Mary as literary representations than as historical figures.

Second, unlike Witherington, Brown, and Schüssler Fiorenza, I am not Christian but Jewish. These texts do not undergird the theology or social structure of my religious community, nor can they be used for feminist critique and the empowerment of women within that community. What does concern me is the manner in which the New Testament, the Mary and Martha stories included, has been used to legitimate anti-Jewish attitudes and a supercessionist theology. While I am concerned about the roles of women within the Jewish community and can offer a critique of their ambiguous portrayal in Judaism's foundational documents, I deplore superficial and apologetically motivated attempts to demonstrate the superiority of Christianity to Judaism on the basis of the respective roles they accord women.

In evaluating the process of historical reconstruction attempted above, we must consider whether we have in fact resurrected Martha and Mary from their fixed places in the gospel texts. Have we been able to move from literary analysis to historical reconstruction of the sisters on the one hand, and of the first-century women who read and heard about them on the other? The answer, despite the hesitations expressed in this paper, seem to be a qualified yes, that is, as long as certain assumptions are maintained.

To reconstruct the sisters as historical figures, we must assume that the third and fourth gospels bear witness to an early and authentic tradition. Since the portraits are for the most part complementary, we can with some imagination create a composite picture of two sisters living with their brother Lazarus near Bethany. Martha, the head of the household, and possibly the elder sister, has charge of such duties as greeting visitors and preparing and serving meals; however, she expects her younger sister to help. The three siblings have come to believe that Jesus is the messiah, although they continue to develop in their understanding of his message. As disciples, they are confident of his affection for them, and consequently they do not hesitate to ask him for help or to organize social functions in his honor. This latter function may indicate their presence in his inner circle as well as their leadership and influence over others outside the circle. Moreover, although their allegiance to Jesus is no secret, they are fully integrated into the Jewish community of Bethany, and they rely on and benefit from

process of historical reconstruction, see Brooten, "Early Christian Women," 67-69.

that community's emotional support in times of need. It is not therefore inconceivable that their example may have influenced other Jews in Bethany to follow Jesus as well.

The evangelists told their tales not to address women only but to deepen the theological understanding of all readers. Nevertheless, women readers in the early church especially would likely have identified with Martha and Mary. For these readers, the sisters may have demonstrated the possibility that women independent of male supporters such as fathers and husbands could be active in the world. In addition, they may have affirmed the activity of women not only in the rank and file of the church but also in its inner circle of authority. Finally, Martha and Mary may have been seen as models of integration, according to which it was possible for women to view their belief in the Christ and active participation in the church as compatible with, and complementary to, other important elements of their lives.

This highly tentative reconstruction requires, in addition to many assumptions, an active historical imagination. Nevertheless, it seems that the process of which this double-focussed and rather blurry picture is the result may indeed lead to new insights, not only about the history of the early church but also about the narratives — their implied authors, their theological and social agendas, and their literary ploys — from which we try to recreate that history.

Women in the Third Gospel
and the New Testament Apocrypha

Stevan Davies

Until recently I thought it possible to make the case that the Gospel of Luke and the Acts of the Apostles were written by a woman.[1] Along with many scholars, I assumed both that the two-volume work advocated raising the social status of women and that the third evangelist presented Jesus as showing exceptional concern for women. In the effort to creating a convincing case, however, the whole house of cards collapsed. Indeed, together with the unstable peak of the house, its base — my set of assumptions about Luke's particular concern for women — crumbled as well. Not only do I no longer think Luke can be shown to have been a woman (although she may nevertheless have been one), I no longer believe that Luke can be shown either to have been intent on presenting Jesus as particularly sympathetic to women or to have encouraged the liberation of women in any significant sense.

The Elevation of Women's Status

To speak of a text's showing sympathy for a category of person or striving to effect the liberation of an apparently marginal group, one's analysis must meet certain methodological criteria. Specifically, if an author advocated the elevation of a particular class from subjugation, then one would expect to find in the literary product evidence of both the subjugation and the liberation. Should it be claimed that the subjugation is so obvious that it requires no demonstration (e.g., we know that women could not enter certain areas of the Jerusalem Temple), then its obvious presence should be evident from contemporary texts or from common human experience. For example, one does not need to prove for Luke the poor had a more limited opportunity than the rich to acquire the necessities of life. One does, however, need to demonstrate that Luke portrayed Jesus as speaking sympathetically of the poor as such, and that Luke further portrayed him as seeking to change their situation. This proof is easily established through gospel material such as

---

[1] Cf. Leonard Swidler, *Biblical Affirmations of Women* (Philadelphia: Westminster, 1979), 161-93, 278-81, who argues that "proto-Luke" was probably compiled by a woman.

1:52-53; 6:20-26; 19:1-10; etc.

In the case of women no subjugation is stated or implied. Luke depicts women, without needing Jesus' intervention, as self-reliant. The widow who demands justice from the unjust judge eventually achieves her goal (18:1-8); Anna, Elizabeth, and Mary the mother of Jesus act independently and with self-confidence; and so forth. There is no specialized motif here; rather, Luke simply presents the common view that women are capable people. Although some assert "that Luke will stress again and again that women are among the oppressed that Jesus came to liberate,"[2] this assumption, unsupported by the evangelist's specific mention of women's oppression and liberation, must be termed erroneous.

It might be argued from Lk 10:38-42 that Jesus' approval of Mary's listening in contradistinction to Martha's objections is a liberation of women from the role of men's domestic servers and to the role of diligent learners. To make this claim, however, one must generalize from a single case to a class and from a single instance to a theme. One must dismiss from serious consideration the fact that it is another woman who objects to Mary's listening role; one must overlook the fact that listening to a man is far from an unusual or liberated role for a woman; and one must regard as irrelevant the fact that in each of the gospels Jesus speaks publicly to crowds of male *and female* listeners. Moreover, one needs to determine whether Luke's Jesus is approving "listening" or, specifically, "women listening." That is, were the characters Jacob and Joshua, the point of the story would be unchanged. Some have argued that for Jesus, a rabbi, to have taught women would be an exception to traditional and so expected practice.[3] This argument, based in part tendentiously on evidence adduced from the substantially later Mishnaic literature (which itself represents a much different cultural context), would hold only if it were also true that Luke portrays Jesus primarily as a rabbi or, in less technical terms, as a teacher and sage. This is not the case. The evangelist depicts Jesus as a wonder-worker (Acts 2:22; 10:38) and a spirit-inspired prophet (Lk 4:14-22). Unless it can be shown that such charismatic individuals normally refused to instruct women, then the portrait drawn in the corpus simply reflects reality as Luke knew it.

---

[2]Ben Witherington III, *Women in the Earliest Churches* (SNTSMS 59; Cambridge: University Press, 1988), 128.
[3]Cf. Swidler, *Biblical Affirmations*, 154-57, who appeals particularly to *m. Sotah* 3:4; Constance Parvey, "Women in the New Testament," in R. R. Ruether (ed.), *Religion and Sexism* (New York: Simon and Schuster, 1974), 141-42.

To a greater or lesser degree[4] the evangelist seems to have a dim view of marriage: "Wives" are added to lists from Mark (18:29) and Q (14:26) of those whom itinerant disciples are to desert; all identifiable women who prophesy (Jesus' mother, Anna, Philip's virgin daughters) are unmarried or widowed; divorce is permitted (Luke deletes Mk 10:1-9); remarriage after divorce is forbidden (16:18). Women who follow Jesus (8:2-3) are not accompanied by their husbands, and one — Joanna, the wife of Herod's steward Chuza — may have deserted her husband (given that she had been possessed by demons, he may not have regarded her desertion as much of a loss).

The combined social effect of encouraging men to desert their wives, of approving of women who travel unaccompanied by their husbands, and of permitting divorce while forbidding divorced women to be remarried is that the number of socially marginal if not destitute women will increase. This is an effect one intent on elevating women's social status would not wish to achieve. Yet even the admonition that male disciples should desert their wives is sometimes taken to reflect "Luke's interest in and concern for women."[5]

I see no elevation of women's status in Luke. Unless one presumes the society of the time to be pathological to the extent that women were regarded as despised,[6] disreputable, beyond the pale of respectable society,[7] and so forth (as some scholars do although Luke, Mark, Matthew, Paul, John, Josephus, etc., do not), then Jesus' actions in regard to women are nothing unusual. One might even go so far as to argue that Luke intentionally suppressed information which would have encouraged women's assumption of leadership roles in the church. Elisabeth Schüssler Fiorenza writes that Luke "mentions women prophets and the conversion of rich women but does not tell us any instance of a woman missionary or leader of the church. He seems to know of such functions of women, as his references to Prisca or Lydia indicate, but this knowledge does not influence his portrayal of early Christian history."[8] If Luke's Jesus liberates women from anything, he liberates them

---

[4]Depending on whether one believes Luke 20:34-38 applies to those who, while living, are "accounted worthy" or whether the verses apply only to those who have died.

[5]Witherington, *Earliest Churches*, 129.

[6]Werner Georg Kümmel, *Introduction to the New Testament* (Nashville: Abingdon, 1975), 139.

[7]Joseph Fitzmyer, *The Gospel According to Luke I-IX* (AB 28; New York: Doubleday, 1981), 192.

[8]*Memory*, 50.

from what Luke explicitly notes he liberates them from: demonic possession (4:39; 8:2-3; 13:10-13).

Jesus' Exceptional Concern for Women

If Luke sought to portray Jesus as acting in an exceptional way towards women, then the text should tell us that Jesus' actions were regarded as exceptional. The gospel will explicitly state either what its author thought exceptional, or what the author thought Jesus' contemporaries would have thought to be exceptional. If Jesus' behavior is to be regarded as obviously anomalous, then either contemporary texts or general human experience must support the assertion. It is, for example, clear that Jesus' claim to have the power to forgive sins is considered exceptional, for Luke so informs the reader. Further, one may conclude from general human experience that Jesus' resurrection is not in the normal course of events.

The third gospel informs us that, as he did with men, Jesus healed women, included women in his audience, accepted them as followers, forgave their sins, used them as characters in parables. However, not gynocentric proclivities but Jesus' divinely given capacities are Luke's point (Acts 10:36-39). One may justly conclude that Jesus therefore generally dealt with men and women on an equal basis. Yet this conclusion is trivial unless it can be shown that a prophetic wonder-worker of the time would normally have acted otherwise, and this has never been shown.

Moreover, Jesus' relationship to women is never shown to be thought odd by anyone, except Martha. When Luke adds to Mark's account the story of a handicapped, possessed woman (13:10-17), the peculiarity of the incident is that Jesus healed the woman *on the Sabbath*, not that he healed *a woman* (cf. 14:1-4). Luke adds the story of the sinful woman (7:36-50), but the character's remarkable feature is not that she was *a woman*, but that she was *sinful*: onlookers find it odd that Jesus would let himself be anointed by a sinner (cf. 5:17-26).

One might adduce the datum of the gospel's paired passages featuring a man and a woman respectively to assert Luke's concern for women.[9] But more obvious motives should take precedence. For example, one of Luke's christological perspectives is that Jesus is a prophet in the manner of Elijah or Elisha.[10] Jesus' introductory

---

[9]Witherington, *Earliest Churches*, 129; Swidler, *Biblical Affirmations*, 181.
[10]Fitzmyer, *Luke I-IX*, 213-15; Craig Evans, "Luke's Use of the Elijah/Elisha Narratives and the Ethic of Election," *JBL* 106.1 (1987): 75-83; R. E. Brown,

sermon in Nazareth is evidence for this claim, and from that sermon one might expect Jesus to raise the son of a widow as did Elijah and to heal a leper as did Elisha.[11] Luke does add to Mark a story of the raising of a widow's son (7:11-17) similar to 1 Kings 17:17-24, and the story of Jesus' healing of ten men with leprosy (17:12-19). Thus the pericope depicting the widow of Nain cannot to be adduced as evidence of the evangelist's concern for women in general or widows in particular; it is primarily an attestation of Jesus' likeness to Elijah.

Luke follows Mark (and may have adopted the technique from Mark) in pairing the healings of a man and a woman (Lk 4:33-39// Mk 1:23-31). The third evangelist adopts from Q a saying which reiterates its message with examples appropriate to both sexes (17:34-35): the parable of the shepherd (15:1-7) is reinforced by the parable of the woman with the lost coin (15:8-10); quite possibly, however, this pair was originally in Q.[12] Luke thus does nothing different from Mark in pairing stories and nothing different from Q in reiterating points using first one and then the other sex.

Luke once more than Mark indicates that women accompanied Jesus from Galilee to Jerusalem (8:2-3), but their following him is not a specifically Lukan motif. The third evangelist adopted it from Mark, and neither they nor Matthew indicate that anyone found the women's presence odd. Mark shows Jesus teaching his disciples about his prospective resurrection (Mk 8:27-33); since Luke understands "disciples" to be Jesus' followers of either sex, then — if Jesus had women followers (as Mark claims), and if Jesus taught his disciples — Jesus taught the women among them as well as the men. Luke's report in 24:6-9 that Jesus revealed his future to women does not aggrandize them, for they evidently forgot this teaching. Rather, it reiterates at a crucial time that Jesus predicted the passion and resurrection. Mark's account (14:3-9) of the woman who anticipates the resurrection and so proleptically anoints his body for burial, an action for which she is enthusiastically praised, Luke deletes.

Regarding Luke's affirmations of the virtues of Jesus' mother, in a convincing study, Brown et al. conclude that Luke's "interest was not primarily in Mary as a person but in Mary as a symbol of

---

"Jesus and Elisha," *Perspective* 12 (1971): 85-104.

[11]One might further expect that the widow and the leper would not dwell in the land of Israel, but, since Luke depicts Jesus as coming first to Jews, this expectation is unmet.

[12]J. Lambrecht, *Once More Astonished: The Parable of Jesus* (New York: Crossroad, 1981): 24-56, cited in *Memory*, 131.

discipleship."[13] Luke specifies, in a passage found in no other canonical gospel, that Mary's role as Jesus' mother is no reason to hold her in high regard: "A woman in the crowd raised her voice and said to him, 'Blessed is the womb that bore you, and the breasts that you sucked!' But he said, 'Blessed rather are those who hear the word of God and keep it'" (11:27-28). It is Mary's discipleship that receives praise, not her motherhood, and the content of her discipleship is to hear and to obey. Thus, she and her sons are evidently among those praised as people who "hear the word of God and do it" (8:21). The "word of God" which she obeys is, in turn, simply "the message transmitted by Luke's book."

If we may conclude with Brown and his colleagues that Mary is a symbol of discipleship, particularly the discipleship of women, then the nature of that discipleship is clear. Women are to hear and obey. One might hope for more from an author credited with being exceptionally sympathetic to or concerned with the liberation of women. Apart from these two tasks, the only specific role women have in the mission of Jesus is to provide financing (8:2-3). In turn, the third gospel devalues both their biological role (11:27-28, cf. 23:29: "Behold, the days are coming when they will say, 'Blessed are the barren, and the wombs that never bore, and the breasts that never gave suck'") as well as their primary social role, namely, being wives.

Judging by the fact that none of the characters in the gospel takes Jesus' actions toward women to be out of the ordinary, one cannot argue that Luke sought to show that Jesus had an extraordinarily positive attitude toward women. Furthermore, no such extraordinary attitude can be inferred from our knowledge of the status of women in the society of the time. There is a simple solution to the problem of why Luke's gospel contains more stories about women than the others: Luke was writing for an audience wherein women were numerous. Points made regarding men are also made in regard to women, but not to insist that women could be taught, healed, forgiven or that they were among Jesus' followers (all this is assumed in Luke's own sources). Rather, the evangelist seeks to capture the attention of the female portion of the audience.[14] And Luke's competence in writing to engage the attention of his audience has recently been exhaustively demonstrated.[15]

---

[13]Raymond E. Brown et al. (eds.), *Mary in the New Testament* (Philadelphia: Fortress, 1978), 162.
[14]Parvey, "Women in the New Testament," 140-42, suggests this as well.
[15]Richard I. Pervo, *Profit With Delight: The Literary Genre of the Acts of the*

Luke/Acts and the Apocryphal Acts: Points on a Trajectory

In a recent study, Richard Pervo argues persuasively that the Acts of the Apostles should be considered an historical novel akin to ancient romances rather than an attempt to write history.[16] Further, he shows both that in style and literary quality the Acts of the Apostles are comparable to the Apocryphal Acts and that "the literary disparity that exists between the various Apocryphal Acts and between Acts and the Apocryphal Acts is not so great as that among the romantic novels."[17] Regarding Luke's gospel, Pervo generally remains silent. Nevertheless, the last page of his book refers the reader to a footnote which observes: "Because my study has concentrated upon the various Acts, I have not taken the genre of [the Gospel of] Luke into question, apart from noting some differences between Luke and Acts. 'Biographical novel' may be an appropriate characterization of the Gospel type."[18] If one takes the genre of Luke's first volume into question when following Pervo's argument, it is clear that his points made in regard to Acts and their kinship to ancient novels, both pagan and Christian, apply well to the gospel narrative.

The overall similarities between Apocryphal Acts and Luke's gospel may be obscured by differences in titles; were the Gospel of Luke entitled the "Acts of Jesus," the similarities between the "Acts of Jesus" and the Apocryphal Acts might be more readily apparent. Indeed, if one looks to Luke's own summaries of his "Acts of Jesus" (Acts 2:22-24; 10:37-41), one can see the author has presented more a compendium of tales about a divinely empowered miracle-working martyr than the theologically sophisticated treatise we scholars are trained to read the gospel to be.

I believe for three principal reasons that Luke's "Acts of Jesus" is more akin to the form of the Apocryphal Acts than is the Acts of the Apostles. First, the initial twelve chapters of Acts focus on no single hero. Discrete segments provide accounts of Andrew, Saul/ Paul, Peter, Stephen, Philip, etc. Only the latter sixteen chapters have a single hero: over the course of Acts, the character Paul develops. He is a persecutor of Christians, then the recipient of a vision, next an effective apostle with some difficulties vis-à-vis the Jerusalem church, and finally the prime promulgator of the faith. In the Apocryphal Acts, on the other hand, there is usually one hero

Apostles (Philadelphia: Fortress, 1987).
[16]Ibid.
[17]Ibid., 129.
[18]Ibid., 138 n. 5.

who is flawless from the outset and hence whose character remains static. In the "Acts of Jesus," the only principal character is similarly flawless, and similarly does not develop.

Second, the Apocryphal Acts conclude with lengthy and climactic stories of the martyrdom of their heroes; frequently, this martyrdom is occasioned by the hero's having offended an official by requiring sexual continence of the official's wife. Those women are, at the time of the martyrdom, often the heroes' principal associates.[19] At the conclusion of the Acts of the Apostles, Paul teaches without hindrance in Rome. Conversely, the "Acts of Jesus" concludes with the martyrdom of the hero. Although their presence is not a motive for his opponents, the women in his entourage are mentioned more in the crucifixion account than at any other point in the narrative.

Third, the Apocryphal Acts are replete with stories featuring the excellence of women in general and the difficulties encountered by continent Christian women in particular. The "Acts of Jesus," far more than the Acts of the Apostles, contains stories wherein women play a role even though their roles are far from central to the narrative. The virtues of sexual continence, an obsessive concern of the Apocryphal Acts, are not discussed by Luke. However, if one notes his devaluation of marriage and, further, assumes an opposition to intercourse outside of marriage, an underlying ethic of continence may be inferred. Such a supposition is more difficult to make from the canonical Acts (cf. Acts 18:1-28; 21:5) than from the gospel wherein the only cohabiting married couple are the Baptist's parents. Still, in contradiction to historical fact (I Cor 9:5), the gospel never depicts the apostles as married, and much less as travelling with their wives; neither do the Apocryphal Acts.

Luke's first two chapters, unlike other stories mentioning women in the two volumes, are intriguingly similar to accounts of women found in the Apocryphal Acts. Rather than being incidental characters, Elizabeth and Mary are the focus of attention. Elizabeth acknowledges God's message; Zechariah fails to do so. Mary acknowledges God's message, while Joseph — partly as a consequence of that message — is little more than a cipher. Thus the two women, particularly in light of their response to God, surpass the men to whom they are married or betrothed; the same point is made regarding the heroines of several Apocryphal Acts.[20]

---

[19]Cf. Stevan Davies, *The Revolt of the Widows: The Social World of the Apocryphal Acts* (Carbondale: So. Illinois University, 1980), 50-69.
[20]Ibid.

Scholars have long known that these introductory chapters differ stylistically from the remainder of Luke/Acts, and they have surmised that Lk 3:1-2 may have once been the introduction to the gospel. According to Fitzmyer, it is "imperative to acknowledge the independent character of the infancy narrative and its telltale qualities of a later addition."[21] This observation suggests that "Luke composed his Gospel, beginning with 3:1-2, and having written it (and Acts too, if R. E. Brown's evidence for the dependence of the infancy narrative on Acts is accepted), he composed the infancy narrative."[22] It is possible that Luke wrote the gospel with the partial intent of holding the attention of the women in a mixed congregation, but that the infancy narrative was designed for another audience, one *predominantly* female. Even if this is not the case, the evidence still stands that the first two chapters of the gospel especially foreshadow themes later developed in the Apocryphal Acts.[23]

Luke's two volumes in their entirety are grammatically, doctrinally, and even in terms of word choice similar to the pastorals, and the bond between the works has long been noted.[24] The epistles are designed, in part, to insure that women and especially widows (I Tim 5:3-16) submit to the authority of the male church leaders; Luke implicitly advances a similar view. If Luke's volumes advocate principally that women should hear and obey the word of the Lord as transmitted by men (e.g., Jesus and Paul; i.e., Luke), and if one judges Paul's letters to reveal the existence of women apostles and teachers (whose accomplishments Luke passes over in silence), then the evangelist may be thought to advocate women's having a more subordinate role in the Christian community than the positions some of them formerly enjoyed.[25]

The conflict between Christian men and women that Dennis MacDonald locates beneath the proto-Acts of Paul and the pastorals may to a lesser degree also underlie Luke/Acts. MacDonald makes the case that the tales about Paul and about Thecla which appear in

---

[21]Fitzmyer, *Luke I-IX*, 310.
[22]Ibid., 311; cf. Raymond E. Brown, *The Birth of the Messiah* (New York: Doubleday, 1977), 242-43.
[23]Similarly, Luke 2:40-50 foreshadows the legends written into Apocryphal Infancy Gospels.
[24]See John Drury, *Tradition and Design in Luke's Gospel* (Atlanta: John Knox, 1976), 18, who adds that the connections may even "support theories of common authorship."
[25]*Memory*, 50.

this collection first circulated orally.[26] He concludes that these stories "were 'old wives' tales,' told primarily by celibate women outside the οἰκία, hostile to Rome, and alienated from Asia Minor society."[27] Further, "the author of the Pastoral Epistles knew these stories, knew they were told by women, and knew that there was no more effective way of silencing them by writing in Paul's own name."[28] MacDonald sees the pastorals as a reaction against the women who told such tales about Paul as are preserved in the Acts bearing his name.

The Apocryphal Acts are not concerned with the intra-Christian institutional problems evident in Pastorals. The Acts rather show women accepting the norm of Christian life — i.e., complete sexual continence — because they have heard and obeyed the words of charismatic apostles. Sexual continence is depicted as freeing women from secular male domination based on marital roles. Accordingly, the central conflict is between pagan men wishing to insure that women be subordinate to their individual authority and apostles wanting the same thing. The Acts contain lengthy episodes wherein women who seek Christian excellence are restrained by their husbands and fiancés; they usually conclude with an apostle's martyrdom caused by his insistence that wives should subordinate themselves to his message rather than to that of their husbands. The conflict between husband and apostle is the setting upon which the principal characters make decisions and accept the consequences of those decisions; these principal characters are the women who choose the Christian mode of life. Having so chosen, the women do not remain under the authority of the apostle: the itinerant missionary cannot exercise continuing control.[29] Rather, they are freed from marital authority to enter a lifestyle wherein they rely primarily on one another.[30]

Virginia Burrus observes that the episodes showing women successfully struggling to adopt and maintain sexual continence — episodes she calls "chastity stories" — form the basis of the principal surviving parts of the Acts of Paul, Peter, Andrew, John, and Thomas.[31] She has suggested that women produced and trans-

---

[26]Dennis Ronald MacDonald, *The Legend and the Apostle: The Battle for Paul in Story and Canon* (Philadelphia: Westminster, 1983).
[27]Ibid., 53.
[28]Ibid.
[29]Paul tried to do so by letter, but he seems to have enjoyed only limited success.
[30]Davies, *Revolt*, 110-29.
[31]Virginia Burrus, *Chastity as Autonomy: Women in the Stories of the Apocryphal Acts* (Toronto: Edwin Mellen, 1987).

mitted these stories orally, and she proposes in addition that "(1) the stories originated independently of the Hellenistic romantic novel; (2) the stories emphasize the assertiveness and independence of their heroines; and (3) the stories were most likely oral folkstories told by women and thus reveal aspects of the historical situation of these women."[32] Although their methodologies differ, both Mac-Donald and Burrus use techniques drawn from folklore study, and both reach a similar conclusion: the Apocryphal Acts did not arise solely from the imaginations of the novelists who composed them but originated in oral stories developed and transmitted by women. MacDonald's adventures of Paul and Burrus's chastity stories constitute the majority of the material contained in the surviving sections of the five earliest Apocryphal Acts.

I have argued that the *Acts of Paul* most evidently, and the other four collections also, were probably written for and by Christian women called "widows"; their community memberships included virgins and women who had left their husbands.[33] It appears that MacDonald and Burrus have substantiated my research. Not only can I continue to infer from the Acts themselves the character of their female authors, but I can add to my earlier lines of reasoning another factor: if one is convinced by MacDonald or Burrus, or both, it is *prima facie* reasonable that the sort of person who invented and transmitted the tales of the apostles is also the most likely sort of person to have written them down.

MacDonald, however, disagrees with my position on two principal grounds.[34] First, he argues that men could have written down the traditions developed by women; thus one cannot be *certain* of the Acts' female authorship. As I claimed only probability rather than certainty for my hypothesis, all I can do is agree with MacDonald and note that his own study has raised the level of the probability to a somewhat higher degree.[35] Second, MacDonald defends the veracity of Tertullian's report in *De Baptismo* that a presumptively male elder of a church in Asia Minor authored the *Acts of Paul and Thecla* (although he denies the veracity of Tertullian's assertion that said elder invented the Acts; it is his conclusion that they were largely transcriptions of previously circulated stories).[36] I have since made

---

[32]Virginia Burrus, "Chastity as Autonomy," in D. R. MacDonald (ed.), *The Apocryphal Acts of Apostles* (=*Semeia* 38 [1986]): 101.
[33]Davies, *Revolt.*
[34]Dennis Ronald MacDonald, "The Role of Women in the Production of the Apocryphal Acts of the Apostles," *Iliff Review* 40 (1984): 21-38.
[35]Davies, *Revolt.* 110.
[36]MacDonald, "Role of Women," 24-25.

the argument that Tertullian was commenting on a now-lost pseudepigraphical Pauline letter and not the Acts of Paul. An otherwise unknown letter fits the circumstances of Tertullian's argument far better than does the Acts in question.[37] With MacDonald, I observe that the person of whom Tertullian speaks is credited with inventing the document in question, rather than with transcribing tales, and take this observation to support the thesis that the document in question is not the Acts of Paul but something else entirely.

We are left, alas, with the usual uncertainties inevitable in our sort of historical inquiry. But all we can do is try.

Conclusion: A Trajectory

Rather soon after Jesus' death Christians wrote down collections of miracle stories to show the powers of their proclaimed savior, in whom they saw a prophet after the mode of Elijah and Elisha. Some of these stories can be recovered from the gospels of Mark and John.[38] Mark created the gospel format in part to make a case against believing Jesus to have been primarily such a miracle-working prophet.[39] In turn, Luke revised Mark in part to show that Jesus' powers as manifested through the miracles indeed evince his exceptional, God-given status as a miracle worker, to reveal his likeness to the ancient prophet, and to capture the attention of the women in his audience. Luke subsequently wrote the Acts of the Apostles, a work Pervo has demonstrated to share features with Apocryphal Acts. Finally, Luke wrote an introductory birth narrative that focuses on the actions and words of two women; in its broad features, these first two chapters of the gospel are especially reminiscent of portions of the Apocryphal Acts.

Not very much later, women — perhaps influenced by the tales of Paul found in Luke's second volume — told tales about the apostle to the gentiles among themselves, and in these tales their particular concerns as Christian *women* play a central part. An author akin to Luke composed the pastorals in opposition to such tales and their tellers. Subsequently, women dedicated to sexual continence began

---

[37]Davies, "Women, Tertullian and the Acts of Paul," in *Semeia* 38 (1986): 139-43.
[38]Cf. Paul J. Achtemeier, "Toward the Isolation of Pre-Marcan Miracle Catenae," *JBL* 89 (1970): 265-91; R. Fortna, *The Gospel of Signs* (Cambridge: University Press, 1970).
[39]Theodore Weeden, *Mark, Traditions in Conflict* (Philadelphia: Fortress, 1979).

to tell among themselves chastity stories which featured the relationship between continent women and itinerant apostles. In the mid-second and the third centuries, those tales of Paul and chastity stories were written down, quite likely by women, in a format inspired both by the romance novels of the period and by the biographical novels known today as gospels, primarily the Gospel of Luke.

Did Ancient Women Write Novels?[1]

Mary R. Lefkowitz

If anyone had asked this question, at least until very recently, the answer would have been *no*. We have no record of any novels or romances attributed to women writing in ancient Greek and Latin, though women wrote poems, treatises and memoirs. But now it has been suggested that certain stories in which women play important roles may have been written by women: perhaps the Book of Ruth,[2] and, of texts written in Greek, the non-canonical story of *Joseph and Aseneth*, certain chapters of the *Testament of Job*, and perhaps also portions of *The Acts of Paul and Thecla* found in the New Testament Apocrypha.

These rather disparate texts have in common an interest in and sympathy for the lives and experiences of women, concerns that are not otherwise especially prominent in biblical literature. What more logical way to account for their anomalous character than to suggest that the works were composed in whole or in part by women? Behind the suggestion that texts sympathetic to females were written by female authors lies an assumption that is becoming increasingly common in present-day critical and historical theory: that writers put themselves into whatever they write; otherwise put: directly or indirectly one writes about what one is. Thus (in simplest terms) men will write about the concerns of men; women about women, etc. In any works where women show initiative or qualities that might at times seem contradictory to the roles ordinarily assigned them in patriarchal society, the case for female authorship may seem stronger. Presumably, male authors would not wish to write what might encourage such independent and even "uppity" behavior.

There are two basic problems with the assumption that only women can write sympathetically about women, especially about women who take initiative. The first is familiar to students of classical literature: content is not always a sure or reliable means of determining authorship. For example, theories about the composition of the Homeric poems necessarily assume that content pro-

[1]My thanks to Roger Beck, Michael Coogan, and Leofranc Holford-Strevens for advice and criticism. All translations unless otherwise noted are my own.
[2]Cf. S. D. Goitein, "Women as Creators of Biblical Genres," trans. M. Carasik, *Prooftexts* 8 (1988): 31.

vides a key to authorship, since no reliable biographical data about
the author(s) exist. Some scholars speak of him (supposing, with
the ancients, that he was a male) as if he were a tradition rather
than a flesh-and-blood human being. According to this approach,
the bard, instead of freely choosing his own words and determining
his own subject matter, responds with traditional phrases to the
stimuli provided by the material of his song. But such notions of
Homeric composition, which concentrate on the generic aspects of
epic song, often fail to consider the power of an individual artist to
develop or even to break with inherited tradition. What makes
"Homer" (whoever he was and whenever he wrote or composed)
different from other, later epic bards? What explains distinctive
qualities of style or content? To these questions the poet's gender,
nationality, or race cannot in themselves provide an adequate
answer; unless some account can also be taken of the contribution of
an individual's originality, then presumably any number of Greek
bards could have written an *Iliad*.

It follows that sympathy for women alone, in the absence of
other kinds of evidence, does not constitute proof that a text was
composed by a woman. Almost any anomaly can be explained as an
act of individual genius. And even were we to accept that it is at least
theoretically possible for a male author to write sympathetically
about women, is it *likely* that he would do so? I cannot speak with
authority about other literary traditions, but I can demonstrate that
in ancient Greek literature, there is an established tradition of men
writing with sympathy and concern for women's experience. The
practice begins with Homer and is taken up by other male writers,
most conspicuously by the Attic dramatists.

Not only do these male authors frequently express sympathy
for women and women's lot, they also describe women who take
initiative. Even in resolutely patriarchal cultures, there is nothing
necessarily wrong with women who make decisions or assume
responsibility for their actions; what matters is why the initiative is
taken. In certain cases the end justifies the means, for example, in
cases where initiative is taken to help a fiancé or husband, or to
protect family and children.

To take a famous illustration of women's initiative from
ancient Greek literature written by or attributed to a man:
Andromache in the *Iliad* 6 advises her husband Hector not to
continue his offensive against the Greeks but to remain on the tower
and station his men at the weakest part of the wall, at the place
where the best Greek fighters have already made three attempts to

enter Troy (431-39). Hector refuses because he would be ashamed to be thought cowardly by the Trojans for staying outside of the battle, even though he knows well that ultimately Troy will fall and that Andromache will end up in servitude to some Achaean woman (447-65). He tells her to go inside and see to her own work, the loom and the distaff; "the war will be the concern of the Trojan men, all of them, and especially to me" (492-93).

Is Hector putting Andromache down for stepping out of her place in a patriarchal society? One prominent feminist scholar has thought so and has argued that Andromache's advice displays the precise knowledge of strategy appropriate to women in a matriarchal society.[3] But surely the situation is much more straightforward. Andromache has asked Hector to leave the fighting altogether so that he will not be killed; this he cannot do, not only because he is the best fighter among the Trojans but also, to withdraw would betray both his male comrades as well as the women and children of Troy: "My wife, all this (i.e., my family life) is a concern to me also; but I would be dreadfully ashamed before the Trojan men and Trojan women with their trailing dresses, if like a coward I avoided the fighting" (441-42). If later he tells Andromache to go inside and look to her own work, he is not criticizing her for giving him advice but rather is reminding her that he too must do his duty (cf. 493). Nor is he trying to put her in her place when he tells her: "See to your own work, the loom and the distaff, and order your women to go about their work." Compliance would distract her attention from the war, and from his role in the fighting.

Andromache in the *Iliad* fails to persuade Hector to play it safe, and she cannot save her son when the Greeks decide to execute him. However, after she is taken to Greece to be a slave in the household of Achilles' son Neoptolemus and bears him a son, she is able to save that son from Neoptolemus's wife Hermione and her father Menelaus by seeking refuge at the altar of the goddess Thetis. In Euripides's drama *Andromache*, by stating her case courageously, she saves her child, lives to marry again, and sees her son by Neoptolemus king over the Molossians. In having a woman take moral initiative, Euripides was following a pattern well established by earlier epic.[4] According to Hesiod's *Theogony*, which describes how Zeus obtained power, new dynasties are brought into being among the

---

[3]S. B. Pomeroy, "Andromaque: un exemple méconnu de matriarchat," *REG* 88 (1975): 15-19. But cf. M. R. Lefkowitz, "The Heroic Women of Greek Epic," *American Scholar* 56 (1987): 507-9.
[4]Cf. M. R. Lefkowitz, "The Powers of the Primeval Goddesses," *American Scholar* 58 (1989): 586-91.

gods by the action of goddesses. Earth decides that she can no longer endure her husband Heaven's placing each of their newly born children back inside of her so that none will succeed him. She contrives a plan which will enable her youngest son, Cronus, to castrate his father and thus both to succeed him as ruler of the gods and to release his brothers and sisters from captivity. But when Cronus in turn swallows his children to prevent future succession, his wife Rhea — on the advice of Earth and a now more cooperative Heaven — hides the infant Zeus in a cave and gives Cronus a stone to swallow in his place. In each case, females take initiative and act independently to protect their children, even if their action means opposing or harming their husbands or sons.

Although the plots of myth clearly show males, whether gods or mortals, behaving aggressively, assuming control, and making judgments (often with disastrous results), it is the females who tend to call the attention of the male characters and ultimately, of the audience, to the most sensible and equitable means of solving disputes and problems. To take a now little-known but in its time influential example: in a recently discovered fragment of a long poem the lyric poet Stesichorus[5] describes how Oedipus's mother and wife (Sophocles calls her Jocasta but she may have had a different name in Stesichorus's version) tries to avert the seer Tiresias's prophecy that her two sons, Eteocles and Polynices, would kill each other in a duel. Resorting not to entreaty or lamentation but to experience and reason, she says to Tiresias and her sons:[6]

> For the immortal gods have not established strife firmly among mortals on the holy earth nor indeed friendship, but the gods determine men's intentions on the day. But may Apollo who works from afar not bring all your prophecies to pass.

> but if it is fated for me to see my sons killed by one another, and so the Fates have spun, then straightway may the end of hateful death come to me, before I see ... with sorrows, sad ... my children dead in the hall and my city taken.

> But come, my dear children, [obey] my words, for in this way I reveal to you a solution: one of you keeping the palace live

---

[5]Although his name does not appear on the papyrus, virtually all scholars attribute this poem to Stesichorus; cf. P. Parsons, "The Lille 'Stesichorus,'" ZPE 26 (1977): 7-36. We know of no women authors who wrote on this subject or in this dialect.

[6]Text in J. M. Bremer et al., *Some Recently Found Greek Poems* (Mnemosyne Suppl. 99; Leiden: Brill, 1987), 131-33.

[beside the streams of Dirce], and the other go into exile, taking the wealth and all the gold of your father, whichever of you first draws the lot that is shaken on behalf of the Fates.

this I think will be a release from an evil outcome foretold by the holy prophet ... [if in truth] Zeus [will save] the family and city of Cadmus and postpone for a long time the evil that is fated for the race [of the kings].

Thus spoke the noble lady, speaking with gentle words, trying to keep her children from fighting in the hall, and Tiresias along with her, and they were persuaded.... (Lille 76Aii+ 73i., 201-34)

The problem, at least in this version of the story, is that Oedipus's inheritance must be divided among two sons; according to custom, land and/or dominion cannot be divided. The solution Jocasta proposes is so far as possible equitable, and it occurs in a number of other myths where there are two sons.[7] Perhaps Oedipus is absent, incapable, or unwilling to propose a solution himself; in any case, his wife (and mother) is the peacemaker who is prepared, though without impiety, to avoid the prophesied outcome.

We do not know what happened in the rest of Stesichorus's poem. Sophocles, of course, tells a different story, though even in his *Oedipus the King* Jocasta settles a quarrel as soon as she comes on stage. This Jocasta kills herself when she realizes that her husband is in fact her son whom she had believed dead. But in his *Phoenician Women* Euripides again shows Jocasta alive, trying to mediate between her two sons, though now just as Polynices is preparing to attack Thebes and wrest the throne from Eteocles. This portrait of Jocasta is particularly interesting for our purposes, since the *Phoenician Women*, although now rarely studied, seems once to have been extremely popular: more scraps of papyrus from this work (i.e., manuscript copies from the early centuries of the Common Era) have come down to us than from any other ancient play.[8]

Despite its title and many characters, the *Phoenician Women* concentrates on the fates of Jocasta and her children with Oedipus. But in this version the solution Stesichorus has her propose is not practical: Eteocles and Polynices had agreed to take turns ruling Thebes rather than live together in the same house and thus run the risk of fulfilling the curse of Oedipus that they would kill each other.

---

[7]Bremer, *Greek Poems*, 166-68.
[8]E. Craik (ed.), *Euripides: Phoenician Women* (Warminster: Aris and Phillips, 1988), 52.

Eteocles ruled first, but when his turn came to relinquish the throne he refused. Meanwhile Polynices, who had hated his time in exile, arrives with an army organized by his father-in-law to attack Thebes. Jocasta asks Polynices to come to her under safe conduct to talk with Eteocles.

In this scene the men behave irrationally and threaten violence while Jocasta is calm and reasonable. Perhaps surprisingly, in contrast to Hecuba in the *Iliad* or Clytemnestra in the *Oresteia*, Jocasta does not use a mother's arguments or make the traditional gesture of baring her breast to remind her sons of their obligations to her. Instead she claims the authority of old age ("experience can speak more wisely than the young" [529-30]), and she uses philosophical arguments.[9] She asks Eteocles why he devotes himself to the goddess Ambition, who has destroyed so many families and cities. It is better, she says, to honor Equity (Isonomia), the goddess who invented weights and measurements and who made the day and night "move equally through the course of the year: neither of them when defeated bears ill-will to the other" (535-45). After drawing this analogy from nature, she offers basically the same argument about the instability of glory and wealth that the statesman Solon made in his famous elegy (7.9-10West): "Mortals do not have possessions of their own, but we get them from the gods and look after them; when they want them, they take them back again. Wealth is not secure, but ephemeral" (555-58).[10] Then Jocasta turns to Polynices and asks him to consider the reputation he will have if he attacks his own city and how his allies will resent the lives they will lose on his behalf.

This time neither son wishes to obey his mother. Perhaps the traditional breast-baring would have been more effective, but Jocasta does not succumb to her emotions until she learns her sons are dying. At this point, she throws herself on their bodies while "lamenting the great labor of her breasts" (1434-35); she then picks up one of their swords and drives it through her own throat (1455-58). Her death here seems more courageous than that in Sophocles's *Oedipus the King*. Here, after she discovers that she has married her own son, Jocasta goes on living and tries until the last to save her sons.

Equally impressive, though in a different way, is the courage and determination shown in the *Phoenician Women* by Jocasta's

---

[9]Cf. ibid., 197-98, who compares the arguments used by Theseus in Euripides's *Suppliants* 409-62.
[10]Cf. also Theognis 719-28West. See Craik, *Euripides*, 197-98, for the use of similar ideas in political and philosophical contexts; the point is that *men* would readily use these arguments.

daughter Antigone. Appearing first as an observer from the city walls, Antigone learns from an attendant the names of the leaders of the Argive army. Seeing the enemy, she states that if they win, she will never serve as a slave in Mycene. The same promise is made (and kept) by other young women in Euripides's dramas: Polyxena in the *Hecuba* and Macaria in the *Children of Heracles*, both of whom willingly offer themselves as sacrifices in order to avoid a life of slavery.[11] Antigone goes with her mother to try to intervene between her two brothers, and she returns to tell her blind father about their deaths as well as Jocasta's. The play ends with her defying her uncle Creon, first because he proposes to banish Oedipus from Thebes, and then because he refuses to allow her to give Polynices proper burial on the grounds that he attacked his homeland. Even though she does not explicitly defy Creon's orders about burying Polynices, as in Sophocles's play, Antigone confronts her uncle by refusing to marry his son Haemon and by insisting she will accompany her father into exile.

Although parts of this final scene may have been rewritten by actors after Euripides's death, it is for our purposes notable that — whatever the playwright's intentions — in later times actors and audiences considered Antigone's defiant behavior to be as significant as her father's incest or her brothers' mutual hatred.[12] The ending of Aeschylus's *Seven Against Thebes*, the earliest surviving treatment of the legend, also appears to have been rewritten to give Antigone a more prominent role; although in the original version she may have appeared only to join her sister Ismene in a formal lamentation, in later versions of the play, she tells the messenger who announces Creon's edict concerning Polynices's corpse that whatever the consequences she intends to bury her brother.[13]

It is not anomalous — at least in Greek literature — that the female characters in the most popular dramas are active, brave decision-makers. Along with the *Phoenician Women*, two others of Euripides's plays were selected for special study in the schools: *Hecuba* and *Orestes*. In both women have important roles, make significant decisions, and confront danger and death with extraordinary courage. But the closest analogy to Jocasta in the *Phoenician Women* is Hecuba; she also learns of the death of two of her children,

---

[11]Cf. M. R. Lefkowitz, *Women in Greek Myth* (Baltimore: Johns Hopkins, 1986), 99-102.

[12]Cf. G. O. Hutchinson (ed.), *Aeschylus: Septem Contra Thebas* (Oxford: 1985), 209-10; Craik, *Euripides*, 51-52. For the popularity of Sophocles's *Antigone*, cf. Dioscurides, *Anth. Pal.* 7.37.9-10 (=HE 1606-67).

[13]Cf. esp. Hutchinson, *Aeschylus*, 210-11.

but she manages to take revenge on the murderer of her son.

Recently it has been argued that Hecuba plots revenge because her previously good character has been corrupted by the suffering inflicted on her: first by the sack of her city Troy; then by the fate of her daughter Polyxena, who is offered as a sacrifice to the ghost of Achilles; and finally by learning how her trusted friend Polymestor has murdered her last surviving son, Polydorus.[14] But this interpretation appears to impose modern and essentially Christian values on the ancient work. If the sudden news that her son's body has been washed up on the shore changed Hecuba's sense of right and wrong, Euripides gives no indication of it. Hecuba hesitates to ask Agamemnon to punish her son's murderer not because she feels it would be wrong to take revenge, but because she is afraid that Agamemnon will reject her plea. Nonetheless, she asks for and receives at least his passive cooperation.

As in the case of Jocasta, Euripides shows Hecuba acting with cool rationality rather than appealing to emotion. She argues that even though she is a slave, the laws of the gods apply to all. Consequently, hosts who murder guests should be punished, even if the guest is the son of a slave; "stand at a distance, like a painter, and look at me and see how badly I have been treated" (799-808). She then reflects on the power of persuasion and wishes that mankind paid more attention to this "sole tyrant among men" (816). She states what she herself has lost, but then makes her final and most persuasive argument: Agamemnon has taken her daughter Cassandra as his concubine; she is in a sense his mother-in-law. She concludes her speech by wishing that her arms, hands, hair, and feet each had a voice; this bizarre notion vividly emphasizes her present isolation, with husband and all male children dead.[15]

Hecuba's speech persuades Agamemnon to allow her to act without interference, and she plots a particularly gruesome revenge. She asks Polymestor to come to her tent with his two sons so she can give him a secret message; he agrees to enter without his armed guard because, she explains, she wants to reveal the location of hidden treasure. But once he enters, her women attendants take his children away as if to play with them, and then they draw hidden swords and kill them. They next restrain Polymestor and put out his eyes with the pins of their brooches. Hecuba defends her actions

---

[14]M. C. Nussbaum, *The Fragility of Goodness* (Cambridge: University Press, 1986), 406.
[15]Contrast ibid., 415, who regards Hecuba's use of this metaphor as further evidence of the corruption of her character.

most effectively, and she receives Agamemnon's support. Although Polymestor prophesies that Hecuba will fall from the ship that takes her to Greece, be turned into a dog, and die, undaunted she replies: "I don't care what happens, now that you have been punished by me" (1274).

If the *Phoenician Women* and the *Hecuba* were relatively obscure works, it might be possible to argue that most ancient Greeks would have found Jocasta and Hecuba's actions unusual; but on the contrary, the Greeks seem to have expected women to behave decisively and courageously, and to understand and debate issues of great moral importance. In many myths, women delegate the more active roles to men, but in the *Hecuba* — when no men are willing or available to do the dirty work — the women not only make the plans but enact the necessary violence. If we now find Hecuba's action morally repulsive, we may be imposing on the Greeks notions of appropriate conduct that properly belong to Christian women; for the Greeks revenge was "terrible" but necessary.[16] When Greek women turn the other cheek upon being wronged, it is only because they have no better choice, like Hecuba in Euripides's the *Trojan Women*, where she endures and laments without a ready means of revenge.

Although no Greek dramas (or comedies) are attributed to women, ancient audiences were accustomed to hearing from male authors about active, rational, violent women. Other examples from drama abound: Antigone defies an edict although she knows she might die for it; Electra in Sophocles's play plans to kill her father's murderer herself; Helen concocts an escape plan for herself and her husband Menelaus; Iphigenia masterminds such a plan for herself and Orestes.[17] It would not have occurred to the Greeks that only women could write about women's experience, any more than they found it remarkable that Homer and the dramatists could write about the conversations of the gods on Mt. Olympus.

Nor are such sympathetic portrayals of active women confined to the classical period. Because drama, especially the adventure plays of Euripides, was the primary inspiration for both for ancient comedy and what we now call ancient "novels", audiences would not have been surprised to see women taking active roles in these genres also, even though no comedies or novels in the Hellenistic period are

---

[16]Cf. Sophocles, *Electra* 221-22, where the chorus remonstrates with her about her hostility towards her mother and Aegisthus: "I am compelled to dreadful deeds by dreadful deeds; I know it well, my passion does not escape me."

[17]Cf. Lefkowitz, *Women in Greek Myth*, 102.

known to have been written by women.[18] But since some women in
the Hellenistic world could and did write, it is theoretically possible
that some of them wrote novels. What we do know about Hellenistic
women writers is summarized below.

Epigrams by several highly professional women poets are
preserved in the collection of ancient epigrams known as the
Palatine Anthology (*AP*).[19] To judge by the extant literature, these
female poets are few in number and much less productive than their
male contemporaries. For example, the largest preserved oeuvre of a
female poet, Anyte of Tegea, is twenty-four epigrams; that of of a
male poet, Leonidas of Tarentum, ninety-two epigrams. Erinna also
wrote a poem in hexameters, said to have been some three-hundred
lines long (i.e., about half of an ordinary "book"); preserved are large
fragments mourning her childhood friend Baucis.[20] Hedyle of
Samos (or Athens — the sources are quite uncertain), herself the
daughter of a female poet, Moschine of Attica, and mother of the
male poet Hedylus, wrote a poem about the love of Glaucus for the
female monster Scylla; Boeo of Delphi wrote a hymn to Apollo.[21] In
Greek we also have a fragmentary text of an incantation against
headaches attributed to Philinna of Athens, and a rather dreary
poem about Rome probably written by Melinno around the time of
Hadrian.[22] In Latin, we have several attractive love poems by Sulpicia (1st c. B.C.E.), the grand-daughter of the great Roman jurist.[23]
The poet Martial (1st c. C.E.) speaks of a different "Sulpicia" who wrote
"chaste" love poetry suitable for married couples, which (to judge
from the two surviving lines) was suggestive if not pornographic.[24]

---

[18]On the development of the ancient novel from adventure drama and New
Comedy, see esp. S. Trenkner, *The Greek Novella in the Classical Period*
(Cambridge: University Press, 1958).
[19]Anyte, Erinna, Moero, Nossis: epigrams in *HE*, *The Garland of Meleager*.
Literal prose translations in W. R. Paton, *The Greek Anthology* (Loeb Classical
Library; Cambridge: Harvard, 1918); selected poems in *WLGR*. Cf. esp. J. McI.
Snyder, *The Woman and the Lyre* (Carbondale: So. Illinois University, 1989),
64-98.
[20]Erinna: fragmentary text of *The Distaff* in *SH*; trans. D. L. Page, *Select Papyri
III* (Loeb Classical Library; Cambridge: Harvard, 1970); *WLGR* #9.
[21]Hedyle: 5 lines preserved by Athenaeus, quoted in *SH* 456. Boeo: Pausanias
x. 5. 8; J. U. Powell, *Collectanea Alexandrina* (Oxford: Clarendon, 1925).
[22]Melinno: text in *SH* 541; cf. M. L. West, "Die griechischen Dichterinnen der
Kaiserzeit," *Kyklos* (Festschrift R. Keydell; Berlin: De Gruyter, 1978), 101-15.
Philinna: *SH* 900.
[23]Cf. Snyder, *Woman and the Lyre*, 128-36. On her identity, see R. Syme,
Roman Papers (Oxford: Clarendon, 1979), I, 290; III, 1420; her poems are
preserved in the ms. of her contemporary (and friend?) Tibullus, 4.7-12;
translation in *WLGR* #s 132-33.
[24]Cf. Martial 10. 35, 38; for her poetry, see O. Jahn, F. Buecheler, and F. Leo,
Persii Flacci, D. Iunii Iuvenalis, Sulpiciae Saturae, Ed. 5 (Berlin: Weidmann,

Limited as this *Nachlass* may seem, we know even less about Hellenistic women prose writers. We know the names of and some anecdotes about certain women philosophers: Plato's pupils Lastheneia and Axiothea, Hipparchia (3d c. B.C.E.), Magnilla (2d/3d c. C.E.), Sosipatra (3d c. C.E.), and Hypatia (5th c. C.E.), but virtually nothing about what they might have written.[25] In a list of 235 names of the followers of Pythagoras in the Greek cities of southern Italy, seventeen (or about seven percent) belong to women.[26] Works said to be written by two of these, Pythagoras's wife or daughter Theano, and his daughter Myia, survive, along with letters and treatises attributed to women who do not appear in Iamblichus's list: Pythagoras's daughter Arignote, Melissa, Periktione (incidentally, also the name of Plato's mother), and Phintys.[27] But they and the other writings attributed to women of Pythagoras's school are probably not original or even written by women; rather, they consist of rhetorical exercises and treatises composed by men at different times and places.[28] Certainly the content of what they wrote concerns topics particularly dear to men: women's duties,[29] women's chastity,[30] how to behave when one's husband acquires a mistress (put up with it cheerfully).[31]

1932), 281-85. It seems unlikely that she wrote the complaint about "the state of Rome and the times of Domitian" attributed to her. Perhaps this is a scholastic *declamatio* of the fifth century C.E.; see W. Kroll, "Sulpicia no. 115," PW II, 4A (1932): 880-82.

[25] Women philosophers: Lastheneia and Axiothea: see Lefkowitz, *Women in Greek Myth*, 144; Hipparchia: *WLGR* #43; Magnilla: *WLGR* #168; Hypatia: *Women in Greek Myth*, 107-11, and Snyder, *Woman and the Lyre*, 113-21; Sosipatra, Eunapius, *Vit. Philos.* 467-70. Perhaps we should also include Arete of Cyrene, who educated her son, the philosopher Aristippus (Diogenes Laertius 2.86); Menexene, Argia, Theognis, Artemesia, and Pantaclea, daughters of the philosopher Diodorus Cronus; and Themista, the wife of Epicurus's disciple Leontes (Clem. Alex., *Strom.* iv. 19; cf. Snyder, *Woman and the Lyre*, 101-5). But no writings are attributed to any of them.

[26] For the list, from the fourth century C.E. Neoplatonist Iamblichus, see H. Diels and W. Kranz, *Die Fragmente der Vorsokratiker* (Berlin: Weidmann, 1934), I, 448 s.v. Pythagoreische Schule 58a.

[27] For texts and testimonia (in alphabetical order), see H. Thesleff, *The Pythagorean Texts of the Hellenistic Period* (Acta Academiae Aboensis, Humaniora 30.1; Abo: Abo Akademi, 1965).

[28] Cf. esp. H. Thesleff, *An Introduction to the Pythagorean Writings of the Hellenistic Period* (Acta Academiae Aboensis, Humaniora 24.3; Abo: Abo Akademi, 1961).

[29] For a translation of Periktione's treatise on women's duties, see S. B. Pomeroy, *Goddesses, Whores, Wives, and Slaves* (New York: Schocken, 1975), 134-36; cf. also Melissa's letter to Cleareta.

[30] For a translation of Phintys's treatise on chastity, see *WLGR* #107 (Thesleff, *Texts*, 151-54).

[31] Two letters about coping with mistresses are attributed to Pythagoras's wife Theano: #3 (Thesleff, *Texts*, 197), and #5 (198-200), which contains the sober advice: "tragedy teaches you to control your jealousy, through the exam-

We know even less about other women who wrote prose treatises. Though none of her work survives, Pamphile of Epidaurus (1st c. C.E.) was said to have written historical memoirs in thirty-three books, a three-book epitome of Ctesias's history of Persia, and "many epitomes of histories and other books, about controversies, sex, and many other things" — though some ancient sources apparently claimed that these books were written by her husband Socratidas.[32] Courtesans were said to have authored pornographic works: for example, a few papyrus scraps survive of a treatise attributed to the fourth-century B.C.E. courtesan Philaenis about how to flatter women. Again, some ancient authors claimed that this work was written by a man.[33]

Treatises are also attributed to two women alchemists from Roman Egypt in the early centuries C.E. — Mary the Jewess and Cleopatra — though their precepts about chemical procedures survive only in quotation in writings by men.[34] Since nothing whatever is known about them except what they are said to have said, it is possible that they never existed.[35] Even their names are suspicious. At Jesus' crucifixion, next to his mother Mary stood Mary of Cleopas (or in Greek, κλωπᾶ; John 19:25) — were these names chosen because they were endowed (as in certain Gnostic writings) with mystical significance?[36]

---

ples of the dramas, in which Medea disobeys the law." Cf. Snyder, *Woman and the Lyre*, 108-13.

[32] Pamphile: Suda P 139 (I 4 15 Adler), *WLGR* #166. The treatise on sex may have been attributed to her simply because of her name (Athenaeus mentions a courtesan Pamphile, xiii. 591d); cf. L. Holford-Strevens, *Aulus Gellius* (Chapel Hill: University of No. Carolina, 1989), 21 n.13.

[33] Courtesans Philaenis, Astyanassa, Elephantine: references and bibliography in *WLGR* 160 n. 4. The witty sayings of other courtesans are recorded in Athenaeus, Deipnosophistae bk. XIII. Cf. esp. the poet Machon's accounts of remarks by Gnathaena, her daughter Gnathaenium, and also Lamia, Mania, Lais, Hippe, Phryne, and Nico; A. S. F. Gow, *Machon* (Cambridge: University Press, 1965).

[34] For Mary's precepts, cf. M. Berthelot, *Collection des anciens alchimistes grecs* (Paris: G. Steinheil, 1888) II, 93, 102, 103, 146, 149, 152, 157, 173, 182, 192, 193, 196-97, 198, 200, 201, 236-37, 351, 356, 357, 382, 404; Cleopatra, 293, 298-99. On the practical contributions they are said to have made to the science, cf. F. Sherwood Taylor, "The Origins of Greek Alchemy," *Ambix* 1 (1937): 30-47.

[35] Perhaps the female gender was important for some mystical purpose, cf. Mary's repeated precept: "Join the male and the female and you will find what you seek; without the association of this union, nothing can be done right" (Berthelot, *Coll.* [n.34] II, 102, 201). Three women are listed among twenty-six philosophers of the divine science and art: Mary, Theosebeia, and Juliana; cf. M. Berthelot, *Introduction a l'étude de la chimie* (Paris: G. Steinheil, 1889), 26.

[36] Clopas is a standard abbreviation of both Cleopas and Cleopatros. Cf. M.

As for Roman women writers of prose, we have from the 120s B.C.E. excerpts from a letter by Cornelia to her son Gaius Gracchus that urges him not to stand for the tribunate. Like the general and formally rhetorical letters attributed to the female Neopythagoreans, the work is probably a composition written after her death.[37] We have summaries of a speech given in 42 B.C.E. by Hortensia, daughter of a famous orator.[38] Agrippina the Younger, the mother of the Emperor Nero, wrote (perhaps in Latin) "the story of her life and the misfortunes of her family," which Tacitus cites in his *Annals*.[39] But odd as it may seem to those of us who think of the novel as a "women's genre", we know of no woman who wrote either fictional romances or their prototypes, romantic dramas and comedies.

It is not easy to know why, since no ancient author, male or female, discusses the question. The genres most congenial to women writers — at least the ones we know something about — are lyric and elegiac poetry.[40] Perhaps this preference was to some extent determined by the conditions of publication: lyric and elegiac poems could be performed at private parties or at symposia, perhaps in certain cases by the women themselves. Epigrams and epitaphs would be inscribed on stone tablets placed where the public could read them by themselves (though presumably out loud). Comedies and dramas were performed by actors, who were always male; in some instances, one of the actors might be the play's author. Women appeared only in mimes, but these actors — unlike the female poets and writers of treatises whose names have been preserved — were not respectable women. Longer works, like prose treatises, would be read out loud by trained readers, their authors, or male slaves; the settings might be formal or intimate: when the emperor Augustus was unable to sleep he summoned readers rather than reading to himself.[41] Since even in Rome women did not ordinarily give public addresses, presumably it would have been inappropriate for a woman to read out a novel or treatise she might have written. However, there is no

---

Berthelot, *Les origines de l'alchimie* (Paris: G. Steinheil, 1885), 173. On her identity (the wife or daughter of Joseph's brother, and perhaps also the mother of James and Joses), cf. HSW I, 426-27.

[37]The letters are preserved at the end of the mss. of Cornelius Nepos (fr. 2 Winstedt, fr. 59 Marshall); text and translation in the Loeb Classical Library: *Florus and Cornelius Nepos*, ed. J. C. Rolfe. But Snyder, *Woman and the Lyre*, 124-25, and A. S. Gratwick, in *Cambridge History of Classical Literature* (Cambridge: University Press, 1982), II, 145-47, argue for their authenticity.

[38]Cf. Snyder, *Woman and the Lyre*, 125-27.

[39]Agrippina (lst c. C.E.): *WLGR* #167; cf. Snyder, *Woman and the Lyre*, 128.

[40]Cf. Snyder, ibid., 155.

[41]Suet. *Divus Augustus* 78.2; cf. W. V. Harris, *Ancient Literacy* (Cambridge:

reason why her work could not have been presented by a slave.

Could it then have been the case that no novels are attributed to women writers because the genre derived from long epics and dramas, the types of works women did not write? To some extent the content of novels may also have been considered inappropriate for respectable female authors: most are romances in which enemies and/or misfortunes separate a loving couple so that the consummation of their marriage, long anticipated, is excitingly postponed.[42] The heroines, as in Greek comedy, are faithful to their fiancés; they are also often more interesting and courageous than the men with whom they strive to be reunited.[43] Discussions and descriptions of physical passion, when they do occur, are expressed from the man's point of view.

On the other hand, there is considerable reason to think that when novels were read aloud, women comprised a large part of the audience. Papyrus fragments indicate that the audiences included people outside of large cities, and they show that copies, both more and less expensive, were made of the novels. Indeed, novels are among the first literary works copied in codex form as opposed to the papyrus roll that continued to be used for epic and drama.[44] Women presumably liked the novels for many of the same reasons that men did: they were accessible, rooted in the familiar world rather than the remote past but at the same time larger than life, with idealized characters, exciting adventures, and romance.[45] But ancient readers would not have found in their novels the characters' internal insights or personal reflections that appeal to their counterparts in the nineteenth and twentieth centuries.

If any ancient novels were written by women, they were written pseudonymously. But this possibility is both unproven, and probably unprovable.[46] The suggestion seems unlikely for two reasons. First, there was no taboo on women publishing in their own names. And second, the descriptions of the women in the novels do not emphasize or — as far as I can see — even refer to those aspects of women's life apart from men occasionally described by ancient women writers: love for other women, particularly childhood con-

---

Harvard, 1989), 226.
[42]Cf. esp. E. L. Bowie, "The Greek Novel," in *Cambridge History of Classical Literature* (Cambridge: University Press, 1985), I, 684-85, with list of surviving or known ancient novels.
[43]Cf. T. Hagg, *The Novel in Antiquity* (Oxford: Blackwell, 1983), 96.
[44]Ibid., 93-95; E. Rohde, *Der griechische Roman*, 3d ed. (Leipzig: Teubner, 1914; repr. Hildesheim: G. Olms, 1960), 73-77.
[45]Cf. Bowie, "Greek Novel," 684-85.
[46]Hagg, *Novel in Antiquity*, 96.

temporaries, the joys of childhood, and love for a daughter. On the contrary, the authors' tendency to describe the heroine's sexuality from a man's point of view leaves the impression that these ancient novels were written by the kind of writers who normally wrote this type of narrative: men.

For example, the young couple Anthia and Habrocomes are separated shortly after their marriage and are reunited only after many dangers and much mental and physical suffering. When they are at last together in bed, Anthia lists for her "husband and master" all the attempts on her chastity that she has resisted: has he also been chaste? Unlike Odysseus, who tells Penelope about Circe and Calypso, Habrocomes says (truthfully) that he has been faithful, but he does not mention specific situations (5.14). Now that the long-postponed consummation is imminent, it is the events of Anthia's life that the audience is meant to recall, such as the robber Anchialos's attempt to rape her. He had thrown himself on her and tried to take her by force, but Anthia seized a knife and killed him (4.5.5). No Hellenistic audience would have been surprised to think that a male author could write about such an ingenious, courageous, and clever, not to mention beautiful and chaste heroine. But where heroines in tragedy take action in order to right wrongs done to members of their family, in the novel the heroine's efforts are devoted to preserving herself for her husband.

What then would such novels have sounded like had women written them? The question would be easier to answer could we with any certainty identify distinctive qualities of female authorship in Hellenistic literature. Many of the extant poems by women are by their very nature indistinguishable from those written by men: these women poets were professionals who wrote epitaphs and dedicatory epigrams to their clients' specifications. But occasionally, when their patrons were women, they wrote about aspects of women's lives that we know about also from epigrams of the archaic and classical periods: a mother's grief for a daughter who died before marriage;[47] a woman's grief for a childhood friend.[48] These poems by women about women can be distinguished from men's poems about women by their tendency to describe women's thoughts about aspects of their lives not connected with marriage or sexuality, and to say little or nothing about *men*. Male patrons, by contrast, even in

---

[47]Mother and daughter: Anyte, *WLGR* #s 13 and 14; cf. the anonymous 5th c. B.C.E. epigram for Bitte, *SEG* xv. 548 = *WLGR* #24.
[48]Erinna, *WLGR* #9 (above, n. 2), 10 = *AP* VII, 710, 712; cf. the mid-5th c. B.C.E. anonymous epigram for Biote, *IG* II2 10954 = *WLGR* #25; cf. Snyder, *Woman and the Lyre*, 97-98.

poems written by women, tend to call attention to themselves, usually poignantly, in expressing their sorrow over a dead wife or daughter; sometimes they include self-praise along with praise for their wives, like the tombstone inscription by the physician Glycon for his physician wife Panthia, which indulgently states: "Although you were a woman you were not behind me in skill."[49] Were I to specify any characteristic that distinguished poetry about women by or for men from that by or for women, it would be the tendency in men's poetry to call disproportionate attention in describing women's lives (however sympathetic the authors' or patrons' intentions) to the importance of men or to those aspects of women's lives that are specifically concerned with men, like marriage.

Although no prose known to be by women survives from the first centuries C.E., we can perhaps get some idea of what women's writing might have been like from the narrative attributed to Perpetua of Carthage, who was executed by the Romans in 203 C.E.[50] An account of her martyrdom almost to the day of her death, describing her imprisonment and trial, is included in the *Acts of SS. Perpetua and Felicity*. Perpetua's narrative has been considered genuine because it is so anomalous.[51] As in the case of poems by and about women, this prose account places unusual emphasis on Perpetua's own thoughts and emotions. In prison, she records: "I was terrified (*expavi*), because I never had before experienced such darkness" (3.5); she "was undone" (*tabescebam*) by seeing how her family suffered on her behalf" (3.8). She grieves for her father and tries to comfort him (5.6). When her baby appears to have been weaned, "my breasts did not bring on a fever, so that I was not tortured by concern for my baby or pain in my breasts" (6.8). This concentration on the experience of a nursing mother is unique in ancient literature.[52] We should also note that in her narrative, Per-

---

[49]Panthia (2d-3d c. C.E.), *WLGR* 175 = H. Pleket (ed.), *Epigraphica II: Texts on the Social History of the Greek World* (Leiden: Brill, 1969), #20; cf. 1st/2d c. C.E. husbands' epitaphs for physician wives, without self-praise, *WLGR* #171 (= Pleket #26), 172 (= H. Dessau, *Inscriptiones Latinae Selectae* [Berlin, 1892; reissue Chicago: Ares, 1979], #7804).

[50]I am assuming that the letter of Mary of Cassobola to Ignatius (no. 13 in Ignatius, *Epistulae Spuriae*, in F. X. Funk and F. Diekamp [eds.], *Patres Apostolici*, 3d ed. [Tübingen: Laupp, 1913]) is a forgery; did it seem especially characteristic of a woman to propose that young men should be bishops (13.5)?

[51]"Passio Sanctarum Perpetuae et Felicitatis," in H. Musurillo (ed.), *Acts of the Christian Martyrs* (Oxford: Clarendon, 1972), #8. Cf. E. R. Dodds, *Pagan and Christian in an Age of Anxiety* (Cambridge: University Press 1965), 47-53; P. Brown, *The Body and Society* (New York: Columbia University, 1988), 73-74.

[52]Cf. the 3d-2d c. B.C.E. letter attributed to Pythagoras's daughter Myia, which is concerned strictly with the effect of the nurse's habits on the baby, in

petua mentions the men in her life only insofar as they concern her. She feels sorry for her father when he is thrown to the ground and beaten, "just as if I myself had been beaten" (6.5), but she does not praise him (understandably, since he objected to her martyrdom). She speaks kindly but very briefly of "those blessed deacons who looked after us" (3.7, cf. 6.8), and she refers in passing to Satyrus, who was later along with her thrown to the wild animals (4.4).

A verbatim account by this same Satyrus of a vision he had while in prison is included in Perpetua's martyrology (11-13), and it is instructive to compare his narrative with hers. Satyrus concentrates on what he saw when he and Perpetua "were free of the world" (11.4). When he speaks of emotion at all, it is briefly and as experienced by a group: "we were moved and embraced them" (13.3); "all of us were sustained by an indescribable scent which satisfied our hunger; and then I woke up rejoicing" (*gaudens*, 13.8). Perpetua, recounting the vision she had before she was to fight the beasts, concentrates on herself: "And I looked at the large crowd who were astonished ... I was amazed that no beasts were sent after me ... my clothes were stripped off and I became a man..." (10.5-7).[53]

In the narrative about Thecla in the *Acts of Paul and Thecla* (which has been compared to a novel), there is no such concentration on the heroine's reactions. After she miraculously survives being bound by the feet to bulls, Thecla delivers a homily about God to the governor (37) and goes to stay with her protectress Tryphaena. "But Thecla yearned for Paul and sought after him, sending in every direction." Unlike Perpetua, she constantly seeks a man's approval for her actions.[54] The suggestion that the story of Thecla in the *Acts of Paul and Thecla* may have been written by a woman seems to me curious; the narrative displays many features characteristic of novels attributed to pagan male authors: dramatic escapes and rescues, sadistic persecution, lively interest in the heroine's sexuality.[55] The only difference is that the expected marriage between the hero (Paul) and the heroine (Thecla) is never consummated. Instead, Thecla remains a virgin, and she denies her femininity so far as possible by

---

Thesleff, *Texts*, 123-24 (=*WLGR* #111); or the advice of the 1st c. C.E. physician Soranus, *Gynaecology* I. 19-20 (=*WLGR* #178).
[53] On the significance of her vision, cf. M. R. Lefkowitz, *Heroines and Hysterics* (London: Duckworth, 1981), 53-58.
[54] Paul and Thecla: translation in HSW II, 353-63 = *Maenads* #114.
[55] Cf. S. Davies, *The Revolt of the Widows* (Carbondale: So. Illinois University, 1980), 58-61; D. R. MacDonald, *The Legend and the Apostle: The Battle for Paul in Story and Canon* (Philadelphia: Westminster, 1983), 34-53. Cf. also Hagg, *Novel in Antiquity*, 160, who notes that "the erotic element lies all the while beneath the surface." Finally, cf. the angel's visit in *Asen.*, which pro-

wearing men's clothes and preaching sermons.[56]

Odd as the ending of Thecla's tale would seem to a pagan audience, it made a lasting impression on pious Christians. The virtuous mother of SS. Macrina and Gregory of Nyssa dreamt when she was pregnant with her first child that an angel had addressed the baby as Thecla, "meaning Thecla about whom there was so much talk among the virgins."[57] So although the child was called Macrina after a Christian ancestress, her private name was Thecla. "It seems to me," Gregory wrote, "that the vision was not so much guiding the mother to the right choice of name, as predicting the life of the young girl, and by the name to hint at the similarity in her vocation." Like Thecla, Macrina remained celibate and became an ascetic; eventually, she used her family's land and wealth to found a monastery.[58]

Because the *Acts of Paul and Thecla* was one of the more popular early Christian legends, Gregory would have known at least the outlines of the story of Thecla's adventures; the later versions of her life retain the emphasis on her celibacy. According to one account, even when Thecla is very old, men sent by pagan doctors jealous of her healing powers threaten to rape her, but she is miraculously protected by a rock wall.[59] Stevan Davies, in his ingenious book *The Revolt of the Widows*, argues that the *Acts of Paul and Thecla* were more likely to have been written by a woman because a male author would have been required to have "an almost pathologically negative sexual self-image" combining "sympathy with sadistic imaginings." But sympathy for women, along with sadistic imaginings, may be found almost at random in any ancient novel written by (pagan) men.[60]

Other scholars have suggested that among the Hellenistic texts in the Pseudepigrapha are works which may have been written or at least inspired by women authors. On the basis of what we know about the Greek and Latin texts by women authors, I see little reason to think that women would have written all or even the most sympathetic sections of *Joseph and Aseneth* (*Asen.*) and the *Testa-*

---

vides the spiritual foreplay to Aseneth's actual marriage to Joseph.

[56]Lefkowitz, *Women in Greek Myth*, 130-31.

[57]St. Gregory of Nyssa, *Life of St. Macrina*, 962a-c, ed. V. Woods Callahan, in *Gregorii Nysseni Opera Ascetica*, 3d ed. (Leiden: Brill, 1986).

[58]Cf. esp. A. Momigliano, "Macrina, una santa aristocratica vista dal fratello," in G. Arrigoni (ed.), *Le donne in Grecia* (Roma-Bari: Editori Laterza, 1985), 333-34.

[59]Lefkowitz, *Women in Greek Myth*, 110-11.

[60]Cf. Davies, *Widows*, 107.

ment of Job (T. Job).[61] Since the author of *Asen.* writes in a plain style similar to *koine* Greek and seems acquainted with the novel genre, he (*sic.*) seems to have intended his work for an audience that was not highly educated.[62] The novel concentrates on the emotions of the Egyptian heroine Aseneth, who falls in love with Joseph and is eager to convert to Judaism in order to marry him. But I would argue that Aseneth behaves more passively than a Greek woman would under similar circumstances, and that the process of her conversion places an emphasis on her physical desires that is absent from the one conversion narrative attributed to a woman author we possess.

The differences in approach may best be demonstrated by direct comparison between the narrative of the angel's visit to Aseneth in *Asen.* and Perpetua's account of her vision in which a heavenly figure offers her a symbolic drink. While Perpetua is in prison with her brother, he begs her — because she is "in great favor" (*in magna dignatione*) — to ask for a vision, so that they will know whether they will be condemned or freed. She responds that she knows she can speak "directly with the Lord, in whose great blessings I was already experienced" (4.2). She then dreams of carefully climbing a ladder to heaven, avoiding all danger, confident that she will not be harmed by the dragon lying at the ladder's foot. When she reaches the top an old man dressed as a shepherd gives her "something like milk" to drink from her hands; then she wakes, still tasting something sweet. "I told this at once to my brother. And we understood that we would be executed, and we began to give up all hope in this life" (4.8-10).

In *Asen.*, by contrast, a "man" from heaven (or an angel) gives Aseneth explicit instructions and tells her both that her repentance has been accepted and that she will marry Joseph; his speech throughout places emphasis on her virginity. Aseneth expresses her gratitude to him and to the Lord, and she offers to prepare a meal for him. He in turn produces a magic honeycomb for her, tastes it himself, and puts a morsel into her mouth for her to eat (16:9). The man explains to her the honeycomb's symbolic significance, makes it burst into flames, and then disappears in front of her eyes. She sees a vision of a chariot of fire going towards the east, and she realizes that she was talking with God himself: "Have mercy on your

---

[61]*Joseph and Aseneth:* citations from Greek text in M. Philonenko, *Joseph et Aseneth* (Leiden: Brill, 1968); English translation (incorporating variants from texts in other languages) by C. Burchard; *Testament of Job:* trans. R. P. Spittler, in *OTP = Maenads* #113, #119.
[62]Bowie, "Greek Novel," 685.

slave, Lord, because I spoke mischievous words in your presence"
(17:7). Whereas in her vision Perpetua receives a drink that initiates
her into eternal life and indicates her impending execution, the
sacrament Aseneth receives endows her with physical strength and
beauty to make her ready for immediate marriage to her Jewish
bridegroom. Aseneth's love for Joseph is the primary motivation for
her conversion and is involved in every aspect of her religious
experience; like Psyche searching to find and win back her husband
Cupid in Apuleius's *Metamorphoses*, she is courageous and willing
to endure extreme physical hardship. She is overcome both emo-
tionally and physically at the sight of Joseph: "Her soul was pene-
trated strongly, and her entrails were crushed and her knees were
loosed and her whole body shook and she was terrified and moaned"
(6:1, cf. 8:8). Further, she is willing to abandon her previous way of
life: she rejects her gods, her idols, and Egyptian food.[63] But
Perpetua climbs the ladder to heaven alone. Her husband never
appears and is not even mentioned by name in the narrative, nor
does she note any prospect of a heavenly bridegroom.[64]

Perpetua is concerned about her brother in prison, but she
asks neither for his help nor for that of any man in deciding what
she should do. She does not allow her father to persuade her to
abandon her faith, though she loves him and is sorry that he suffers
on her account. When, after she is condemned to death, she dreams
that she will win a wrestling match against an Egyptian man, she
immediately realizes the dream's significance: "I understood that I
was going to fight not with the wild beasts, but with the devil, and I
knew that I should win the victory" (10.14).

One looks in vain for similar independence on the part of the
women in either *Asen.* or *T. Job.* Job's three daughters do speak up
for themselves: "Are we not also your children? Why then did you
not give us some of your goods?" (46.2). But it is their father who
must explain why his spiritual gifts to them are better than the
material inheritance which ordinary women would expect.[65] Only
when they bind on the phylacteries their father gives them are they
able to sing hymns in the language of the angels. Conversely,

---

[63]Cf. S. West, "*Joseph and Asenath*: A Neglected Greek Romance," *Classical
Quarterly* 24 (1974): 73, 76.
[64]Perpetua's husband: *Vibia Perpetua, honeste nata, liberaliter instituta,
matronaliter nupta* (i.e., not a concubine) *habens patrem et matrem et fratres
duo, alterum aeque catechumenum, et filium infantem ad ubera* (2.1-2). Since
she appears to be living in her father's household, and her father appears in
court as her guardian, perhaps Perpetua was separated or divorced from her
husband.
[65]Job's daughters: P. W. van der Horst, "The Role of Women in the Testament

Perpetua needed no assistance either to see her vision or to interpret it. Perhaps the ability of Job's daughters to speak in tongues and to forget earthly things (48.2, 49.1, 50.2) indicates that in the Jewish group to which the author of *T. Job* 46-50 belonged women "played a leading role."[66] Perhaps this group allowed or even encouraged women to speak in tongues and even to prophesy, like the early Christians in Corinth (I Cor 14:34-35) or the Montanists Maximilla and Priscilla whom Epiphanius and Eusebius mention with such disdain.[67] But in *T. Job* itself, we do not see women assuming any authority on earth or even taking the initiative in the development of their own spirituality.

Certainly the focus of *Asen.* and *T. Job* 46-50 is on women, and the authors of these texts attribute to women an ability to experience the highest spiritual values of Judaism. But in all other respects Aseneth and Job's three daughters play conventional female roles. Aseneth prays: "Make me into his slave, so that I may wash his feet and serve him and be a slave for him and serve him all the days of my life" (13:12, cf. 20:3). In *T. Job* it is certainly remarkable that Job's wife acquires a name and Job's three daughters some personality; their prominence in the narrative may reflect the relatively higher status accorded to women in the Hellenistic World. Perhaps the prayers attributed to Job's third daughter, Amaltheia's Horn, were concerned exclusively with praise of God (50:2-3), but the narrative that describes her spirituality gives the credit for this religiosity to the wisdom of her father. The women in both pseudepigrapha remain subordinate to and dependent on men; if they had some of Perpetua's independence and initiative, I might be persuaded that the two texts were written or at least inspired by women, but then only because these Jewish documents could not have been written by a "pagan" man.[68]

---

of Job," *Nederlands Theologisch Tijdschrift* 40 (1986): 282.

[66]Ibid., 289.

[67]Eusebius, *EH* v.14-19 (quoting Apolinarius and Apollonius); Epiphanius, *Panarion* 49; cf. *Maenads*, 102-6. Even the learned pagan philosopher Sosipatra was renowed primarily for her accurate prophesying and for her "inspiration" (*enthousiasmos*; Eunapius, *Vit. Philos.* 469).

[68]But cf. A. Brenner, "Female Social Behaviour: Two Descriptive Patterns within the 'Birth of the Hero' Paradigm," *VT* 36.3 (1986), on narratives where women are "seen as strong and constant characters, and the male role is kept to a skeletal minimum. Proving female authorship for all three stories which belong to this category — Exodus 11, Ruth, and Luke 1-11.7 — would have been quite to my personal taste. However, this is not warranted by any further evidence of the texts themselves; and here we should let the matter rest, and regrettably so."

Women's Authorship of Jewish and Christian Literature in the Greco-Roman Period

Ross S. Kraemer

Introduction

Not very long ago, an article so titled might reasonably have been expected to be blank. It is unfortunate but true that we currently possess no literary texts *known* to have been authored by Jewish or Christian women before the writings of Faltonia Betitia Proba in the late fourth century C.E.[1]; the sole exception is, perhaps, a portion of the early third century martyrdom account of Vibia Perpetua.[2]

Before the current surge of feminist scholarship, scholars of early Judaism and early Christianity rarely if ever remarked on this absence; they were seemingly content to believe that we possess no texts authored by women because no women authored texts. Were we confident of the authorship of those surviving early Jewish and Christian writings, such a position might be plausible. But in reality, a significant portion of this early literature is either anonymous or pseudonymous, and thus the assumption that the authors were invariably male is rendered premature at the very least. Recently, several scholars have begun both to consider the possibility that some of these texts may have been authored by women and to explore the grounds on which such an attribution might be proposed.

In this paper, I first consider what little we do know about women writers in the Greco-Roman world; then I examine women's authorship within the context of writing and its dissemination at

---

[1]See Elizabeth A. Clark and Diane Hatch (eds.), *The Golden Bough, The Oaken Cross: The Virgilian Cento of Faltonia Betitia Proba* (Chico, CA: Scholars Press, 1981). Another translation of Proba appears in Patricia Wilson-Kastner et al., *A Lost Tradition: Women Writers of the Early Church* (Lanham, MD: University Press of America, 1981). For discussion of Proba within the context of a study of women writers in Greek and Roman antiquity, see Jane McIntosh Snyder, *The Woman and the Lyre: Women Writers in Classical Greece and Rome* (Carbondale: So. Illinois University, 1989).

[2]A translation of Perpetua by Rosemary Rader appears in Wilson-Kastner, *Lost Tradition*; the version in *Maenads* #53 is excerpted from that of Herbert Musurillo, *Acts of the Christian Martyrs* (Oxford: Clarendon, 1972). For discussions of Perpetua, see Mary Lefkowitz, "The Motivations for St. Perpetua's Martyrdom," *JAAR* 44 (1976): 417-21; Ross S. Kraemer, *Gender, Cult and Cosmology: Women's Religions Among Pagans, Jews and Christians in the Greco-Roman World* (New York and Oxford: Oxford University Press, forthcoming).

the time. The third section explores methodological problems of
identifying the gender of the author behind the production of anonymous and pseudonymous literature, and the fourth treats the
explicit debate over women writers in a fourth-century anti-
Montanist work.[3] The final section considers in more detail possible
explanations for the apparent absence of works by women and the
implications of women's authorship for the study of Judaism and
Christianity in the Greco-Roman world.

Evidence for Women Authors

In the Greco-Roman World. A handful of women writers are
attested in Greek and Latin literature. At best, only fragments of
their work are extant; in some cases, only a brief notice that a
woman wrote survives in the work of a male author. Nevertheless,
women are known to have composed poetry, epigrams, letters
meant for public circulation, philosophical treatises, and so forth.[4]

In Jewish Circles. Two references in Jewish sources from the
Greco-Roman period allude to women writing. In his treatise on the
monastic, contemplative Therapeutics,[5] Philo of Alexandria reports
that the daily routine of members included not only study of
scripture and allegorical commentaries, but also the composition of
hymns and psalms. As I have elsewhere discussed at length, Philo is
unequivocal in asserting that female Therapeutics, or *Therapeutrides*, share in all respects the contemplative calling of their male
counterparts. Their activities must therefore have included education and study, and by analogy, composition as well. Certainly,
nothing in Philo's presentation suggests that the women did not
write such hymns and psalms. Whether the Therapeutics, male or
female, wrote anything else is unknown. Some scholars have
imputed the authorship of *Joseph and Aseneth* — which is more
appropriately called *The Conversion and Marriage of Aseneth*
(*Asen.*) — to a member of this community; such arguments, while

---

[3]*The Debate Between a Montanist and an Orthodox:* Greek text and English
translation in Ronald E. Heine, *The Montanist Oracles and Testimonia.* North
American Patristic Society Monograph Series 14 (Macon, GA: Mercer University, 1989), 112-27, using the text of G. Ficker, *ZKG* 26 (1905): 446-63.
[4]Excellent summaries and discussions of women writers in Greek and Roman
antiquity appear in Snyder, *Woman and the Lyre;* see also the contribution in
this volume by Mary Lefkowitz.
[5]For detailed discussion of the women members of this community, see Ross
S. Kraemer, "Monastic Jewish Women in Greco-Roman Egypt: Philo of Alex-

intriguing, are by no means definitive.[6]

In the enigmatic *Testament of Job* (*T. Job*), a work whose authorship, date, provenance, and even Jewish origins are not firmly established,[7] the three daughters of the title character receive as their inheritance the ability to prophesy. The hymns each composes and recites while in an ecstatic state are said to have been written down by her observing sisters and, as a safety precaution, by Nereos, the brother of Job (*T. Job* 51). The pseudepigraphon claims that the reader may find these in the *Hymns of Amaltheias-Keras* and the *Hymns of Cassia* (*T. Job* 49-50), but such works are otherwise unknown to us. Whether they ever existed and did in fact represent the writings of women prophets is similarly unknown. All we can say is that the *Testament of Job* presents such works as plausible.

In the Early Christian Communities. The earliest Christian writing now thought to have been composed by a woman is the prison diary of Vibia Perpetua (ca. 203 C.E.), which is incorporated within the *Martyrdom of Saints Perpetua and Felicitas*.[8] The preface supplied by the unknown Montanist editor[9] states explicitly that Perpetua wrote down the account in her own words (*Perpetua* 2). No other writing by a Christian woman is known to us with certainty until the well-known late fourth-century Latin *Cento* of Faltonia Betitia Proba and the fifth-century travelogue of Egeria.

That other Christian women wrote is nevertheless unquestionable. The Montanist prophets Priscilla and Maximilla are said to have written books of their own prophecies,[10] and sayings attributed to them as well as to a third prophet named Quintilla are preserved in several sources.[11] Indeed women writing books in their

---

andria on the *Therapeutrides*," *Signs* 14.1 (1989): 345-80.

[6]Translation of *Asen.* in *Maenads* #113. On the question of authorship, see Kraemer, "Monastic Jewish Women," 361-63; see also M. Delcor, "Un roman d'amour d'origine therapeute: Le Livre de Joseph et Asénath," *BLE* 63 (1962): 3-27.

[7]Excerpted in *Maenads* #119.

[8]See above, n. 2.

[9]Timothy D. Barnes doubts the veracity of this attribution: *Tertullian. A Historical and Literary Study* (Oxford: Clarendon, 1971), 265. Wilson-Kastner asserts it without discussion in her introduction to *Lost Tradition*, xi; R. Rader refers simply and more judiciously to the "redactor" in the introduction to her translation of *Perpetua* in the same volume.

[10]See *Maenads* #102; Heine, *Montanist Oracles*.

[11]Sayings attributed to Maximilla, Priscilla, and Quintilla are found in Heine, *Montanist Oracles*, and *Maenads* #105 and #106. On the attribution of these sayings, see Douglas Powell, "Tertullianists and Cataphrygians," *VC* 29 (1975):

own names was a source of controversy between the Montanists and their opponents.[12] Women were also active participants in correspondence with certain male Christian authors, notably Jerome and Chrysostom.[13] Although not unsurprisingly none of the letters of Olympias to Chrysostom, or of Paula or her daughter Eustochium to Jerome has survived, we have ample evidence from the men that these women's letters were equal in sophistication and erudition to their own.[14]

All of this evidence has received some notice in recent scholarly discussions. One curious text, however, has apparently gone unremarked in the attempt to assess women's authorship in early Christian circles. Among the corpus of letters considered falsely attributed to Ignatius of Antioch[15] is one entitled *Mary the Proselyte to Ignatius*; an alleged reply of Ignatius to Mary also is extant.[16] This text is particularly relevant to the discussion of women authors not simply because it purports to have been written by a woman, but

---

33-54.

[12]See below on the *Debate Between a Montanist and an Orthodox*.

[13]Samples of the correspondence from Jerome to several women and from Chrysostom to Olympias appear in *Maenads* #70-75. See also E. A. Clark, *Ascetic Piety and Women's Faith: Essays in Late Ancient Christianity*, Studies in Women and Religion 20 (Lewiston, NY: Edwin Mellen, 1986); idem, *Jerome, Chrysostom and Friends*, Studies in Women and Religion 2 (Lewiston, NY: Edwin Mellen, 1979); and A. H. Ewing, *Women of the Roman Aristocracy as Christian Monastics*, Studies in Religion 1 (Ann Arbor: UMI Research Press, 1987). Other instances of letters to Christian women include *Ptolemy to Flora* (late 2d-early 3d cent. C.E.).

[14]For example, Jerome extols the ease with which Paula learned Hebrew; indeed, he claims that she surpassed his own knowledge (*Jerome to Eustochium* 27). He also dwells at some length on the intricacies of her arguments against persons and doctrines he considered heretical (23-26).

[15]Ignatius himself is usually dated to the late 1st-early 2d century, on the basis of the references in Polycarp. Robert Joly, *Le Dossier d'Ignace d'Antioche*, Université Libre de Bruxelles 69 (Brussels: Editions de l'université, 1979), has suggested, however, that the references to Ignatius in Polycarp's letter to the Philippians are interpolations. He would place Ignatius considerably later. For a summary of these problems and additional bibliography, see William R. Schoedel, *Ignatius of Antioch*, Hermeneia Commentary Series (Philadelphia: Fortress, 1985), esp. 4-7.

[16]The history and problems of the Ignatian corpus are many, complex, and largely outside the scope of this paper. See Schoedel, *Ignatius*, for a comprehensive survey; see also his review essay, "Are the Letters of Ignatius of Antioch Authentic?" *RelSRev* 6.1 (1980): 196-210. Even though Roberts and Donaldson observed over a century ago that such texts were worthy sources of later Christian conflicts and communities (*ANF* I:106 n. 1), *Mary the Proselyte to Ignatius* appears to have been universally rejected as authentically Ignatian, and so the alleged correspondence between this Mary and the bishop has been deemed of little further interest. The Greek text with Latin translation and notes is found in *PG* ser 2, vol. V: 873-80. Greek with Latin is found in William Cureton (ed.), *Corpus Ignatianum* (London: Francis and John Rivington, 1849), 119-27. English translation in *ANF* I, 120-23.

because it explicitly expresses awareness of the potential offense such a letter might seem to be.

Extant in Greek, the letter is relatively short and concerns primarily the appropriateness of ordaining young men to priestly office. Mary writes to reassure Ignatius that certain men who have recently attained priestly office (προσφάτῳ νεότητι ἱερωσύνης ἀστράπτοντες πολιάν) are well qualified, despite the fact that they are very young. In support of her claim, she offers numerous examples from Scripture of men who, although young, were nevertheless wise and pleasing to God, and who were entrusted with priestly, prophetic, or royal office: these include Daniel, Solomon, Josiah, and David.

At the conclusion of the letter, Mary assures Ignatius that she writes not to instruct him, but rather only to bring these testimonies to his remembrance. It is difficult not to see in this disclaimer an allusion to I Tim 2:12, in which women are prohibited from either teaching men or having authority over them.

I will later return to the possible relationship between this correspondence and Montanist-Orthodox debates over women's writing as the equivalent of having authority over men. For the moment, we shall consider several other implications of this fascinating, neglected text.

Whether the actual author was a woman seems impossible to determine on firm ground. Reinoud Weijenborg suggests that not only this letter but also its reply, together with much of the rest of the pseudo-Ignatian material was actually written by Evagrius Ponticus in the fifth century.[17] He proposes that the figure of Mary camouflages Evagrius's own sister, the figure of Hero represents Evagrius himself, and Ignatius represents Evagrius's father. The letter titled *Hero to Ignatius* (9) does mention a Mary who is apparently the same Mary as the alleged author. But Weijenborg's solution to the problems of the Ignatian corpus has been widely rejected in the subsequent scholarly literature; we have little foundation for his association of Evagrius with the pseudepigrapher.[18]

---

[17]Reinoud Weijenborg, *Les Lettres d'Ignace d'Antioch. Étude de Critique Littéraire et de Théologie* (Leiden: Brill, 1969), 399, 410-11; cf. his "Is Evagrius Ponticus the Author of the Longer Recension of the Ignatian Letters?" *Antonianum* 44 (1969): 339-47.

[18]See Schoedel, *Ignatius* and the review essay. Elizabeth Clark, who has been engaged in a detailed study of Evagrius, finds no indication in the style or theological content of *Mary to Ignatius* to support Weijenborg's hypothesis (personal correspondence, 12 April 1990).

Regardless of the author's actual identity, the fact remains
that someone composed a letter in the name of a woman, addressed
to a bishop, which concerns issues of authority and politics in some
Christian community before the sixth century. At another point, I
hope to explore further the ramifications of this correspondence; for
now, it is sufficient to suggest that the author of this work did not
think a letter in the name of a woman to be at all implausible, provided that the woman presented herself as cognizant of the apostolic
restraints on women "teaching." Further, the author of *Mary to
Ignatius* depicts this woman as learned in Scripture and savvy in
matters political, while the author of *Ignatius to Mary* (possibly but
not certainly the same?) acknowledges her as intelligent, learned,
and of the highest repute (1, 4). Next, the author of *Ignatius to Hero*
(5) presents her as the head of a church in her house. And finally,
the letter of reply depicts Mary and Ignatius as friends for whom the
exchange of correspondence is an adequate though not ideal sub-
stitute for each other's companionship (*Ignatius to Mary* 1). We may
conclude, then, that women who wrote letters addressing important
theological and political issues were not unknown to the author's
community, and thus not inherently unacceptable.

Women's Authorship in Context

No discussion of women's authorship, whether Jewish,
Christian, or "pagan," can be divorced from questions about the
context of writing in antiquity. Such questions include patterns of
literacy, the production and dissemination of written materials —
especially, but not only literature — and the connections between
literacy and authorship.

Literacy in Antiquity. Scholarly estimates of literacy rates in
the Greco-Roman world vary considerably. While literacy may have
been in general the prerogative of the aristocracy, it was by no
means correlated only with class: male slaves were often able to read
and write well enough to transact business for their owners, educate
children, and copy manuscripts.[19] Recent feminist scholarship
seems agreed that while fewer women than men were likely to have
been literate, meaningful numbers of women — regardless of class —
learned to read and write, if this is in fact what we mean by
literacy.[20] And scholarship in general seems agreed that the vast

---

[19]William V. Harris, "Literacy and Epigraphy, I," *ZPE* 52 (1983): 87-111; and
idem, *Ancient Literacy* (Cambridge, MA: Harvard, 1989).
[20]Sarah B. Pomeroy, *Goddesses, Whores, Wives and Slaves: Women in Classical*

majority of people in antiquity were illiterate; the writing skills of many were limited to the ability to scrawl their names on required legal documents.

The Production and Dissemination of Literature. Stereotypes concerning the production and dissemination of written work in antiquity, particularly of what we tend to class as literature as opposed to commercial, governmental, or even personal documents, all too easily obscure the realities of the processes. A recent article by Raymond J. Starr illuminates the processes of both literary composition and literary dissemination in the Roman world.[21]

Roman authors apparently both physically wrote compositions themselves and dictated them to secretaries (who were likely to have been slaves). Once a work was drafted, authors commonly circulated a copy to one or two close friends, who would annotate and then return the manuscript. Writers assumed that such preliminary versions would not be circulated without their authorization, but apparently confidentiality could be a problem, and unauthorized manuscripts were sometimes more widely disseminated than their authors wished.[22] When an author was sufficiently satisfied with a draft, he might circulate a few more copies or invite a limited group of friends and associates to hear the work read aloud.[23] Afterwards, copies might be given to close friends, who might in turn permit their friends to make copies. Starr suggests that at this point, when it "became possible for people unknown to the author to acquire a text," we may consider the work published, that is, made public or released.[24] The distribution of authorized manuscripts was thus part of the commerce of friendship and influence in ancient society. Starr suggests that little dissemination took place by commercial means until at least the first century C.E., and even then private distribution remained a major channel of dissemination. The use of public booksellers to distribute one's

---

Antiquity (New York: Schocken, 1975), 137; cf. idem, "Technikai kai Musikai: The Education of Women in the Fourth Century and in the Hellenistic Period," *AJAH* 2 (1977): 51-68; and Susan Guettel Cole, "Could Greek Women Read and Write?" *Women's Studies* 8 (1981): 129-55, reprinted in H. Foley (ed.), *Reflections of Women in Antiquity* (London: Gordon and Breach, 1981), 219-45.

[21]Raymond J. Starr, "The Circulation of Literary Texts in the Roman World," *CQ* 37 (1987): 213-23.

[22]Ibid., 218.

[23]The use of the gendered pronoun here is intentional. Starr's portrait is drawn solely, if understandably, from male authors; I consider below its ramifications for women's writing.

[24]Starr, "Circulation," 215.

works was considered declassé in many circles.[25]

While the implications of this study for textual issues in early Jewish and Christian literature are considerable — they suggest, *inter alia*, that even in antiquity there was no such thing as an *original*, not always even such a thing as an *autograph* — I am particularly interested here in the ramifications of his thesis for women's writing. The location of both the composition process and the initial dissemination within the relatively private sphere suggests that women with sufficient education and leisure time could indeed have produced literary works and could have shared them with others, probably mostly other women. But the writings of many women authors might never have circulated beyond such small gatherings.

Starr's article also serves to remind us that connections between literacy and authorship are only indirect. One need not have been technically literate[26] in order to have composed a written work; one only need have access to a secretary.[27] While it seems unlikely that an individual could have authored a complex literary work without some formal education (including not only reading, writing, and grammar but also rhetoric), it may not have been impossible. Susan Cole points out that Aspasia, the mistress of Perikles, reputed to have been an accomplished orator in fifth-century Athens, may not have known how to read and write.[28] Cole's work, which suggests that a skilled speaker could dictate a skilled piece without necessarily having the ability to write it down, may have substantial implications for our assessment of women's ability to author texts.

Women's Education. On the assumption, however, that for most people some degree of formal education was a prerequisite for the ability to compose literary materials, we should next briefly survey what we know about women's education in the Greco-Roman

---

[25]Ibid., 223.
[26]Cole, "Could Greek Women Read and Write?" (in Foley, *Reflections*, 219), defines "literacy" as "knowledge of the alphabet and the ability to write one's name and to read simple formulaic expressions."
[27]Cole (ibid., 220), points out that in antiquity, reading and writing were separate skills and that "ability in one does not automatically imply ability in the other." For a discussion of the use of professional scribes, see ibid., 234-35: the fully literate, the barely literate, and the illiterate all used scribes — some of whom themselves were only marginally literate — for various reasons. A mummy ca. 200 C.E. bears the inscription of a woman γραμματική (so ibid., 236 and 244 n. 107).
[28]Ibid., 225.

period.

In the Greco-Roman world generally. In the classical period, Greek girls regardless of class were unlikely to receive any formal education beyond instruction in domestic arts. It is, however, possible that a few were taught their letters at home.[29] By the Hellenistic period, formal education began to be acceptable for at least some girls in Greek families; this shift correlates with the emergence of Greek women poets such as Erinna.[30] The curriculum for girls was apparently limited to reading, writing, and poetry; mathematics and rhetoric were not included. Among elite Roman families, formal education for girls seems to have been quite acceptable, and not only at the elementary level.[31] Pomeroy points out that girls had less opportunity to study at the advanced level, since they usually married at an age (12-15)[32] when boys were still studying with philosophers or rhetoricians.[33] As evidenced by numerous references to highly educated courtesans and freedwomen, women skilled in philosophy, poetry, music, and mathematics, among other disciplines, were not limited to the Roman elite. A snippet from Juvenal's vicious satire on women, quoted by Pomeroy, illustrates at once that educated women were no longer a rarity and that many Roman men had mixed emotions about that fact:

> Still more exasperating is the woman who begs as soon as she sits down to dinner, to discourse on poets and poetry, comparing Virgil with Homer: professors, critics, lawyers, auctioneers — even another woman — can't get a word in. ... Wives shouldn't try to be public speakers; they shouldn't use rhetorical devices; they shouldn't read all the classics — there ought to be some things women don't understand. I myself can't understand a woman who can quote the rules of grammar and never make a mistake and cites obscure, long-forgotten poets....[34]

The Education of Jewish Women. Regrettably, but typically, the limited discussions of the education of Jewish women in the

---

[29]Ibid., 226.

[30]Ibid., 231. Cole's evidence is mostly from the Greek cities of Asia Minor, including Teos, Pergamon, and Dorylaion.

[31]Pomeroy, *Goddesses*, 170; and "Technikai," 51-68.

[32]On the relationship between average age at marriage and education for girls, see R. Kraemer, "Jewish Women in the Diaspora World of Late Antiquity," in Judith Baskin (ed.), *Jewish Women in Historical Perspective* (Detroit: Wayne State, 1991), 43-67.

[33]Pomeroy, *Goddesses*, 170.

[34]Juvenal, *Sat.* 6.434-56, cited in Pomeroy, *Goddesses*, 172.

Greco-Roman period have relied heavily, if not exclusively, on rabbinic sources for evidence. Equating education with the study of
Torah, authors like Leonard Swidler have concluded that Jewish
women were more or less prohibited from attaining any meaningful
degree of education.[35]

In reality, of course, educated Jews in this period, especially in
the diaspora, undoubtedly studied far more than Scripture and its
interpretation, as we know from writers as diverse as Jesus ben Sira
and Philo.[36] As we have already seen, the women who joined the
contemplative Therapeutics possessed a sophisticated education
which must have been similar in content to Philo's own, and we
know that Philo received all the elements of a classical education as
well as the study of Scripture and exegesis. A handful of Jewish
inscriptions, primarily from Rome, attest to the education of Jewish
women.[37] It seems reasonable that many, if not all, of the women
who held various synagogue offices would have possessed sufficient
formal education to carry out the responsibilities of their offices.[38]

The Education of Christian Women. Little research has been
done on the specific question of the education of Christian women.
Since in the period under consideration many Christians were not
born such, it may be helpful to distinguish between the educational
opportunities for girls born into Christian households and those
who became Christians after the traditional age of education for
children. For the latter group, we have already in effect surveyed
their circumstances.

The emphasis on Scripture and its interpretation so prevalent
in early Christian communities, coupled with the pervasive evidence
for women's participation in the spread of Christianity, strongly
suggests that women who became Christians must have received
some formal training in the study of Scripture. Whether they would
have taken up the study of letters without previous education, or
whether women who functioned as teachers would have already had

---

[35]Leonard Swidler, *Women in Judaism: The Status of Women in Formative
Judaism* (Metuchen, NJ: Scarecrow, 1976), esp. 114.
[36]See, for example, Ben Sira 34:9-12. The breadth of education which at least
some diaspora Jews must have had is evident throughout Philo's writings.
[37]In *CIJ* 215 a man named Sempronius Basileus commemorates his wife,
Aurelia Caelerina, as *discipulina bona.* In *CIJ* 132 a woman named Crispina is
eulogized as φιλέντολος, a term which is also used to commemorate men, and
in its denotation of love for the commandments may imply formal education
and study. Crispina's inscription is likely to have been commissioned by her
husband, Procopius.
[38]On which see Bernadette J. Brooten, *Women Leaders in the Ancient
Synagogue,* BJS 36 (Chico, CA: Scholars Press, 1982).

some knowledge of reading (and writing) cannot be determined from the available sources, at least for the first century or two. The account of Priscilla, who is credited in Acts 18:26 (together with her husband, Aquila) with the proper instruction of the sophisticated Alexandrian Apollos, suggests that Priscilla herself was sufficiently educated to have some credibility with one schooled in allegorical exegesis. Similarly, one might argue that the figure of Thecla could not have been expected to function so effectively as a teacher had she not possessed some formal education.

Finally, there is the intriguing reference in Eusebius that as Origen dictated his commentaries on Scripture, he had the services of seven shorthand writers, seven copyists, and numerous girls skilled in calligraphy. Whether these girls were Christians, and if so, whether from birth, we do not know.[39] It is important to remember that the more we deal with converts, the more the likelihood their education is intertwined with their circumstances prior to their becoming Christians.

Problems of Method:
Anonymous and Pseudonymous Literature
and the Identification of Authorial Gender

We have seen that at least some Jewish and Christian women in Greco-Roman antiquity possessed the educational skills necessary to author more than brief personal letters such as those preserved on papyri. As I remarked at the outset, no women are identified as authors of extant works, yet a vast amount of early Jewish and Christian works are in fact either anonymous or pseudonymous. Are there any viable criteria which can be used to identify the sex of these authors?

Stevan Davies tackles this issue in his study of early Christian apocryphal acts.[40] In support of his thesis that many of these texts were authored by women, Davies points to several key characteristics shared by the various documents: (1) women play central roles; (2) women are not denigrated; (3) men do not play central roles. Comparing the portrayal of women in the apocryphal acts collectively with works he considers roughly contemporaneous — particularly the virulently misogynistic *Pseudo-Clementines* — Davies proposes that the texts known to have been authored by men

---

[39]Eusebius, *EH* 6. 23.
[40]Stevan Davies, *The Revolt of the Widows. The Social World of the Apocryphal Acts* (Carbondale: Southern Illinois University, 1980).

assign central roles to men and denigrate women. He concludes that
women therefore wrote the apocryphal acts. In a somewhat similar
vein, Elisabeth Schüssler Fiorenza has considered the possibility
that women wrote both the Gospel of Mark and the Gospel of John;
she bases her thesis on the portrayal of women characters in the
texts as well as on the relative importance of women characters in
Mark and John as compared to the other two canonical gospels.[41]

Given the frustrations involved in identifying the authors of all
this anonymous and pseudonymous literature, including the canonical gospels and acts, the suggestion that attitudes towards
women and men reliably differentiate writings by women and men
might have some appeal. However, this suggestion is a methodological minefield. Corollary to Davies's hypothesis is the argument
that men in antiquity could not, or would not, write non-miso-
gynist, non-androcentric literature, even if women were intended as
recipients. I am strongly inclined to agree with Davies that whoever
wrote the *Pseudo-Clementines* did not write any of the apocryphal
acts, but there is no reason to conclude therefore that a more
sympathetic male could not have been their ultimate author.
Certainly we know of at least some ancient male authors who
demonstrated such sensitivity.[42] Davies, and perhaps others who
have made similar proposals, would seem to be claiming that men
could not, or would not, write works in which women played central
roles, unless perhaps the women were at some point denigrated; in
such a case, we might conclude that the combination of central
female characters and the absence of misogyny points strongly to a
woman author. This hypothesis would make numerous ancient
Jewish and Christian writings, including Judith, Susanna and the
Elders, and *The Conversion and Marriage of Aseneth*, candidates for
female authorship. With regard to the apocryphal acts, at least, I
find more satisfactory the suggestion of Dennis MacDonald that
while the works contain stories told by women, in their current form
they are perhaps more likely to have been collected and edited by a
number of men.[43]

Davies's hypothesis contains another corollary: women are

---

[41]*Memory*, 316-33.
[42]Musonius Rufus, for example, advocated the advanced education of women
and seemed generally sympathetic; see his *That Women Too Should Study
Philosophy*, text and translation in Cora E. Lutz, "Musonius Rufus, 'The Roman
Socrates,'" *Yale Classical Studies* 10 (1947): 38-43; and A. C. Geytenbeek,
Musonius Rufus and Greek Diatribe (Assen: Van Gorcum, 1965), 51-62.
[43]In *The Legend and the Apostle: The Battle for Paul in Story and Canon*
(Philadelphia: Westminster, 1983).

unlikely to have authored works in which men are the central characters or in which women are portrayed in a negative light. Yet much feminist research has demonstrated the degree to which many if not most women inculcate the dominant, misogynist values and perspectives of their own cultures into their self-understanding. At the risk of invoking modern analogies, we have only to consider the case of Phyllis Schlafly, or perhaps more kindly, the perspectives of modern Orthodox Jewish women, to see the extent of the dilemma. Two-thousand years from now, will some scholars of late twentieth-century American culture argue that Schlafly must have been a man writing under a woman's name, because no women would write such things?

The criteria proposed by Davies and a few others are ultimately inadequate in part because of their logical deficiencies and in part because we lack the controls to verify their claims. Classicist Mary Lefkowitz has wisely tried to approach the problem from the other side: she takes those few known literary writings (as opposed to personal letters) by women and attempts to analyze their characteristics to see in what significant ways they differ from the writings of men in the same genre.[44] The known writings by women tend to fall into certain categories, principally poetry, epigrams, some historical memoirs, and a few philosophical treatises (no longer extant). Lefkowitz points out that no women are known to have written novels or fiction, despite the modern association of these as female genres. Although she observes that professional women poets wrote epigrams which are indistinguishable from those of professional male poets, Lefkowitz concludes that women's writings from the classical Greek, Hellenistic, and Roman periods all emphasize details of women's lives apart from men: women's love for other women, especially their devotion to childhood companions; the joys of childhood; the love of daughters; and so forth. These traits are particularly obvious in the epigrams the poets wrote for their women patrons.

Lefkowitz then analyzes in some detail the prison diary of Vibia Perpetua, and she concludes that the roles of men are downplayed, particularly in Perpetua's references to her own salvation which is achieved largely through her own efforts. Autonomous female action characterizes the diary. By contrast, Lefkowitz analyzes two texts which some scholars, myself included, consider

[44]See her contribution to this volume. My comments here are based on a presentation to the Hellenistic Judaism section of the Society of Biblical Literature (1987 Annual Meeting, Boston). Professor Lefkowitz was kind

candidates for female authorship: *The Conversion and Marriage of Aseneth* and (portions of) the *Testament of Job*. She emphasizes the centrality of the male figure or angel in *Asen.* as well as the importance of Aseneth's marriage to Joseph as evidence that this pseudepigraphon does not display similarities with known women's literature; her discussion of *T. Job* is similar. Lefkowitz concludes: "The women in both pseudepigrapha remain subordinate to and dependent on men; if they had some of Perpetua's independence and initiative, I might be persuaded that the two texts were written or at least inspired by women."[45]

Although I applaud Lefkowitz's attempt to proceed from the known to the unknown, her analysis is susceptible both to critique and to nuancing. In the case of *Asen.*, we must confront some intriguing textual problems. Lefkowitz relies primarily for her discussion on the translation by Christopher Burchard, which in turn is based on his own reconstruction of what he calls an "eclectic text."[46] Further, there are some disputes between Burchard and Philonenko over the text of *Asen.*[47] which are particularly germane to the discussion of women's authorship. Sexually explicit language, which may been seen to denigrate the character of Aseneth, is present only in Burchard's reconstruction.[48] Philonenko's version presents Aseneth as chosen by God before her birth and thus it places her in the company of numerous distinguished biblical males, whereas Burchard's text differs subtly but significantly: it is God's people who were chosen before all things came into being.[49] Father imagery is much stronger in Burchard's version.[50] While in Philonenko's text Aseneth confesses that she has incurred her parents' wrath because she destroyed their gods, Burchard has Aseneth offend her family not only by her rejection of their gods but also by her hatred of men and her rejection of marriage.[51]

These examples and others strongly suggest that more is at issue here than strict text-critical questions of which reading is more likely to be the earlier, and therefore the "original." In our

---

enough to provide me with a copy of her remarks.

[45]See above, this volume, p. 219.

[46]OTP 2: 177-247; text in Christopher Burchard, *Joseph und Aseneth. Jüdische Schriften aus hellenistisch-römischer Zeit* (Gütersloh: Gütersloher Verlagshaus Gerd Mohn, 1983).

[47]Marc Philonenko, *Joseph et Aseneth: Introduction, texte critique, traduction et notes* (Leiden: Brill, 1968).

[48]Philonenko 8:4; Burchard 8:5.

[49]Philonenko 8:11; Burchard 8:9.

[50]Philonenko 12:7; Burchard 12:8.

[51]Philonenko 12:11 versus Burchard 11:3b-6; 21:18-21.

discussion of the production and dissemination of ancient texts, we have seen that such concepts are too simplistic and that they do not take full account of the ways in which Greek and Latin authors wrote and rewrote their own works. But in the case of *Asen.*, the textual differences clearly have contextual ramifications. While these observations are preliminary, I do not think one pushes the evidence too far to suggest that Burchard's reconstruction, whether it more accurately represents earlier versions of the text or later revisions, represents the concerns of a male audience and a male author, while the text proposed by Philonenko remains a much better candidate for female authorship or editing.

Even if we were to accept the emphasis on men and the denial of female autonomy Lefkowitz detects in *Asen.* and *T. Job*, I think it is important to observe that both works are constrained to some extent by the biblical materials on which they are probably based. The conclusion of *Asen.* must certainly be that Aseneth marries Joseph: this is virtually all that Genesis tells us about her, except that with Joseph she has two children, Manasseh and Ephraim. To argue that this is not a women's text because it glorifies marriage fails to comprehend the framework in which such a story evolves.

Lefkowitz also raises a problem similar to that discussed earlier in the context of Davies's study: the assumption that women could not write work reflecting their subordination. On this point, all we say can is that anonymous and pseudonymous texts, let alone texts written in the names of women, which manifest some acceptance of prevailing cultural androcentrism and misogyny cannot, on those grounds alone, be rejected as candidates for women's authorship.

On this question of the relationship between context and authorship, Lefkowitz's own criteria complicate if not contradict her analysis. Her assessment that women are unlikely to have composed either *Asen.* or *T. Job* relies heavily on the predominant roles that male figures, both human and angelic, play in both texts. Yet in her evaluation of work known to have been written by women in antiquity, Lefkowitz suggests that women's writing is characterized by a reflection of the minutia of women's lives. The story of Aseneth, though perhaps not the Testament, is replete with such details. The author provides elaborate descriptions of interior spaces, of Aseneth's many rooms, her clothing, and her food. Lefkowitz observes that known writing by women exhibits strong affection for other women and for childhood companions. In *Asen.*, the author pays significant attention to the seven women who were born on the

same night as Aseneth and who have been her constant companions since then.[52] When Aseneth retreats in grief and misery to her
chamber, the seven companions attempt to comfort her, but feign-
ing a headache she kindly turns them away (10:2-8). After her
mystical initiation by the angelic figure, Aseneth seeks and obtains
blessings for these seven women (17:4-5). Philonenko's version in
particular emphasizes her love also for both her parents. Interiority
is thus a key aspect of this text, which is set largely within the house
of Pentephres and mostly within either Aseneth's own chambers or
viewed from her balcony. All of these details accord well with
Lefkowitz's own observations about the perspectives and concerns
of known women writers.

Inverse Problems — The Pseudo-Ignatian Material.   The
problematic letter of *Mary to Ignatius* presents methodological
difficulties of an inverse order. Either a male author wrote the letter
in the name of a woman, or a woman wrote it. But since there can be
virtually no doubt that the letter is not an authentic epistle to the
early Christian martyr, in either case someone fabricated a document in the name of a woman and expected it to be accepted as such.
Does such a document offer any insight then into contemporaneous
perceptions of the ways in which Christian women might have
written, or the topics they might have engaged?

It is perhaps premature to attempt to address these issues
fully; one should first undertake a detailed study, with these concerns in mind, of the entire pseudo-Ignatian corpus. Those scholars
who have studied the material extensively have primarily been interested in determining an authentic Ignatian corpus, but to the extent
that they have accidentally addressed questions related to women,
none has singled out *Mary to Ignatius* as stylistically unusual.[53]

Even if we assume that this particular letter was written by a
male author who composed much if not all of the pseudo-Ignatian

---

[52]*Asen.* 2:10-11 (in *Maenads* #113, based on Philonenko).
[53]For example, in their original introduction to the *ANF* translation (I, 106 of
the reprint), Roberts and Donaldson remark on the idiosyncratic style of
Ignatius to Mary, but they say nothing about *Mary to Ignatius.* In his effort to
test the usefulness of linguistic and stylistic criteria to detect forgeries in the
name of an author whose authentic works are known, Milton Perry Brown
excluded any study of Mary to Ignatius on the grounds that it was merely
addressed to Ignatius, not attributed to him. See his *Authentic Writings of
Ignatius* (Durham, NC: Duke, 1963), xi, 120. Brown found no significant
stylistic differences between *Ignatius to Mary* and the other Pseudo-Ignatian
letters, and he concluded that the same author is likely to have written all of
the texts, most probably in the mid-fourth century C.E.

corpus,[54] we are left with the observation that a letter written in a woman's name did not differ in either style or content from those written in the name of men. One could argue that such is precisely the give-away that a woman did not write the letter. But again, we are confronted with the inescapable fact that the author thought a letter written in the name of a woman credible, unless we wish to suppose a far more devious forger, who sought to undermine the causes defended in this letter by attributing them to a woman. There is, however, no evidence to suggest such a devious forger, nor has anyone who has studied the correspondence proposed such an explanation on any grounds. Thus it seems not unreasonable to take the letter as evidence that Christian women were thought capable of writing letters addressing matters of concern to the whole community and displaying no characteristics which could reliably be attributed to the gender of the author. But one critical exception to this observation remains: the allusion to the proscription of I Tim 2:12 against women teaching men.

Certainly, from the correspondence of men like Jerome and Chrysostom, we know that Christian women in the fourth and fifth centuries could and did write letters. What makes *Mary to Ignatius* so intriguing is, first, simply that it is extant: none of the correspondence of Olympias to Chrysostom or of any woman to Jerome has survived. Second, *Mary to Ignatius* is presented not merely as the personal correspondence between friends, although it is also that: it is presented as an authoritative response to a difficult political-ecclesiastical situation.

The Conflict Over Women's Authorship in Early Christianity

The *Letter of Mary to Ignatius* raises one further issue, namely, the possibility that Christian women who wrote, at least for public consumption, wrote pseudonymously. There seems little doubt that, even if the author was female, whoever wrote *Mary to Ignatius* was not, in fact, a woman named Mary who lived in the eastern portion of Asia Minor no later than the second century.

Although the question of why anyone wrote pseudonymously in late antiquity, particularly among Jews and Christians, is complex,[55] it is easy to surmise why women would have done so.

---

[54]As does Brown, *Authentic Writings*.
[55]On pseudepigraphy, see Kurt Aland, "The Problem of Anonymity and Pseudonymity in Christian Literature of the First Two Centuries," *JTS* n.s. 12 (1961): 39-49; Bruce Metzger, "Literary Forgeries and Canonical Pseudepigrapha," *JBL* 91 (1972): 3-24; Martin Rist, "Pseudepigraphy and the Early

Women in societies far less restrictive than those of late antiquity have nevertheless found it much easier to gain public acceptance by writing under a male pseudonym. But such suggestions, however likely they may be to approximate reality, fail to meet the requirements of rigorous scholarship.

Fortunately, we possess some evidence that at least some early Christians did actually discuss the appropriateness of women writing in their own names. In an enigmatic document entitled *The Debate Between a Montanist and an Orthodox*, such an explicit discussion appears. The Montanist asks whether the Orthodox do not accept Priscilla and Maximilla as prophets because they think women may not prophesy. The Orthodox replies that this question has nothing to do with the issue of acceptance: he agrees that women may prophesy, and he cites the famous example of Mary the mother of Jesus, who foretells the future when she proclaims "Henceforth all generations will call me blessed" (Lk 1:48). But, relying on the classic constellation of I Cor 14:33b-36, I Tim 2:12, and I Cor 11:5, the Orthodox continues:

> We do not allow [women] to speak in the assemblies, nor to have authority over men, such that ultimately even books are written in their own names. For this is what it is for women to pray and prophesy uncovered: this, then, is what has dishonored [her] head, that is, [her] man. For was not the holy God-bearer Mary able to write books in her own name? But she did not, so that she did not dishonor her head by exercising authority over men.[56]

The astonished Montanist then asks whether the statement about praying and prophesying uncovered is really a statement about writing books, and the Orthodox assents again. To the Montanist's suggestion that Mary herself prophesied openly and without covering, the Orthodox responds that Mary had the evangelist for her veil: she did not write the gospel in her own name. The Montanist remains unimpressed by this allegorical interpretation and pointedly rejects the offering of allegory as dogma.

After an additional exchange on whether Scripture is to be read allegorically or literally, with the Orthodox illustrating the absurdities into which the Montanist must fall if he persists in his literal readings, the Montanist returns the subject to women writing. Is it,

---

Christians," in D. E. Keene (ed.), *Studies in New Testament and Early Christian Literature: Essays in Honor of Allen P. Wikgren* (Leiden: Brill, 1972), 75-91.
[56]Heine, *Montanist Oracles*, 124-27; translation mine.

he asks, because Priscilla and Maximilla composed (συνέταξαν) books that the Orthodox reject them? The Orthodox concedes that it is for this reason, and also because the women were false prophets.

This fascinating text thus indicates that at least in some circles I Cor 11:5 and I Tim 2:12 were interpreted allegorically to prohibit women from writing books in their own names. We may assume that these members of these circles were not sympathetic readers of the *Gospel of Mary*; more pointedly, we may assume that these persons were not sympathetic readers of *Mary to Ignatius*. However, both *Mary to Ignatius* and the *Debate Between a Montanist and an Orthodox* are usually dated to the fourth century, and both have links to proximate geographic regions in Asia Minor.

The stance of the *Debate Between a Montanist and an Orthodox* provides at least one possible motivation for Christian women in the fourth century, if not earlier, to write pseudonymously. The Orthodox protagonist is insistent that it is not women's writing per se, but their writing *in their own names*, a phrase he repeatedly uses, that is the core of the offense. He even suggests that the evangelist (in this case, Luke) is really writing Mary's work, but in his name, not hers. Women like Priscilla and Maximilla could clearly write in their own names, as we know they did, and gain acceptance in their own Montanist communities. It is probably not insignificant that Perpetua herself was a member of the New Prophecy (that is, of Montanism) in North Africa.

The *Letter of Mary to Ignatius* demonstrates that not all non-Montanists interpreted I Cor 11:5, let alone I Tim 2:12, in such an allegorical manner.[57] But Christian women who wished to write, at least in some circles such as those represented by the so-called Orthodox, could clearly deduce that pseudepigraphy would have to be the order of the day.

Accounting for the Paucity of Evidence

A variety of explanations may be offered for the total absence of known writings by Jewish women and the virtual absence of known writings by Christian women prior to the early medieval period. The simplest is that women lacked the education and skills to write. As demonstrated above, however, ample evidence contradicts such

---

[57]Unless one wants to argue on precisely this ground that the letter is Montanist! I am unaware if anyone has proposed this identification on other grounds.

sweeping generalizations. At least some Jewish and Christian women in late antiquity did have the necessary education and skills.

Conceivably, Jewish and Christian women produced no literature of any kind because they lacked the opportunities to write. If we concede that the prerequisites for writing included not only sufficient education and familiarity with literary language, but also both the time and space needed for composition, we may have a more plausible explanation. Virginia Woolf's contemporary observation that women writers require both financial autonomy and a room of their own might not be too far off the mark for antiquity as well. But at least a small number of elite women in the Greco-Roman world did possess both the financial resources and the leisure time as well as the kind of education conducive to writing. Further, it is significant that all the Jewish and Christian women we have tentatively described as authors (the daughters of Job, the Montanist prophets, the Therapeutrides, Perpetua) are depicted as free from the traditional obligations and responsibilities of women in late antiquity and thus were more likely to have had the ways and means to write. The daughters of Job are not depicted as wives and mothers who devote the vast majority of their time to women's traditional pursuits. The Montanists Maximilla and Priscilla are said to have left their husbands to join the New Prophecy; in so doing, they would have abandoned the daily obligations of most women.[58] There is no question that Therapeutic women possessed all the prerequisites for writing: education, lack of financial constraints, and virtually all the time in the world. As for Perpetua, it is precisely when she is stranded in prison and has delivered her infant son to the care of her family that she composes the account of her suffering. Whether it was her only work is something we are unlikely ever to know.

It is also intriguing that the Christian candidates for authorship are all presented as proselytes. The Letter of *Mary to Ignatius* is actually titled *Mary the Proselyte to Ignatius*. Why this is the case is uncertain, particularly in a forgery, unless the title is meant to lend some credence or some clue of identity. Possibly the ascription is meant to be a subtle critique of I Timothy's dislike of proselytes as community leaders, even as the letter itself may be read as a subtle critique of I Timothy. Perpetua is explicitly described as a catechumen, a recent convert, and Priscilla and Maximilla may also have been new to the faith, as Eusebius's source contends.[59] Conceivably, pagan women were more likely to have been educated as children

---

[58]Apollonius *apud* Eusebius, *EH* 5.18.3.
[59]*EH* 5.16.6.

and taught to write, and less likely, as converts, to accept positions such as those advocated by the Orthodox opponents of Maximilla and Priscilla or even to convert into such churches in the first place. Our pseudepigraphical Mary may also be presumed to have had the time to write, for she is not described as married, or having children; in *Ignatius to Hero* she is described as the head of a church in her house.

Other Jewish and Christian women, particularly elite women with education, money, and leisure time, conceivably also composed literary works. Why we do not know of such women may be attributed in part to factors of dissemination. As noted above, ancient authors relied on relatively informal although structured processes of dissemination to "publish" their work. Women who wrote may have lacked the mechanisms for such dissemination. Perhaps they had the support of other women writers to provide comments and criticisms, or they had the opportunity to read their writings to a sympathetic circle of other women. But numerous factors may have contributed to the likelihood that women's works were not copied and disseminated, except perhaps anonymously or pseudonymously; these factors would include general male disapproval of women writers, the lack of funds to pay for copies, the lack of time to make copies, and the lack of availability of secretaries (slaves or otherwise) to prepare the copies.

Even if Jewish and Christian women did write and were able to circulate their compositions in a limited manner, numerous plausible explanations exist for why their writings were not subsequently transmitted. Copies of women's writings, identified as such, might simply never have moved from women's circles to the male mainstream of transmission. Monks who were subsequently responsible for the transmission of much ancient literature might not have bothered, malevolently or otherwise, to copy women's works. In at least some Christian circles, works written in women's names were interpreted as "authority over men" and simply unacceptable.

In the case of Jewish women, there are additional twists. In the centuries under consideration, much of Jewish literature was written in Greek, but I have not devoted any consideration to the possibility of women composing in Hebrew or Aramaic. Further, all of that early Jewish literature written in Greek depended for its survival not on Jews, who relinquished if not repudiated much of Greek Judaism, but on Christians, who in turn transmitted only that Greek-Jewish literature which they found acceptable to their ecclesiastical and theological concerns. Thus even writings by

Jewish women would have had to pass muster by Christian standards, which as we have seen, was not a system conducive to the transmission of writings acknowledged to have been authored by women, at least before the medieval period.

On balance, I think we are justified in concluding that Christian women certainly and Jewish women probably wrote in the Greco-Roman period, but their works are either lost or preserved almost exclusively under the cloaks of pseudonymity and anonymity. Identifying works written by women among the large corpus of Jewish and Christian anonymous and pseudonymous literature from late antiquity is nevertheless exceedingly difficult for precisely the kinds of reasons explored above in response to Davies and Lefkowitz. The few extant works in the names of women simply complicate our efforts.

But such difficulties do not exempt us from the need to be sensitive to the possibility that some of our texts may not have been written by men. We should not therefore draw conclusions from those texts which assume male authorship without some assessment of the probabilities for each and every work. Given the lack of controls available to us from the ancient texts, we must remain alert to studies from other periods and cultures which attempt to assess gender-based differences in literature; such investigations might fruitfully, if judiciously, be applied to ancient works. Yet this method too is highly problematic. The use of such studies from other settings might be taken for belief in the proposition that differences in the writing of women and men are rooted in biological differences that may then be observed cross-culturally and transhistorically. Such a theory has contemporary ideological ramifications which are patently dangerous, and I have no wish to support them in any form.

On the basis of my research, I am much more comfortable with the hypothesis that identifiable differences in the writings of women and men can be attributed to the different social realities which women and men experience in virtually all cultures: the utility of such work transhistorically or cross-culturally depends, then, on the similar distinctions of female and male experience in different cultures and historical periods. And the same can be said for religion![60]

---

[60]This thesis is central to my forthcoming *Gender, Cult and Cosmology*.

Index of Sources

Authors Cited

Classical Authors

(See also names of individual texts in the Index of Sources)

List of Contributors

Betsy Halpern-Amaru
  Department of Religion
  Vassar College
  Poughkeepsie, NY 12601

Beverly Bow
  School of Religion
  University of Iowa
  Iowa City, IA 52242

Claudia V. Camp
  Department of Religion
  Texas Christian University
  Fort Worth, TX 76129

Randall D. Chesnutt
  Department of Religion
  Pepperdine University
  Malibu, CA 90265

Stevan Davies
  Department of Religious Studies
  College Misericordia
  Dallas, PA 18612

Ross S. Kraemer
  Department of Religious Studies
  Franklin and Marshall College
  Lancaster, PA 17604

Mary R. Lefkowitz
  Department of Greek and Latin
  Wellesley College
  Wellesley, MA 02181

Amy-Jill Levine
  Department of Religion
  Swarthmore College
  Swarthmore, PA 19081

George W. E. Nickelsburg
School of Religion
University of Iowa
Iowa City, IA 52242

Richard I. Pervo
Seabury-Western Theological Seminary
Evanston, IL 60201

Adele Reinhartz
Department of Religious Studies
McMaster University
Hamilton, Onatario L8S 4K1
Canada

Robin Darling Young
Department of Theology
Catholic University of America
Washington, DC 20064

Judith Romney Wegner
Department of Judaic Studies
University of Massachusetts
Amherst, MA 01003

862887

Printed in Great Britain by
Amazon.co.uk, Ltd.,
Marston Gate.